YO' MAMA!

YO' MAMA!

NEW RAPS, TOASTS, DOZENS, JOKES and CHILDREN'S RHYMES from URBAN BLACK AMERICA

Edited by
Onwuchekwa Jemie

TEMPLE UNIVERSITY PRESS
Philadelphia

Temple University Press, Philadelphia 19122
Copyright © 2003 by Onwuchekwa Jemie
All rights reserved
Published 2003
Printed in the United States of America

⊗ The paper used in this publication meets the requirements of the American National Standard for Information Sciences—Permanence of Paper for Printed Library Materials, ANSI Z39.48-1984.

Library of Congress Cataloging-in-Publication Data

Yo' mama! : new raps, toasts, dozens, jokes and children's rhymes from urban Black America / edited by Onwuchekwa Jemie.
    p. cm.
Includes bibliographical references.
ISBN 1-59213-028-3 (cloth) — ISBN 1-59213-029-1 (pbk.)
    1. African Americans—Folklore.   2. Urban folklore—United States.
I. Jemie, Onwuchekwa, 1940–

GR111.A47 .Y64
398'.089'960?3–dc21   2002040858

For black folks everywhere

We hold it as an article of faith
that every person of African descent
should visit the Motherland, Africa,
at least once in their lifetime
and take at least
one African name

CONTENTS

Contents

Contents

Contents

Contents

xiii

Contents

PREFACE

These versions of African-American urban folklore were collected over a period of four years (1969–1973), primarily from the metropolitan areas of New York and Philadelphia, but the informants were from all over the United States and a few were from the Caribbean. Starting with an informal committee of friends, and including some three hundred African-American students from three universities, the material was gathered through an expanding chain of contacts. Some of it was tape-recorded live, candid and unstaged on front stoops, sidewalks, street corners, schoolyards, playgrounds, handball and basketball courts, bars, barbershops and pool halls. The rest was gathered through interviews.

Those were the turbulent early years of African-American Studies. Like most of my contemporaries I had been trained exclusively in European and Anglo-American literatures, from Nigeria's colonial schools to Columbia and Harvard. I was now in the process of discovering, two steps ahead of my students, African-American literature as a whole; the poetry of Langston Hughes, which was to become my particular interest; African-American folklore through Langston Hughes and Arna Bontemps's landmark anthology *The Book of Negro Folklore;* and the contemporary "street poetry" of signifying, dozens and toasts through Roger Abrahams's pioneering study *Deep Down in the Jungle.* Many of my students had grown up with this "street poetry" and were delighted to discover that it was not only "literature" but merited serious critical attention. When therefore I sent them scouring their communities in search of this oral gold, it was for them a labor of love. This magnificent collection is the fruit of that collaborative enterprise.

Those young people dug into their memories of a not so distant childhood and adolescence, and they wrote down what they remembered. Then they pressed their age-mates into service, taking them along on the hunt. They revisited the schoolyards and community playgrounds where another generation of children continued to gather. They interviewed their elders—parents, grandparents, aunts and uncles and senior neighbors. And they tracked the broad talkers, the street-wise and hip, to their favorite haunts and recorded what they heard.

Virtually everyone returned from the hunt with nuggets, gems and forget-me-nots. But as might be expected, the harvest varied widely, in quantity as well as quality. Artists and informants were not always identified and sometimes could not be. And of course there was considerable overlapping, especially with such fragmentary forms as children's rhymes and the dozens.

I have tried to be as exact with sources as the circumstances permit, assigning attributions in four categories: (a) match-ups of collector, artist and work; (b) match-ups of collector and work; (c) multiple collectors of a single text; and (d) a generalized attribution to an undifferentiated list of contributors for the bulk of the dozens, children's rhymes and other fragmentary forms. (Caribbean material, which constitutes a small portion, is not separately noted.) All who went in search of these treasures shared in the thrill of the hunt and the excitement of the find. If their finds could not always be used, an inclusive collective attribution for all the fine work in this book must nevertheless go to every one of the students in my African-American literature classes at the Borough of Manhattan Community College of the City University of New York (1969–1973), Columbia University (1970–1973), and Swarthmore College (1972–1973), and through them to their communities as a whole.

I was in the middle of assembling this collection when I left the United States and returned to Nigeria, where circumstances were such that I could not complete the work. The question might now be asked: what is the justification for publishing a collection of oral literature three decades after it was collected? Well, first of all, it is the beginning of a new century, and every account that could possibly be rendered ought to be rendered, and every lingering activity brought to a close. Secondly, while virtually every item in this collection may have appeared in print somewhere in some form, these particular versions, as far as I know, have not. The soul of oral literature is its infinitude. And its perenniality. The creative variance of its multiplicity is ours to enjoy. We can never have too many versions of "The Signifying Monkey" or "Stagger Lee" or "Titanic," not to speak of "Death Row" or "Doriella DuFontaine," which are not nearly as well known. Jokes, including jokes about preachers and parodies of their sermons, are always in season. And the dozens are fresh and never ending.

In addition, this collection enables us to revisit an important episode of African-American literary history and observe its connections to the contemporary scene. These oral forms exerted an enormous influence on writers of the Black Arts Movement of the 1960s and 1970s. The "black aesthetic" of Amiri Baraka, Larry Neal, Hoyt Fuller, Maulana Karenga, Stephen Henderson and Addison Gayle was fashioned primarily from the whole cloth of the oral tradition. The idiom of the plays of Ed Bullins, Ben Caldwell, Ron Milner, Lonne Elder and Charles Gordone, and of the "performance poetry" of Amiri Baraka, Haki Madhubuti, Sonia Sanchez, Nikki Giovanni, Gil Scott-Heron and The Last Poets was a translation of the sass and spirit of contemporary rapping, signifying, dozens and toasts. Langston Hughes had provided models for such "translation" in his blues and jazz poems of four decades, particularly in *Montage of a Dream Deferred* (1951) and *Ask Your Mama* (1961), and in his practice of reading poetry to musical accompaniment (a practice that the Beat Generation poets learned from him and popularized in the late 1950s). These poetries in their turn provided the verbal and theatrical streams that, conjoined with the musical tributaries of the field holler, talking blues, jazz scat-singing and the recitatives of Isaac Hayes, Millie Jackson and Barry White, finally issued in the sweeping, triumphal, postmodern river that is rap music of the 1980s, 1990s and new millennium. The poets and musicians of the Black Arts era were the fathers and mothers of rap music, and Langston Hughes was its grandfather.

This anthology is therefore intended for that portion of the reading public who relish elegant language, brilliant wit, startling imagery and raucous good humor—a literary feast that some may first have tasted in contemporary rap and hip-hop without knowing who brought the fire, or taught the cooks how to cook.

Scholars, too, and not without laughter, will find in this collection rich and varied new texts for their analysis. Indeed, this is still the first comprehensive anthology devoted to the modern urban folk forms—toasts, dozens, tales, jokes, and children's rhymes. Earlier collections have been more specialized. Bruce Jackson's *Get Your Ass in the Water and Swim Like Me* (1974) and Dennis Wepman, Ronald Newman and Murray Binderman's *The Life* (1976) are devoted to toasts. Roger Abrahams's *Deep Down in the Jungle* (1963, revised 1970) and Daryl Cumber Dance's *Shuckin' and Jivin'* (1978), while wider ranging, display texts that ultimately belong with toasts, tales and jokes. Each of these scholars provides a brilliant analysis of the oral genres and tradition, but children's rhymes and the dozens are notably absent from the texts they display at any length. On the other hand, it is the copious abundance of these two forms that gives our anthology the needed balance as a record of the major contemporary oral genres.

Our understanding of the rhetorical strategies of African-American popular discourse is greatly beholden to dedicated work of the past four decades by these and other folklorists and students of "urban communication," including John Dollard, J. L. Dillard, H. Rap Brown, Geneva Smitherman, Thomas Kochman, Alan Dundes, William Labov, Claudia Mitchell-Kernan, Lawrence Levine, John W. Roberts and Mel Watkins. These fine scholars have built on the foundation set by a generation of giants—collectors, ethnographers, anthropologists and linguists—including Thomas Wentworth Higginson, Joel Chandler Harris, Lorenzo Turner, Melville Herskovits, Zora Neale Hurston, Alan Lomax, J. Mason Brewer, Sterling Brown, Arna Bontemps and Langston Hughes. A third generation, with a new school of applications, might be said to have been inaugurated when Henry Louis Gates adopted the rhetoric of signifying and the figure of the Monkey (whom he read as an avatar of the Yoruba trickster deity Eshu) as critical touchstones for his exploration of African-American literary theory in his book *The Signifying Monkey* (1988), thereby expanding considerably our sense of the uses of pan-African folklore and myth.

One of the major cultural events of the closing decade of the twentieth century was the staging of the Broadway musical *Titanic,* followed by its hugely successful movie sequel, which recreates the beauty and terror of that doomed voyage, oblivious that a fragment of its looming myth is captured in African-American lore in the toasts of "Shine and the Sinking of the Titanic." The relationship of "Shine" and the musical and movie *Titanic* is emblematic of the (sometimes blind) interdependence of cultures. Some of the material in our collection, especially the jokes and children's rhymes, have their parallels and variants in the other American cultures. Some were indeed borrowed from the other cultures. Such lineages are ably traced by the folklorists and are not our concern here. What does distinguish our versions is their cultural stamp, their authenticity, never their exclusivity.

To put it another way, every tale, joke or rhyme in this collection, as in most collections of folk literature, may be presumed in their innumerable variants to be more than "twice-told." Some items enjoy wide currency on this side of the Atlantic, some are known worldwide, and some are very old, hundreds of years old. Who borrowed from whom is not always clear. Indeed, after Stith Thompson's six-volume *Motif-Index of Folk Literature* (1955–1958), which is far from exhaustive, and after Henry Bett's *Nursery Rhymes and Tales: Their Origin and History* (1924), Iona and Peter Opie's *The Lore and Language of Schoolchildren* (1959), Mary and Herbert Knapp's *One Potato, Two Potato . . . : The Secret Education of American Children* (1976), and G. Legman's two-volume *Rationale of the Dirty Joke: An Analysis of Sexual Humor* (1968, 1975), few scholars would find it worth their while to stake claims of originality or exclusivity for folk material under their study in any part of the world. The story of folklore is the story of human culture itself—an infinitely complex maze of creation and re-creation, fusion and diffusion, transmutation and transmission.

It is inevitable that some of the material in our collection will register as dated. References to the Jackson Five, the Osmond Brothers, and Lucky Strike commercials, for instance, locate those pieces properly in their age. It was an age when the homophobia of "The Faggot and the Truck Driver" was not "politically incorrect," when the child abuse implicit in "Felt," "Belly Button," "Coming and Going," and "I Was Walking Through the Park" could still provoke laughter, and when "bitch," "nigger," "motherfucker" and the many other vulgarities that fill these pages were better tolerated. Unsavory language and regressive sentiments are a fact of literary history the world over, and African-American orature is no exception.

I must acknowledge the invaluable assistance of two of my students at Columbia University at the time this material was gathered. Ebele Oseye (Ellease Southerland) and Charles Daniel Dawson worked long hours with me, sifting the mass of written submissions, transcribing audio tapes, retrieving the gold from the chaff. In addition, they produced a sheaf of notes with valuable insights, which I have incorporated into the Introduction. Danny and Ebele were not only my friends but also my teachers. I was, strictly speaking, a stranger to the material I was handling, even though it had affinities with the West African traditions I grew up with. But Danny and Ebele were born in the black communities of metropolitan New York and grew up with these very children's rhymes, dozens, jokes, preacher tales and toasts. And they were gifted with razor-sharp minds—and what imagination! This work is therefore the result of a two-tiered collaboration, first with the students in my classes at those three institutions, and, more specifically, with Ebele Oseye and Daniel Dawson. To them both, and to all the rest wherever they may be today, I extend my grateful thanks.

My sincere gratitude to Daryl Cumber Dance, Robert Hulton-Baker, Jerome Rothenberg, Eleanor Traylor, John Reilly, Barbara Griffin, Tom Clayton, Jon Woodson, Gary Larson, Dolan Hubbard, John Edgar Tidwell, Joseph Asike, Ernest Emenyonu, John Wright, and Chinweizu. They read the manuscript at various stages of its evolution and gave me invaluable criticisms and advice. For source materials and advice on African popular discourses, I am indebted to Adeniran Adeboye (Yoruba), Pathe Sow (Fulani), Mbye Cham (Wolof) and Luis Serapiao (Shona).

I am grateful to the University of Minnesota for a grant for research on this work during its early phases.

I cannot thank enough my editor at Temple University Press, the incomparable Janet Francendese, for her patience and understanding as she waited for this book.

And to Nneka, and our children, who lived in the shadow of this unfinished work for so long, I owe more than words can express.

ACKNOWLEDGMENTS

My greatest debt is to the young people who gathered this material. Their names are in the Contributors list, excluding those who requested anonymity.

Portions of the text and introduction were previously published in *Alcheringa: Ethnopoetics,* Vol. 2, No. 1, April 1976 (and also in *The Coevolution Quarterly,* Spring 1977), and appear courtesy of the publisher.

Every effort has been made to exclude from this collection any rhymes that were previously published and under copyright at the time they were gathered. If any such material should happen to be included, its appearance here is inadvertent and sincerely regretted.

A NOTE ON THE TEXT

Variant versions of the same text are given with the titles originally submitted: for example, "The Tee-Ti-Tanic," "The Three Women," "The Titanic"; "Stag-a-Lee," "Stagolee," "Stackalee," "Stagger Lee"; "Big Pete," "Pete Revere."

Certain words are rendered as pronounced on the original recorded tapes or transcribed by the contributor, especially if this helps preserve rhyme, humor or internal consistency. For instance, some texts use *drawers* for underwear, others *draws; g* and *s* endings are sometimes dropped; and words like *get* and *there* are sometimes rendered as *git* and *thar,* as in the originals.

Gun bores are rendered with their official decimal calibrations: .38, .44, .45, etc., although in the literature they are always pronounced "thirty-eight," "forty-four," "forty-five," etc., without the decimal.

YO' MAMA!

INTRODUCTION

SOME FEATURES OF AFRICAN-AMERICAN ORAL ART

It goes without saying that the nature of a society influences all of its art forms. African-American oral literature (or orature), certainly one of the most fascinating of the black arts, reflects many of the brutal experiences of a life lived in race-stressed America. But what is most remarkable about this literature is its transformational powers—that it so often takes a painful experience, works it through the magic machinery of an inventive imagination, and, still keeping before us the original pain, carries us gently to the point of laughter. Take the following joke in the form of a traffic sign:

Welcome to
Muleshoe, Mississippi
Speed Limit 35
Niggers 90

Or that other well-known sign, which says:

Nigger, read and run
If you can't read,
run anyway

Or the one about a black man arrested for running a red light, and he says to the judge:

Your Honor, I saw all the white folks
driving on the green,
so I figured the red
was for us colored folks!

It is this ironic humor, so richly illustrated in the blues, that brings a triumphant brightness and joy to balance a life weighted with pain. And while the printed page cannot hope to reproduce with any fullness an oral art where the word gains dimension through setting and drama, it nevertheless can increase appreciation for the creative skills alive and laughing in that art.

African-American orature may conveniently be divided into two broad categories—the traditional and the modern. By *traditional* is meant those forms that have been recognized and studied for decades, while the *modern* would embrace those forms that, while they may indeed be as old as some of the traditional, attracted the attention of scholars and were made available in print mostly in the past four decades. The *traditional* would include, for instance, a wide variety of songs, tales and jokes: religious songs such as spirituals, sermons, gospel and shouts; secular songs such as blues, ballads and work songs (cotton-picking songs, lumbering and rowing songs, railroad songs, field cries and hollers, prison camp and chain gang songs); creation myths and explanatory tales; tales of human heroes, such as the John and Ole Massa cycle, and of their analogues in the animal world, such as the Brer Rabbit cycle; and proverbs, superstitions and medicinal recipes. The *modern* would include such forms as children's rhymes and game songs; rapping, signifying and jive (talking shit, talking trash); boasts and threats; dozens (known to the younger generations as sounding, screaming, ranking, woofing, capping, hiking, joning, snapping); toasts (extended verse narratives) such as "The Signifying Monkey," "Stagger Lee," "Shine and the Sinking of the Titanic," "Honky-Tonk Bud," "Dolemite," "Pete Revere," "Mexicali Rose," "Death Row" and "Doriella DuFontaine"); and jokes and parodies, including preacher jokes and inter-ethnic humor.

Clearly, the traditional and modern forms overlap. For instance, new work songs, ballads, sermons and gospel continue to be created, while many children's rhymes are much older than the recent surge of scholarly interest in them. To that extent, the two categories are artificial; and yet it is true that in the main, the forms listed as modern, plus some variants of the traditional, were, for a variety of historical reasons, not widely discussed until the 1960s. The aim of this collection is to make available to the general reader a sampling of the major modern forms.

Perhaps it should be pointed out that many of the features of African-American oral art under consideration are not necessarily unique to it but are present in varying combinations and intensities in oral arts the world over.

African-American oral literature is *drama,* and players, audience and setting are crucial to the total experience. The different oral forms presented here are but different scenes of the same drama, scenes that sometimes overlap and merge, at other times remain distinct—but always, in any moment of the drama, the *word* is the power. The players are actors, conscious of the effect they are having on the audience, and responding to the audience's applause or ridicule (especially in contest situations, such as boasts, threats and dozens). Implicit always in performer–audience interaction is the call-and-response or leader–choral antiphony, which is one of the central features of the oral art of African peoples as a whole, and a dimension difficult to recreate in print.

In its language and imagery, African-American folk poetry is characterized by *virtuosity.* It is unsurpassed in its use of rhetorical devices, including punning, alliteration and assonance, parallel phrasing, internal rhymes and end rhymes, full rhymes and half rhymes, stock phrases and formulas, all suffused with a general playfulness and wit. Eighteenth-century English critic Samuel Johnson might just as well have been speaking of African-American oral poetry when he said of certain English poets of the previous century that they delighted in combining "dissimilar images" and discovering "occult resemblances in things apparently unlike." In this folk poetry, dissimilar images are combined harmoniously, not "yoked by violence together" as Johnson judged them to be in the poetry he was discussing. African-American wit brings together in easy union what Johnson called "strength of thought" and "happiness of language" (S. Johnson 470). An enormous tragi-comic intelligence with a highly developed auditory capacity is at work in the best of this poetry. In its conscious artistry and technical sophistication, its manipulation of language with happy results, its freshness of imagery and mellifluousness of movement, and in its whole and successful devotion to *sound,* African-American oral poetry at its best ranks with the great poetries of the world.

Empowered by their heritage of West African languages, African Americans have bent, stretched, broken, melted down and reshaped the English language, forging for their imagination a malleable instrument capable of carrying their own version of the world.

That instrument is a language of many names. For years it was denigrated as patois, dialect, broken English, bad English, street language, street talk or slang, until gradually it came into its own as Black English, African-American vernacular, African-American language or Ebonics. These transitions parallel the many names of the People themselves over the years, from names of abuse to names of recognition and respect: darky, nigger, nigra, African, Colored, Negro, Black, Afro-American, People of African Descent, People of Color, African American.

Their version of the world may be glimpsed from the folklore in the various modes they have employed in amplifying reality, for instance through wild exaggeration and hyperbole, through the use of complex inversions or flipped polarities, and through the use of words traditionally regarded as obscene and banished from polite discourse in American society.

Hyperbole

Hyperbole is the polished mirror into which the black imagination gazes with every other rhyme, laughing as it sees itself refracted and distorted in a phantasmagorial kaleidoscope. The language of hyperbole amplifies reality by carrying us beyond the boundaries of rational thought, past the limits of the real into the surreal, into a universe in which possibilities are infinite, probabilities unlimited. The images it brings back from that universe are literally far-fetched, unexpected, wild, extraordinary. Their impact is *surprise,* a function of their freshness and power. Hyperbole is perhaps best exemplified in the dozens:

> Your mama's hair is so short she could stand on her head
> and her hair wouldn't touch the ground.
>
> Your mama is lower than whale shit—and that's at the
> bottom of the ocean.
>
> Your father is so low he has to look up to tie his shoes.
>
> You're so low down you need an umbrella to protect yourself
> from ant piss.

These images defy rational understanding and a square, sane conception of space; but they convey, in no uncertain terms, the absolute absence of height. Hyperbole makes extraordinary demands on the imagination: the lines start here, and before you know it they are out there, way out, pushed to their extremest possibility, beyond earth-sense into rare cosmic time-space:

> Your hair is so bad you need to carry a gun just to comb it.
>
> Your mama's so ugly she has to sneak up on a glass to get a
> drink of water.
>
> Your mother's so old, when God said "Let there be light" she
> jumped and cut it on.
>
> You so ugly you scare yourself.

Hyperbole makes its innocent first appearance in the schoolyard:

> You're so stupid you failed lunch.
>
> Your breath is so bad it smells like elephant breath.
>
> Your father is so poor he can't even pay attention.

Then it stretches and deepens with the years:

> Your mother is so skinny she swallowed a pea and swore she
> was pregnant.
>
> Nigger, you'd rather run through hell in gasoline-soaked
> drawers than mess with me.
>
> You would rather let a four hundred pound gorilla suck your
> dick in a telephone booth than fuck with me.

These images are not surreal in the conventional sense, for they are ultimately anchored in reality. They are vivid and concrete, drawing their strength from all five primary faculties—the sensory, visual, auditory, olfactory and gustatory—and often making their impact on several senses at once:

> Your mother is like a cup of coffee: hot, black, and ready to
> be creamed.
>
> Your house is so cold the roaches fart snowballs.

> Nigger, keep messin' with me and I'll slap the cowboy pee
> out of you.
> Mess with me and I'll stick my foot so far up your ass when
> you brush your teeth you'll shine my shoe.

The images manage to capture essential relationships, whether natural/eternal conditions ("the lion stuck on the monkey *like stink on shit*") or historical ones ("Stack stuck on Jesse *like a German on a Jew*").

Inversion

The amplification of reality through *flipped polarities* or *inversion* is well illustrated in such words as *bad, terrible, evil, wicked, mean:*

> He had a little boy who was born to be the baddest mother-
> fucker on land or sea
> And the little boy's name was Stagger Lee.

Not a simple inversion whereby the word takes on the opposite of its conventional meaning, but a complex process whereby it carries simultaneously the conventional meaning and its opposite, with a decided stress on the opposite. Thus, a *bad* man (such as Stagger Lee) is bad in some *good* sense: he is a man of *ability* (power, strength, virtue [Latin *virtus* = strength]), and that ability resides in his talent for badness. If there is one thing he is *good* at, one field of human activity in which he excels, in which his true genius is capable of fulfilling itself, it is in badness, meanness, terribleness, evilness, wickedness. In these realms he is a true champion, and like any true champion (or hero) he exacts a tribute of admiration and awe. To call him by his true name (bad) is therefore to praise him, for he is a person of extraordinary capacity (for badness), and we respect and fear people of extraordinary capacity. This is why "He's a bad motherfucker" is a praise and "I'm a mean motherfucker" is a boast, each implying a warning and a threat—that you know better than to mess with me/him.

A further consideration is that the world of the slave, ex-slave or oppressed is so terrible, wicked, mean, you have to be equally so just to make it. In such a Darwinian jungle it is the *bad motherfucker* who can be counted on to survive. This is probably what Robert Hayden meant by his play on the word *mean* in his great poem "Runagate Runagate." History's most intrepid liberator carried two pistols, and she didn't carry them for decoration. She would shoot the hapless fugitive who proved too tired or timid to keep moving on. Yes, Harriet Tubman was one mean sister. She *means* to be free, that's why she's so *mean*. She had to be mean to get hers, and just as mean to help others get theirs. No wonder in nineteen excursions she never lost a passenger. "Mean mean mean to be free" (Hayden 77).

Harriet Tubman is a *bad motherfucker.* She is the "bad nigger" of tradition who "don't take no stuff off of no white folks." The "bad nigger" was a slave rebel and outlaw, a challenger against the white man's dominance who swears, as in the words of the spiritual:

> *And before I'd be a slave*
> *I'll be buried in my grave.*

The "bad nigger" was "bad" by white (conventional) definition, "good" by black definition. Early commentators on African-American folklore recognized this fracture in sensibility and usage. For example, H. C. Brearley, in a pivotal 1939 essay titled "Ba-ad Nigger," has this to say:

> In all folktales the daredevil is a constantly recurring character. . . .
> In many Negro communities, however, this emphasis upon heroic
> deviltry is so marked that the very word *bad* often loses its original
> significance and may be used as an epithet of honor. . . . In some
> parts of the South, however, there is a change in pronunciation to
> indicate whether or not the word carries approval. If the speaker
> wishes to use the term with the ordinary connotation, he pro-
> nounces it after the manner of Webster. But if he is describing a
> local hero, he calls him "ba-ad." The more he prolongs the *a* the
> greater his homage. (Brearley 580)

Alan Dundes amplifies the point in a 1973 footnote to Brearley:

> The point is that being labeled "bad" by Southern white planta-
> tion owners in the sense of being dangerous, obstreperous, and
> the like indicated to black people that the individual in question
> was unwilling to submit passively to the oppression of slavery.
> Thus "bad niggers" were Negroes who were willing to fight the sys-
> tem. "Bad" didn't mean evil at all. . . . Thus the whites' meant-to-be-
> insulting epithet of "bad nigger" became virtually a badge of honor
> in the black community. If the white slaveowners deemed one a
> "bad nigger," that was high praise indeed. (Dundes 581)

The "bad nigger," says Daryl Dance, "is and always has been *bad* (that is, vil-lainous) to whites because he violates their laws and he violates their moral codes. He is *ba-ad* (that is, heroic) to the Black people who relish his exploits for exactly the same reasons" (Dance, *Shuckin' and Jivin'* 224). She describes the "bad nigger," then and now, as

> characterized by [his] absolute rejection of established authority
> figures—Ole Massa, the sheriff, the judge[—]and his assertion of his
> own power and authority. . . . [His goal is] to attack and destroy all
> that [white authority] holds dear, including its work ethics, its polit-
> ical principles, its moral values. (Dance, *Long Gone* 143, 144, 145)

Elijah Muhammad and his Black Muslims sum it up in one axiom: "The white man's heaven is the black man's hell" (Marvin X 115).

Two black psychiatrists, William H. Grier and Price M. Cobbs, who studied the matter in depth, have called the "bad nigger" "the measure of manhood for all black men":

> The man who fought when threatened and lived to tell the tale became . . . a man among men . . . a man who held his manhood dear, and though his life was likely to be brief had laid hold of the essential task of men and particularly black men—survival and opposition to the foe. (Grier and Cobbs, *Black Rage* 123–124)

Ominously, Grier and Cobbs echo James Baldwin's dictum, that "every black man harbors a potential bad nigger [Richard Wright's Bigger Thomas] inside him" (Grier and Cobbs, *Black Rage* 55).

Fighting the system takes many forms—violent, non-violent; active resistance, passive resistance; physical, verbal, psychological, intellectual resistance. Always, resistance entails danger and demands extraordinary boldness and cunning. And the heroes have not all left the black earth; the "bad niggers" are everywhere still. Virtually every African-American leader down the ages (and, in the broadest sense, every black striver and achiever) may be styled a "bad nigger," one with potential made real. To achieve or lead, in these circumstances, is to wrestle the lion's paws and tear victory from its jaws. Among historical figures, Nat Turner, Denmark Vesey, Gabriel Prosser, Cinque of the *Amistad,* and, in South America and the Caribbean, Toussaint L'Ouverture, Dessalines, Christophe, Clairvaux, Macandal, the Maroons, the heroes of Palmares and all other slave rebels and conspirators—these are the archetypal "bad niggers." Add to these the active resisters—Frederick Douglass, Harriet Jacobs, Harriet Tubman, Sojourner Truth, Ida B. Wells, W. E. B. DuBois, Booker T. Washington, Marcus Garvey, Adam Clayton Powell, Rosa Parks, Martin Luther King, Elijah Muhammad, Malcolm X, Kwame Ture (Stokely Carmichael), H. Rap Brown, Mary McLeod Bethune, Fannie Lou Hamer, Langston Hughes, Richard Wright, Ralph Ellison, James Baldwin, Amiri Baraka, Jack Johnson, Joe Louis, Muhammad Ali, Louis Farrakhan, Jesse Jackson, Randall Robinson—these are some of the "baddest niggers" that ever walked. And this is just a sampling.[1]

The "bad niggers" are role models for the evolution not only of individual manhoods but of the *communal manhood.* In his 1965 funeral oration, Ossie Davis said of Malcolm X: "Malcolm was our manhood, our living, black manhood! This was his meaning to his people" (Davis, "Our Shining Black Prince"). Malcolm spoke the truth that all too many dared not speak. Through his words and acts the community lived.

The community identifies with the "bad niggers" (romanticizes them, as always with heroes), appropriating their badness, boldness, meanness that is their strength. Thus would poet Sonia Sanchez boast in her book title, *We a BaddDDD People,* articulating the collective self-definition: that We, as a

People, are "bad"—mean, wicked, tough, resilient, beautiful, indestructible. Our collective strengths are welded into that single word. Every good thing we ever did, that is, everything we've ever done, sleepwalkingly or by conscious choice, which has worked to our advantage, is "ba-ad," is what makes us one tough mean motherfucker of a nation of people. We in our terribleness. "Our terribleness," writes Amiri Baraka, "is our survival as beautiful beings, any where."

> To be bad is one level
> But to be terrible, is to be
> badder dan nat.
> (Baraka, *Terribleness* n.p.)

And we ain't about to disappear. Nah! "Ain't gonna give up on nothin'" (Baraka). We *are* a ba-ad [*great*] people!

We must bear in mind, of course, that history is one thing, folklore another. Each reflects the other in part, diverging at critical points. But whether in history or folklore, there are at least two traditions of the "bad nigger," one positive, the other conditional, problematic or downright negative. In his masterly study of pan-African cultural resistance, retention and transformation, *From Trickster to Badman* (1989), African-American folklorist John W. Roberts does not speak explicitly of a "positive" and a "negative" tradition, but the division is implicit in his analysis. Roberts prefers the term "bad nigger" for the rebels and outlaws of slave days, and "badman" for those of post-Reconstruction life and lore (Railroad Bill, John Hardy, Harry Duncan, Devil Winston and others, all historical persons to begin with). But the distinction he attempts to make between the two groups of rebels is difficult to sustain, as we shall see later. In any case, Roberts recognizes that rebels of both periods constituted one-man striking forces targeted at slavery, or at white violence, legal injustice and economic strangulation. White people feared and reviled these rebels, but black people relished and revered them. They were heroes, the community's champions, the avengers of black wrong. The slave community could not celebrate them openly, but the free black community of the late nineteenth and early twentieth centuries celebrated them in numerous ballads and stories. However, as the Ku Klux Klan vigilantes of post-Reconstruction, who had evolved from the "patterollers" of slave days, now merged with "legal" police forces, north and south, into a powerful modern twentieth-century law enforcement system "geared toward the protection of white interests in the society," the "badman" hero's acts of legal or economic reprisal, especially when carried out in white communities, became increasingly difficult and then virtually impossible (Roberts 171–173, 198).

Turned back at the white gates, the "badmen" turned on their own communities. Predictably, their formerly whole-hearted adoration became mixed and ambivalent. They continued to be admired as defiers of white law and confronters of white authority, especially as represented by the ubiquitous and brutal police. And they continued to be celebrated, now less frequently in ballads than in the new-found narrative verse form, the toast. But because they now preyed mostly on fellow-victims, they were also feared and hated.

Whether in lore (Stagger Lee, Dolemite, Boothill McCoy) or in real life, the "badmen" who terrorize the black community, robbing and killing, together with their close cousins the pimps, hustlers, dope peddlers and other predators who specialize in corrupting the young—these constitute the negative half of the "bad nigger" tradition. In other words, not every "bad nigger" is *good* for the community. Not every defier of white law is a promoter of black interests. In the final analysis, neither Stagger Lee with all his strength and fearlessness, nor the hustlers and pimps with all their style and cool, could provide a usable model for black manhood or black achievement. Instead, they represent instances of misdirection and perversion of historically positive, creative black energies. Only if they undergo the transfiguration of a Malcolm X, *who was one of them,* could they be honored alongside a Nat Turner, a Harriet Tubman or a Martin Luther King.

But, to return to the phonetics of the term, Brearley was certainly right about "a change in pronunciation" when "bad" means "good." *Tonality,* carried over from West African languages, has been recognized as one of the distinguishing features of African-American speech. As Molefi Asante pointed out,

> African-Americans mean something precise by their pitch, as in speaking such words as *Jesus, man, say.* Vocal color plays a vital role for the black public speaker, particularly the preacher, who utilizes various intonations and inflections to modify or amplify specific ideas, concepts, or emotions. (Asante 25)

Sonia Sanchez intended by her orthography to capture the tone or vocal color, to marry the meaning to the sound of *bad*—a brave effort in a long tradition of contractions, elisions and contortions of the written word, all aimed at replicating the sound of black speech on flat, two-dimensional paper. At its beginnings, that effort gave birth to the grotesqueries of nineteenth-century Southern "plantation dialect," an unreadable travesty of black speech invented and popularized by white minstrelsy, by white novelists and poets such as William Gilmore Simms, Thomas Nelson Page, George Washington Cable and Irwin Russell, and by white collector of black folklore Joel Chandler Harris in his Uncle Remus tales:

> "Tu'n me loose, fo' I kick de natchul stuffin' out'n you," sez Brer Rabbit, sezee, but de Tar-Baby, she ain't sayin' nothin'. She des hilt on, en den Brer Rabbit lose de use er his feet in de same way.
>
> (Harris 7)

> It alluz sets me laughin', when I happens to be roun',
> To see a lot ob gemmen come a-fishin' from de town!
> Dey waits tell arter bre'kfus 'fore dey ebber makes a start,
> An' den you sees 'em comin' in a leetle Jarsey kyart.
>
> (Russell 25)

"Lawd, marster, hit's so long ago, I'd a'most forgit all about it, ef I hedn' been wid him ever sence he wuz born. Ez 'tis, I remembers it jes' likr 'twuz yistiddy. Yo' know Marse Chan an' me—we wuz boys togerr. I wuz older'n he wuz, jes' de same ez he wuz whiter'n me.

(Page 4)

The soul of dialect is *cacography,* the deliberate misspelling of words for comic effect, which is the written equivalent of the malapropism. Mel Watkins, connoisseur of the unerring eye and ear for the comical, ranks cacography "even lower" than the pun, which Europeans have traditionally regarded as the lowest form of humor (Watkins 60).

African-American writers of the nineteenth century were well aware of the malice behind dialect. Dialect represented for them a dilemma: they couldn't work with it, and they couldn't work without it. They needed to be able to transcribe black speech, to capture black thought in its own words. But this powerful convention overflowing with negative stereotypes was already established for such transcriptions, and African-American writers found no way to break out of the cage. Frances Harper, Charles Waddell Chesnutt, James Corrothers, James Edwin Campbell, Paul Laurence Dunbar and others appropriated "dialect" and sought to turn it to positive account. They wrestled with it, attempting to subdue and refine it, to purge it of the white derision and black self-abnegation that oozed from its every pore. But it was a losing battle. Their renditions of black speech remained, to the end, hardly distinguishable from those of their white predecessors or contemporaries:

So nex' mawnin' atter breakfus' Mars Jeems sont fer de oberseah, en ax' 'im fer ter gib 'count er his styoa'dship. Ole Nick tol' Mars Jeems how much wuk be'n done, en got de books en showed 'im how much money be'n save'. Den Mars Jeems ax' 'im how de darkies be'n behabin'.

(Chesnutt 93)

I has hyeahd o' people dancin' an' I's hyeahd o' people singin'.
An' I's been 'roun' lots of othahs dat could keep de banjo ringin';
But of all de whistlin' da'kies dat have lived an' died since Ham,
De whistlin'est I evah seed was ol' Ike Bate's Sam.

(Dunbar 156)

It was this failure to subdue and transform conventional dialect that in 1922 moved James Weldon Johnson, the ablest black critic of his day, to pronounce the doom of dialect, which he said "has only two main stops, humor and pathos," and is incapable of expressing the full height and breadth and depth of authentic black thought and feeling. Johnson, also a gifted poet, had written many dialect poems and experienced firsthand the limitations of dialect. What the African-American writer needed, he concluded, was to find a form that will express the racial spirit by symbols from within rather than by symbols from without, such as the mere mutilation of English spelling and pronunciation. He needs a form that is freer and larger than dialect, but which will still hold the racial flavor; a form expressing the imagery, the idioms, the peculiar turns of thought, and the distinctive humor and pathos, too, of the Negro, but which will also be capable of voicing the deepest and highest emotions and aspirations, and allow of the widest range of subjects and the widest scope of treatment. (J. W. Johnson 41–42)

Johnson's call went largely unheeded. Black writers continued toiling in the coils of dialect deep into the twentieth century, and it nearly strangled them. As late as 1937 the great folklorist and novelist Zora Neale Hurston, at the noontide of her career, could write:

"Ah kin be some trouble when Ah take uh notion. . . . Ah'm uh bitch's baby round lady people."
"Ah's much ruther see all dat than to hear 'bout it. Come on less go see whut he gointuh do 'bout dis town." (Hurston 33)

The same year, Richard Wright, a powerful new voice at the beginning of a great career, wrote:

Awright, Ma, Ahll take the boat back. Hows tha? Wan me t take it back? . . . Whut yuh so scared fer? Ain nobody gonna see yuh wid it. All yuh gotta do is git in n make fer the hills n make fer em quick. Ef Ah hadnt stole tha boat yuh all woulda had t stay here till the watah washed yuh erway. (Wright, "Down by the River-side" 59)

Neither passage is any great improvement over black Chesnutt or white Russell. Hurston and Wright continued rendering black voices in this vein well into the 1940s and 1950s; but, happily, running alongside them were some bolder and more successful experiments at capturing the black voice along the lines Johnson advocated. While reiterating his judgment of plantation dialect in 1931, Johnson had also heralded *a new Northern, urban black language* just then sweeping over the horizon—"not the dialect of the comic minstrel tradition or of the sentimental plantation tradition [but] the common, racy, living, authentic speech of the Negro in certain phases of real life" (J. W. Johnson 4). The prophet of this new day, the master of *light touch,* who was forging a language that worked more by idiomatic suggestion and impressionism than by wholesale orthographic conversion or phonetic transcription—who, in other words, was reaching for "a form that will express the racial spirit by symbols from within rather than by symbols from without"—was Langston Hughes, closely seconded by Sterling Brown:

For I'se still goin', honey,
I'se still climbin',
And life for me ain't been no crystal stair.

> (L. Hughes, *Collected Poems* 30)

Tell all my mourners
To mourn in red
Cause there ain't no sense
In my bein' dead.

> (L. Hughes, *Collected Poems* 250)

Honey
When de man
Calls out de las' train
You're gonna ride,
Tell him howdy.

Gather up yo' basket
An' yo' knittin' an' yo' things,
An' go on up an' visit
Wid frien' Jesus for a spell.

> (S. Brown 48)

Good morning, daddy!
Ain't you heard
The boogie-woogie rumble
Of a dream deferred? . . .

> *What did I say?*

Sure,
I'm happy!
Take it away!

> *Hey, pop!*
> *Re-bop!*
> *Mop!*

> *Y-e-a-h!*

> (L. Hughes, *Collected Poems* 388)

The deft, masterly touch, unmatched by their contemporaries, is a major part of the poetic legacy of Langston Hughes and Sterling Brown. Black poets of the 1960s and 1970s, the next great period of ebullience, appropriated part of that legacy. They too attempt to express the racial spirit, "the imagery, the idioms, the peculiar turns of thought" by "symbols from within." But because their times were different, and the mission of their generation demanded a loud, combative, iconoclastic voice, it was perhaps to be expected that their experiments in orthography as well as verse form would go to such extremes, paralleling the idiosyncratic excesses of Anglo-American poets of their day:

some
    times
        i turn a corner
of my mind
        & u be there
            looooooking
                at me.
& smilen.
        yo / far / away / smile.
               & I moooove
to u.
      & the day is not any day.   & yes ter day
is loooNNg
        goooNNe.
        (Sanchez, *I've Been a Woman* 24).

he didn't say
wear yr / blackness in
outer garments
& blk / slogans fr / the top 10.

he was fr a long
line of super-cools,
    doo-rag lovers &
    revolutionary pimps.
u are playing that
high-yellow game in blackface
minus the straighthair.
                (Madhubuti)

The above samples, from Harris and Chesnutt to Hurston and Madhubuti, represent two centuries of experiment in setting down in writing a brand of English constructed on the structural grid, grammar and syntax of West African languages (Wolof, Akan, Hausa, Yoruba, Lingala, Igbo, etc.). The black (twentieth) century of experimentation differed from the white (nineteenth), but on the whole, it was no resounding success either. Each transcript is different; each writer does his own thing. It might be one of the tasks of the twenty-first century to standardize the African-American language or Ebonics in written form. The "standard" form of any language—standard English, standard French, standard Japanese, standard Ebonics—is simply the totality of grammar, syntax, spelling, punctuation, pronunciation and meaning that is "voted correct" by the elite speakers of that language, the holders and exercisers of political and economic power. The "standard" is only one of the several versions or dialects of a language, but it is privileged by the power elite as the official dialect in which government, education and business are conducted. But having a "standard" never did scuttle experimentation or innovation in language, whether by elite or non-elite speakers or writers; the "non-standard" dialects continue to flourish and to feed and be fed by the "standard" dialect. And given the ancient, pervasive heritage of experimentation and improvisation in the music, rhetoric, lyric poetry and fictional narrative traditions of pan-African peoples, there is no reason at all to fear that the linguistic vehicle, in this case Ebonics, might suffer from standardization.

But, to return to the word. Pronunciation is not the only link of the word *bad* with the ancestral African source. In his essay, Brearley puts forth the commendably bold proposition that

> this use of *bad* as a term of admiration is quite likely an importation from Africa, for [Melville J.] Herskovits has found a similar terminology among the blacks of the Surinam district of Dutch Guiana, among the Negroes of the West Indies, and among the natives of the province of Dahomey in West Africa. (Brearley 580)

But Herskovits, who was co-pilot with Lorenzo D. Turner in the study of Africanisms in the Americas, responded that in his findings

> the use of the word "bad" by Negroes—e.g., "ugly" in Guiana, or *malin,* in Haiti—is much more an expression of admiration for cleverness in a contest of wits than it is for deviltry in action. (Herskovits, Letter 350)

He goes on to say that the "heroic outlaw" of African-American folklore is *not* "a survival of an African tradition":

> The African outlaw is a phenomenon whom I, at least, have never come upon, either in my own field research, or during my reading in literature. (Herskovits, Letter 350)

Herskovits has a point, but Brearley is actually closer to the mark. The "heroic outlaw" of African-American folklore may not indeed be an African import, at least not in his fully finished form; however, the *language* of his praises certainly is.

In his work previously cited, John W. Roberts has plausibly demonstrated the process whereby the "badman" or outlaw folk hero emerged in the 1890s under pressure of post-Reconstruction violence and economic deprivation, shedding the mask of the "trickster" hero whose own evolutionary trail led through human and animal trickster figures of slavery days all the way back to the African homeland. Roberts acknowledges the earlier "bad nigger" of slavery days but then, unaccountably, seeks to divorce him from the "badman" of post-Reconstruction life and lore:

While a black character-type referred to as the "bad nigger" has existed in American society since the days of slavery, whether these figures served as prototypes for badmen heroes in African American folk tradition is certainly debatable. (Roberts 176)

Roberts scolds those scholars who use the terms "bad nigger" and "badman" interchangeably; however, the distinction he seeks to draw proves rather slippery. He bases his distinction on the following grounds: (a) that unlike the "badmen" of a later era, the "bad niggers" of slave days were not celebrated in songs and tales in their day; (b) that their "flagrant disregard for the masters' rules constantly threaten[ed] to bring the masters' power down on the entire community"; and (c) that they were "as likely to unleash their fury and violence on their defenseless fellow sufferers as on the masters" (Roberts 176).

But nothing in their circumstances made the "bad niggers" any more likely than the "badmen" and "oulaws" to prey on their fellow blacks. And except for reprisals following such large-scale assaults as Nat Turner's revolt, there is no evidence of whites punishing the entire slave community for the actions of one "bad nigger." On the other hand, the very possibility of reprisals should explain why the exploits of "bad niggers" went unsung. We need only recall Harriet Jacobs's account of the scale and savagery of the white backlash following Nat Turner's revolt:

> Everywhere men, women and children were whipped till the blood stood in puddles at their feet. Some received five hundred lashes. . . . The dwellings of the colored people . . . were robbed of clothing and everything else the marauders thought worth carrying away. All day long these unfeeling wretches went round, like a troop of demons, terrifying and tormenting the helpless . . . the most shocking outrages were committed with perfect impunity. (Jacobs 393, 396)

Who in those circumstances could weave garlands of song for Nat Turner, Gabriel Prosser or Denmark Vesey? A laurel for Jack Bowler or Peter Poyas? Or a wreath for the many who "died silent"?

In any case, Roberts follows the progress of "bad niggers" from slavery to freedom, right into the 1890s, when the "badman" is supposed to have emerged. Going by his record, the drama does not change. The actions of the emerging "badman" look suspiciously like those of the "bad nigger" before him, and the white reaction doesn't look too different either. As always, the charge is "'putting on airs,' 'sauciness,' 'impudence,' 'disrespect,' 'insubordination,' 'contradicting whites and violating social custom.'" And the response: "acts of violence," "the 'breaking' of recalcitrant 'bad niggers'"—this time through the chain gang and convict lease system of forced labor (Roberts 178). The "bad nigger's" mantle seems to fit the "badman" (Railroad Bill, Harry Duncan, Devil

Winston, et al.) rather nicely. If Roberts is unable to sustain the distinction between "bad nigger" and "badman," it is probably because it is *a distinction without a difference.* (A far more useful distinction is the one Roberts makes between the "badman" of the toasts and of the late-nineteenth-century ballads. We shall consider that distinction later.)

To return to the central issue: the African-American "badman" or "bad nigger" had no African antecedents because his circumstances had no ancient African parallels. *The "badman" or "bad nigger" was born in America; however, the language of his recognition and adulation was made in Africa.*

While noting the common root of "badman" and "bad nigger" in the inversion of the word *bad*, Roberts dismisses Brearley's hypothesis of African origins as "improbable," adding that "it is unlikely that the inverted meaning of 'bad' found in black usage occurred in Africa" (Roberts 180). But the fact is that it did and does occur. Far from improbable or unlikely, the complex inversions of such terms as *bad, evil, terrible, wicked* and *mean* do indeed have their parallels in West African languages, especially in informal praises, boasts and jokes. These usages survived the Middle Passage and came to embrace all of the daredevils, rebels and outlaws (whether historical or fictional) of the black experience in the Americas.

For the West African provenance of *bad* as a term of admiration, let us begin with linguist David Dalby's list of Africanisms in American English:

> *bad* (esp. in the emphatic form *baad*), as used in the sense of "very good, extremely good"; similarly *mean,* as used in the sense of "satisfying, fine, attractive"; and *wicked,* as used in the sense of "excellent, capable." Cf. frequent use of negative terms (often pronounced emphatically) to describe positive extremes in African languages, e.g., Mandingo (Bambara) *a ka nyi ko-jugu,* "it's very good" (literally, "it is good badly"), or Mandingo (Gambia) *a nyi-nata jaw-ke,* "she is very beautiful" (lit. "she is beautiful wickedly"); similarly black West African English (Sierra Leone) *i gud baad,* "it's very good." (Dalby 177)

These Mandingo usages are duplicated in the language of the Igbo (Ibo) people of southeastern Nigeria, as in the statement:

> *O-mara nkirinka mma:* She is a woman of extraordinary beauty (*lit.* she is raggedly beautiful).

Or in the following praise names:

> *Uhoro/Aghugho:* Hip, street-smart, clever guy (*lit.* trickster, artful dodger, slippery fish)

> *Ihe Ojo-o Eji Ose Eri:* Man of Power, Supreme, Indomitable (*lit.* evil thing that must be eaten with hot pepper)

Afo Ojo-o: Man of War, Captain Guts, Commander-in-Chief
   (*lit.* bad belly) (Echewa 203)

Anu Ojo-o: Tough Guy, Clever Woman, "Thick Madam" (*lit.*
   evil animal)

Ototo-o/Nta Muu-Muu: His Majesty, His Awesomeness, the
   Lord of Power (*lit.* monster, ogre, bogeyman) (Echewa
   203)

Ofia Nsii: Evil Forest (*lit.* poison forest); the awesome
   Masked Guardian of the Nation, representative of Divine
   Power (as in Chinua Achebe's *Things Fall Apart* 85–89)

Equivalent usages exist in other West African languages.

Obscenity

Now let us consider those words traditionally regarded as vulgar and obscene:
shit, ass, fuck, motherfucker, etc. These words perform a critical function in the
staging of the drama of modern African-American folklore, and to exclude them
is to shut off part of the tradition's life-giving oxygen. Whereas the flipping of
such terms as *bad, terrible, evil, wicked* and *mean* involves the simultaneous
inversion and retention of meaning, the obscene and vulgar words carry with
them a complex of meanings: each is capable of carrying (sometimes simulta-
neously) the conventional meaning, usually negative; an opposite meaning, which
is positive; a neutral meaning; and a variety of meanings with varying degrees
of negative, positive and neutral, plus a range of emotions and attitudes. Again,
meaning is sometimes dependent on *tone* and *inflection.* Consider the following
examples where the word is used either for primal naming or as an intensifier:

Take your *fuckin* hands off me!   *Negative:* anger

Don't *fuck* with me!   *Negative:* anger

What the *shit* / What the *fuck*   *Negative:* anger
   you think you doing?

Up against the wall, *mother-*   *Negative:* anger, contempt, hate
fucker!

Run, *motherfucker,* run!   *Positive:* affection—a nine-year-old
   to his playmate at stickball
   Negative: same child to same play-
   mate (anger and frustration
   at losing)
   Neutral: football coach to player

Soon as I get my *shit* together	*Neutral: my shit* is my belongings, my act, plan, show, program (cf. Yoruba: *kpanti* [*lit.* trash] = my belongings)
	Negative: self-deprecation—I who have nothing to speak of, I and my raggedy-assed possessions, not worth a damn
That brother's got his *shit* together!	*Positive:* admiration—he is smart, well organized, knows what he's doing, what he's talking about; he's in full control
Nigger, you ain't *shit!*	*Negative:* anger, contempt, defiance— you're nothing, worse than nothing, beneath contempt, and if you don't think so just fool with me, I'll crack your skull, nigger!
It don't mean *shit*	*Neutral:* it's nothing, it's unimportant, nothing to worry yourself about; don't lose any sleep over it

In their close study of the varied meanings of the word *motherfucker,* Nathan and Joanne Kantrowitz write:

> Used alone, as in "He's a motherfucker," the word never has a spe-
> cific meaning, but depends on inflection, facial expression, gesture,
> and context to express extreme distaste or extreme admiration.
> Syllable stress controls the amount of emotional "charge" or "volt-
> age." When used alone, the degree of stress on the first or third syl-
> lable is an index of the emotion—the heavier the stress, the more
> emotion. Emphasis on the first syllable is usually complimentary;
> on the third, it expresses contempt, anger or hostility. Thus, in
> context, the term expresses the highest praise—"Is he smart?"
> "He's a MOtherfucker"—or conversely, the deepest disdain—"Is
> he a deadbeat?" "He's a motherFUcker." (Kantrowitz and Kantro-
> witz 350)

They then proceed to list and demonstrate fourteen adjectives (*good, bad, sweet, fine, rotten, stupid, phoney, dirty, stinking, jive, jazzy, mean, rough, tough*— there are more!) that when hooked with *motherfucker,* and again depending on tone, inflection and context, will produce a vast array of nuanced meanings (Kantrowitz and Kantrowitz 350–352).

The word *nigger* itself, considered a true obscenity by many, is used in its conventional meanings (negative, or neutral) by both blacks and whites; but in addition, it is used by blacks to convey the absolute in positive meanings— as a term of affection between relatives and friends, and of tenderness between lovers. Claude Brown has called it "the most soulful word in the world," a word with "many shades of meaning [and] a unique sentiment . . . exemplified in the frequent—and perhaps even excessive—usage of the term to denote either fondness or hostility" (C. Brown 232):

Lord, how can one *nigger* be so hard to please?	*Positive:* affection, puzzlement, resignation
Nigger, you gonna be the death o' me!	*Negative:* exasperation
He's my *nigger*	*Positive:* affection; he's my best friend (Woman: he's my man) (C. Brown 232)

Or, as one fond father said to his young son, "You my nigger if you don't get no bigger" (McPherson 8).

That these words carry such a burden of complex meanings does not make them any more acceptable in polite company. Quite often they are used deliberately to shock, to register alienation and iconoclasm. Indeed, part of their power, and their virtually limitless potential for generating humor in this literature, comes from the electrifying contact between their rough and ready vulgarity and the smooth, polite fictive milieux in which they are so frequently detonated. A fine example from our text ("Bad Manners") is the putatively polite setting of the classroom in which Little Johnny knocks his cookies and milk to the floor and says to the teacher: "I don't want none of that shit!" The teacher goes into culture shock. More shaken by the language than the act of disobedience itself, she sends for Johnny's mother, who merely compounds her shock by declaring: "If he don't want none, fuck him!" Then there's Little Willie ("Correct English"), who refuses to use the polite term "rectum" to indicate what part of the man's anatomy collided with the truck: "Rectum, my ass! He damn near killed the motherfucker!"

As with the milking of new meanings from old English words through complex inversions, the obscene and vulgar words so common in African-American popular discourse turn out, upon examination, to be common West African usages greatly intensified and molded into jagged, combative formations in the fiery crucibles of the diaspora. Again, examples abound in the language of the Igbo, in their living speech as well as in transliterations by their novelists. In Igbo popular discourse as well as in the formal rhetoric, scatological and sexual references are employed with astonishing frequency, in a casual, unself-conscious manner carrying neither *inhibition* nor *prurience,* and with an equivalent complexity of attitudes and emotions as in African-American popular discourse. There are dialectal and regional variations, certainly, but the phenomenon itself is universal in Igboland.

A few samples from daily usage:

Ri-e nshi! / Ri-e shi! / Ra-a shi! / Ra-a nsi!: Eat shit!

Rigbu-e onwe gi na nshi!: Go to hell! / Go jump in the lake! (*lit.* eat yourself to death with shit!)

I-n'eri nshi!: You're a stupid idiot! / You're full of shit! (*lit.* you eat shit)

A-rasila-m nsi!: Don't insult me! / Don't give me that shit! (*lit.* don't eat that shit near me / don't eat shit in my presence)

O-na ara-ta nsi ike: He/she is a goddam fool / is brash, rude, insolent, full of himself, thinks she is clever (*lit.* he/she eats shit a lot)

Nsi adighi gi na-afo: You're a weakling (*lit.* you don't have shit in your stomach = there's no strength in you. *Compare Ebonics:* you can't do nothin'! / you can't do shit! / you ain't got shit! / you ain't shit!)

Nsi adighi-m na-afo: I feel weak, I don't have an ounce of strength (*lit.* I don't have shit in my stomach = I'm very hungry, I haven't had a thing to eat)

In the deep exchange and synthesis of language and culture-ways that took place among stranger-Africans thrown together in the Americas, it is not too difficult to imagine how the Igbo *nsi, nshi* or *shi,* which just happens to coincide in both sound and meaning with the English *shit,* might have become a staple of African-American speech, serving both for common discourse and for vituperation.

Closely allied to *shit* is *ass.* These two words rank ahead of all others as the omnibus word, the word-of-all-works in all Ebonics. *Get your ass over here. Set your black ass down. I'ma beat your ass. Being Captain's good, while it lasts / But if you can't swim, that's your ass. Money good but money don't last / Shine gotta save his own black ass. When I get through with your goddam face / They're going to kick your damn ass out of the monkey race. If you'll let me get my left nut out of the sand / I'll fight your ass like a natural man / I'll fight your big ass as best I could. They drug his ass out of the sun and laid him in the shade / The animals walked by and viewed his ass like GIs on parade.*

This usage is almost certainly of Igbo origin; if not exclusively so, at least one of its roots is traceable to the peculiar dialect of the Niger Delta Igbo of Ndoki, Akwete, Opobo and Bonny. Instead of the personal pronoun *mu* (I, me), the Delta Igbo use the term *ike-mu* (my buttocks / my ass), and instead of *gi* (you), they say *ike-gi* (your ass):

> *Ike-gi na-akakari anya! Ike-mu na ike-gi anyi bu ogbo?* You
> are very bold and disrespectful! Do you think you are my
> equal? (*lit. Your ass* is very bold and disrespectful. *My
> ass* and *your ass* are they age-mates?)

Among the Igbo, these usages are greeted with laughter, especially by those hearing them for the first time, and speakers of that dialect are teased continuously. Chinua Achebe, the great novelist and scholar of Igbo culture, captures the fun in *Things Fall Apart*. A white missionary has arrived at the village of Mbanta, bringing an Igbo interpreter from the Delta:

> When they had all gathered, the white man began to speak to
> them. He spoke through an interpreter who was an Ibo man,
> though his dialect was different and harsh to the ears of Mbanta.
> Many people laughed at his dialect and the way he used words
> strangely. Instead of saying "myself" he always said "my buttocks."
> But he was a man of commanding presence and the clansmen
> listened to him. . . .
> "Your buttocks understand our language," said someone light-
> heartedly and the crowd laughed. (Achebe, *Things* 134–135)

Then the interpreter spoke of "Jesu Kristi," who he said was "the Son of God." A villager queries him:

> "You told us with your own mouth that there was only one god.
> Now you talk about his son. He must have a wife, then." The crowd
> agreed.
> "I did not say He had a wife," said the interpreter, somewhat
> lamely.
> "Your buttocks said he had a son," said the joker. "So he must
> have a wife and all of them must have buttocks." (Achebe, *Things*
> 136–137)

How did this laughable exception on the mother continent become the rule in the settlements on this side of the ocean? How did this lowly part of the anatomy, elevated to personhood in a comical synecdoche in a remote corner of Igboland, come to usurp the African-American kingdom? The Delta was the corridor through which virtually all Igbo captives passed onto the Middle Passage. The Delta dialect was, as it were, the last word they heard on the Motherland. Was it also *the word* they best remembered? And just think: if Louis XIV spoke Ebonics, *l'etat, c'est moi* would have been something else! . . .

Vulgar and obscene references appear in the most unexpected places in Igbo discourse. In his novel *No Longer at Ease,* Chinua Achebe inserted the following authorial gloss on the unfairness of life:

Ibo people, in their fairmindedness, have devised a proverb which says that it is not right to ask a man with elephantiasis of the scrotum to take on small pox as well, when thousands of other people have not had even their share of small diseases. No doubt it is not right. But it happens. "Na so dis world be," they say. (Achebe, *No Longer* 97)

Elephantiasis of the scrotum is entirely in context with the matter under discussion in the novel, and quite consistent with Igbo rhetoric—but unexpected, and *shocking* all the same.

Just as unexpected though considerably less unpleasant is an example from Achebe's short story "Vengeful Creditor." Mr. and Mrs. Emenike have lost several servants to the free primary education program. Now the gardener too has come to give notice.

> Mr. Emenike tried to laugh him out of this ridiculous piece of village ignorance.
>
> "Free primary education is for children. Nobody is going to admit an old man like you. How old are you?"
>
> "I am fifteen years of old, sir."
>
> "You are three," sneered Mrs. Emenike. "Come and suck breast." (Achebe, *Girls* 53)

Come and suck breast! Just like that? Unthinkable in a British or Anglo-American prose fiction of just about any period!

One way of measuring size or strength among the Igbo is to place the object or person on a sexual scale, that is, to gauge his/her/its ability or inability to perform mature sexual or reproductive duties. Thus:

> *O-si-ghi nne:* He/she/it is very small (*lit.* it can't mount a female; is not big or strong enough to fuck a mother/ woman. *Nne* means *female; full-grown woman; mother.* The verb *si-e* is specific to animals *mounting* their female, but its use in assessing size/strength/capability is extended to humans and all other objects, organic and inorganic)

> *I-toruo-la itunye nwanyi ime!:* You're old enough to impregnate a woman! (a common rebuke to a boy: Behave yourself. You're no longer a child. Don't you know you're old enough to impregnate a woman?)

The Igbo casualness of sexual reference is replicated by the neighboring Yoruba. A boy of comparable age (pre-adolescent, sexually innocent) refuses to run an errand for his older brother's wife. She says to him (even in her husband's presence): *Ti o ko ba jise, fun mi, o ku eniti o ba sun l'ale yi!* If you don't run errands for me, we'll see who will sleep with you tonight! One

Yoruba woman would say to another, casually and sometimes to the hearing of children, her own included: Yours is a small problem compared to mine. *Ohun ti ndo mi nisinsinyi ju oko lo!* What is fucking me now is bigger than a penis! And the Muslims and Christians would exchange playful abuses and lewd jokes on each other's imported religion. All-night Christian vigils evoked this song:

> *Eni ma gbo ti Jesu*
> *Ko ko'di s'oke*
> *A jo ma ba'ra wa sun*
> *T'oju ma i mo kedere*
> *Obo lukuta, oko l'onlo.*

(Those who want to follow Jesus / Must put their asses up / We're going to fuck / All night long / Big vaginas and long penises.)

Sexual references invariably point to the mother. What is surprising is not that the mother is so frequently drawn into the fray (even when studiously avoided, she is always in a closet nearby); what is surprising is that the mother is handled with so much *disrespect.*

Achebe introduces the mother in a comic sally in *No Longer at Ease.* A little boy selling *akara* on the street sees a night-soilman "swinging his broom and hurricane lamp and trailing clouds of putrefaction."

> The boy quickly sprang to his feet and began calling him names. The man made for him with his broom but the boy was already in flight. . . . The night-soilman smiled and went his way, having said something very rude about the boy's mother. (Achebe, *No Longer* 23)

As he plies the roads from market to market, the titular hero of Achebe's short story "The Madman" ruminates on the insults he has suffered—from children "who threw stones at him and made fun of their mothers' nakedness, not his own," and from the lorry driver and his mate who slapped and pushed him off the road saying "their lorry very nearly ran over their mother, not him" (Achebe, *Girls* 2).

The madman's references to the mother are casual and off-handed, nothing as sharp or wounding, presumably, as the night-soilman's measured thrust. A close encounter with his filthy broom would have taught the boy to pinch his nose and shut his mouth, but saying something *very rude* about the boy's mother is evidently vengeance sweet enough to smile. What very rude thing did he say that gave the night-soilman such grinning satisfaction? Let's play hide and seek for a moment. Achebe has "hidden" the answer in a subsequent novel, *A Man of the People.* In a famous scene in an African legislature, the Minister of Finance, "a first-rate economist with a Ph.D. in public finance," is vilified for counseling austerity and other commonsensical solutions to the nation's economic woes. An orgy of abuse is rained on his head:

The entire house, including the Prime Minister, tried to shout him down. It was a most unedifying spectacle. The Speaker broke his mallet ostensibly trying to maintain order, but you could see he was enjoying the commotion. The public gallery yelled down its abuses. "Traitor," "Coward," "Doctor of Fork your Mother." This last was contributed from the gallery by the editor of the *Daily Chronicle,* who sat close to me. Encouraged, no doubt, by the volume of laughter this piece of witticism had earned him from the gallery he proceeded the next morning to print it in his paper. The spelling is his. (Achebe, *Man* 6)

The reference to the mother is remarkable enough for the author to isolate it for comment, probably because it appears in an abnormal context—a legislative chamber run on alien, pan-European protocols (more on this later). The scene nevertheless yields up our answer: the night-soilman heaped specifically sexual insults on the boy's mother, or charged him with incest. Among the Igbo, it could be the simple epithet: *Nne gi!* Your mother! / Yo' mama! Or *Ikpu nne gi!* Your mother's vagina! Or *O-ra nne ya!* Fucker of his mother! Mother-fucker!

Among the Efik or Ibibio (neighbors to the Igbo), it could be *Eyen ntime nsene!* Child of mixed sperm! (i.e., conceived by "more than one father") (Simmons 340). Or the infamous line *Ituru eka afo mmuo-mmuo!* Your mother's vagina is full of water! (is loose, flabby, watery).

Under extreme provocation the Yoruba might say: *Ab'obo'ya gbeko mi tewetewe!* You, whose mother's vagina is big enough to swallow a whole corn meal together with its wrapper! Or: *L'abe odan, oro ndo'ye fa!* Under the tree shade the tree monster is fucking your mother! One Igbo man might say to another: *Hey! Rapu-m aka! . . . Gini ka m-mere gi? . . . M-rara nne gi?* Leave me alone! . . . What did I do to you? . . . Did I fuck your mother? And the Fulani of Mauretania, enraged, would declare: *Jooni mi hoowa yumma!* I am going to fuck your mother!

In a remarkable scene in *Guelwaar,* a film by the great Senegalese novelist and filmmaker Ousmane Sembene, two tides of angry men are fighting over a dead man, a Christian mistakenly buried in a Muslim cemetery. The Christians are determined to open the grave and retrieve the body; the Muslims are determined to prevent such an abomination. They rush at each other. In desperation, a venerable elder freezes the stampeding hordes with a single word: *Hold it! Stop!! If you make another move I'll fuck your mother!!!* So potent is the word.

Scholars have stumbled on similar usages elsewhere on the continent. In the early 1900s, British ethnographer Dudley Kidd found them in Southern Africa:

Boys of the same age tease one another by well-known methods. One boy will say to another, "Your mother is an ugly old thing";

"Your people are all witches and wizards"; "Your mother is a crow," and so on. Strange to say, they do not tease one another much about their fathers, nor about their sisters. The great insults centre round speaking evil of the mother and grandmother. (Kidd 198)

Philip Mayer found them in East Africa in "joking relationships" among the Gusii of Kenya:

The true measure of the unique unrestraint of pals and the climax of their intimacy is to exchange pornographic references to the other's mother and particularly to impute that he would be prepared for incestuous relations with her. "Eat your mother's anus!" is a specimen of this kind, or even the direct "copulate with your mother!" . . .

Though the essence of the relation is that pals do not take each other's insults seriously, it may be part of the fun to pretend to be offended and make some appropriate retort. (Mayer 33)

These usages in popular discourse as well as modern fiction serve to confirm what scholars have long suspected, namely, that African-American dozens has its roots in Africa.

But scholars have also noted parallel usages in Europe and Asia. In his encyclopedic study of scatological and sexual humor, *Rationale of the Dirty Joke* (1968, 1975), G. Legman speculates that African-American dozens might have derived from sexual-insult exchanges in British folk traditions, especially from the "flytings" of Anglo-Scottish bards and the "water wit" of Thames River boatmen of the seventeenth and eighteenth centuries. But he quickly abandons this proposition in view of the weighty countervailing evidence of parallel traditions not only on the African continent but among other non-Western peoples. These include the *poele* or "gross insult" among the Mono people of the Solomon Islands; the Russian "ultimate-insult," which translates "Go fuck your mother"; the mother-sex insult exchange in the works of the Arab rhetorician Al-Jahiz (d. 869 A.D.); and the Turco-Mongolian "grand curses": "Father-killer" and "I urinate on your father's head and have intercourse with your mother" (Legman 1: 171–175). Legman does not suggest (nor, to date, is there textual evidence to suggest) that these or any other traditions of insult-exchange anywhere in the world approach the intensity, complexity, sophistication, pervasiveness and durability of the African-American dozens. Not even the continental African originals can compare.

But why all the *disrespec*ː of the mother? Why these copious references to violation of the mother through seduction, rape or incest—a slew of offenses on which is constructed a whole art form? Is it that what we hold most sacred we vilify—a testimony to deepest ambivalence?

There are two fundamental offenses that human societies have universally tabooed from time immemorial, and it is not clear which should rank first and worst—incest, or the shedding of blood of one's kin. Incest, especially involving the mother, might well in childhood be the primal (male) desire, therefore the deepest (male) fear. And one way to overcome fear is to meet it frontally: embrace the horror, acknowledge it, accommodate it by conscious will; bring it into the open, play with it, consider the possibility, then reject it, trivialize it, make a joke of it, extinguish it with laughter.

A mother's intimate embrace is the child's source of all comfort. To grow and mature is gradually to disengage from that embrace. Boys in particular must be detached neatly and rapidly from the physical and psychological embrace of the mother (and, later, of wives and other mother-surrogates) in order to create space to learn and perform the necessarily hard, sometimes cruel duties imposed on them as guardians of the nation (this is not the place to debate the merits of patriarchy). For boys, then, disengagement may be more like a violent wrenching away.

Every society has invented formulas for enabling the detachment process— a mixed bag of tricks and treats, bribes and threats, sanctions and rewards to bring the young boy to the desired state of feeling. One of the most powerful tricks is to wave before the child the specter of incest, accompanied with prophecies of doom, as in the Efik: *obukpo ana etime ekporo emi abuande ekporo ye eka*—"rottenness will affect the penis which is used in intercourse with the mother" (Simmons 340). It is a preemptive strike against something the child, up to that point, knows little or nothing about. Typically, the agent is a playmate who may be older and bolder but not necessarily worldly-wiser, and the good opinion of one's peers, especially in such confusing, secret matters, is everything.

To be accused is immediately and unequivocally to deny. And denial will follow denial until the child gets in the game and learns to counter-accuse. From then on, it is forward ever, backward never. The twig has been bent—and so will the tree. Imputation of incest, in face of the severe taboo, is society's backhanded way of enforcing detachment. In effect, the child is told: look how you huff and puff and sweat and carry on at an accusation that the accuser and everyone else knows is *false.* How do you think you would feel, what would you do, how could you live *if it were true?* It is reverse psychology applied on a massive scale, a classically simple trick of acculturation or brainwashing, foolproof and fail-safe.

African-American dozens culture represents a circumstantial, culture-specific instance of this remarkable pan-African heritage of male-child rearing. On these western shores, the black male child has needed not only to disengage emotionally from the mother (that, as we have seen, is easy enough), but to stay alive, and sane, in the face of what is done to his mother. In the African homeland, those painted scenes of abuse of the mother were mostly that— painted scenes, unreal, conjured up as a means to preempt and prevent their actualization. But here in the Americas, under slavery, the imagined became real, and the real a nightmare.

Harriet Jacobs long ago set it down as an axiom, that "Slavery is terrible for men; but it is far more terrible for women" (Jacobs 405). Who could possibly argue? The women labored as long and hard in the fields as the men, and suffered the lash with equal virulence. In addition, they were sexually abused, and, to compound the horror, their offspring were snatched and sold away.

Of course, as Toni Morrison has reminded us, the men were sometimes raped by gay white men (Morrison 107–108). Nasty the experience, no matter how small the numbers. But this was not the source of the deepest black male anguish. Far more devastating was the fact that black men stood helpless while white slave traders, slave owners and overseers raped their sisters, sweethearts, wives and *mothers* again and again. Unable to object, strike a blow, or *kill the motherfucker!* What traumas did such radical impotence *not* inflict on the psyche, on the manhood and self-respect? *Powerless to protect his loved ones— that is the ultimate black male nightmare!*

Jacobs provides a glimpse of this male trauma:

> I felt humiliated that my brother should stand by, and listen to such language as would be addressed only to a slave. Poor boy! He was powerless to defend me; but I saw the tears, which he vainly strove to keep back. (Jacobs 391)

Grier and Cobbs state the matter this way:

> By law no slave husband could protect his wife from physical and sexual abuse at the hands of a white man. By law no slave mother could protect her child against physical and sexual abuse at the hands of a white man. (Grier and Cobbs, *Black Rage* 69)

The two psychiatrists paint an equally grim picture of things as they are today:

> The black family [today] cannot protect its members. Nowhere in the United States can the black family extend an umbrella of protection over its members in the way that a white family can. In every part of the nation its members are subjected to physical and verbal abuse, humiliation, unlawful search and seizure, and harassment by authorities. Its members are jailed, beaten, robbed, killed, and raped, and exposed to this kind of jeopardy to a degree unheard of in white families. Thus the black family is prevented from performing its most essential function—its *raison d'etre*—protection of its members. (Grier and Cobbs, *Black Rage* 68)

The African-American male has therefore had to achieve *detachment* of a higher, deeper, tougher quality than his cousin in the homeland, or his counterparts elsewhere in the world. He must not only embrace the horror; he must chew and swallow it, let it work from the inside, tightening the guts, thickening the skin, steeling the bones, petrifying the emotions—and at the same time block the poison from callusing the soul and rendering the total person anar-chic, suicidal, or dead.

How has the African-American male, over the harsh centuries, managed to approximate this tall order? By what routes did he achieve this survival process, this process of pushing back the crushers and enabling the spirit to fly free? The role of music, of religion, and of the affirming sense of community, both in slavery and after, has long been recognized and documented. Now, more recently, the masculine street-game culture of the urban communities has been added to the repertory of protections. When restive youth are corralled into hallways, street corners, playgrounds and bars, the scene is set for the dozens to bloom from bud to flower.

While retaining the form and spirit of the West African original, African-American dozens has elaborated the witty one-liners into complex verbal war games involving huge armories and modes of attack and defense undreamt of in the homeland. It is a case of Darwinian adaptation for survival of the species in the killing jungles of slavery and racism. The mother remains the central figure. By learning to deal with verbal abuse of her, the modern black young-ster learns to endure the historical, real-life abuse. It is as if the system is inoc-ulated with virtual (verbally imagined) strains of the virus, thereby gaining immunity and new health in spite of the reality on the ground.

Grier and Cobbs have suggested that the dozens "introduces the boy to stoi-cism as a requirement of manhood. It insists that he understand that humili-ation may be the texture of his life, but states also that manhood can transcend such onslaught" (Grier and Cobbs, *Jesus* 9).

It is not clear just when or how the relatively limited adolescent African game of sexual-insult exchange burgeoned into the spectacular bloom that is the dozens. But given the unique historical and social environment in which that transformation took place, it is almost certain that African-American dozens is unique, a one-and-only, in world literature. (More on the dozens later.)

In summary, then, the discursive ease with which sex and scatology are han-dled in the cultures and languages of the West African homeland is replicated in African-American culture, so much so that it is virtually definitive of the pop-ular discourse. Parallel instances in the usages of other African peoples on this side of the Atlantic are, similarly, New World updates of ancient (and still con-temporary) usages of the African homeland. When viewed in this light, the phenomenon of vulgarity and obscenity becomes far less startling.

It is now widely acknowledged that American culture is an amalgam mainly of European and African cultures (Native Americans were so systematically excluded and near-exterminated that their overall input is far lower). Ameri-can music consists of the dominant African-American music and its Anglo-American derivatives, plus, more recently, Afro-Latin music of the Hispanic communities. And American English contains large doses of African-American language or Ebonics. In short, white Americans may be transplanted Europeans, but the telling difference between their culture and that of their European motherland is the African real presence.[2]

Ebonics has exerted enormous influence on American popular usage, and some of its vocabulary and styles of expression have become part of standard, formal English. But on the whole, the *formal* written and spoken forms of American English have stuck close to the British originals. *Motherfucker* will not be read in the *New York Times* nor *shit* heard on the floor of the Congress, and *nigger* hasn't been seen or heard in either place for some time. By the 1990s, even in academic settings, the brash sincerity of the 1960s and 1970s had been displaced by a decorous "political correctness" that speaks coyly of "the N-word," "the B-word," "the F-word," and so on. However, out on the street, behind closed doors or among friends, middle-class Americans of all races are just as free and voluble with their vulgarities as any *blood* in the *'hood.* American presidents in particular are notorious for their "colorful language" once closeted with their aides and out of public earshot, but snippets still manage to seep through the listening walls. The most exhaustive record, of course, is the "expletives deleted" from transcripts of Richard Nixon's tapes. And the corporate culture mirrors the political. As one company executive put it, "We met behind closed doors. Voices were raised, and the king's English was abused" (*Newsweek* 42). Abuse of the king's English has been going on in America for ages. The king's linguistic and other property has not been correct around here since way before 1776, and the African presence has had something to do with it.

Every language has its rules of propriety. The overarching prudery of the English language renders inadmissible in polite or formal settings those scatological and sexual references that are perfectly appropriate in the formal rhetoric of the Igbo and other West African peoples and their New World descendants. Middle-class African Americans, growing up bicultural and bilingual, understand the rules and would select their language accordingly. But this is not quite the case with Africans reared in the homeland. Which explains why someone would shout "Doctor of Fork your Mother!" on the floor of an African legislature, where the language and context render it inappropriate, and then compound his gaffe by printing it in the newspaper the next day.

For Africans reared in the homeland but living abroad, the habit of discursive ease with sex and scatology can prove just as treacherous. Once upon a time, and not so long ago, an African scholar, blithely unmindful of the puritan restraints of the English language, and forgetful of time, place and circumstance, concluded his remarks before a professional body in the United States by evoking a time-honored Igbo proverb: "As our people say, when several people urinate on the same spot, it foams" (*Ndi ebe anyi kwuru okwu si, na anyuko-o mamiri ofu ebe, ogbo-o ufufu*). This was his way of celebrating the intellectual ferment (steaming, foaming) he had witnessed at the conference just concluded. As we have seen, this proverb would have been alright at a gathering of Igbos (or Africans generally), or in a story or play set in traditional or modern Africa. However, at an international gathering of scholars or any other formal or polite occasion in the pan-European world, it registers as vulgar and obscene. Such a setting condemns it as language-inappropriate, a case of failed culture-translation and context-transfer.

Which of course is not to say that every demand of a language must be met at all times in all places. If that were the case, we would not have Chinua Achebe's hugely successful and justly celebrated experiments with the English language; nor, for that matter, would African-American English or Ebonics exist, nor the other pan-African creoles. African Americans must of course learn and use "standard English" for any number of reasons, not least of which is economic survival; but really, at the creation of Ebonics, pan-European preferences and norms, whether linguistic, moral or social, had no relevance, no *locus standi,* no presence. Not a thought was wasted on them, nor a backward glance.

LEARNING AND PERFORMING

In attempting to understand their generic interrelationships, the modern forms of African-American oral literature may legitimately be considered from two points of view—in terms of a chronological or real-life progression, and of a dynamic movement or ideal progression. The *chronological real-life progression* would place the various forms in a developmental line corresponding to the life-line from childhood to adulthood, with each form at once anticipating the forms to come and incorporating the forms that went before it—from *children's rhymes* (pre-adolescence) to *rapping, signifying, boasts, threats* and *dozens* (early and middle adolescence) to *toasts* (high school years, late teens and adulthood). The progression is from the simpler to the more sophisticated and complex, paralleling the chronological age of the performers. The more complex forms, insofar as they may be said to exist at all in the early years, exist as the most rudimentary and tentative of presences.

For instance, in early childhood the dozens usually take the form of simple identifications of the mother with some object that is sometimes objectionable for no other reason than that it is *other* ("Your mother is a tree!" or a house, a coconut, a telephone, etc.). The children's rhymes of later childhood are, in a sense, extensions and elaborations of the nursery rhymes learned in early childhood. Children's rhymes provide exercise in development of vocabulary, construction of sentences, and duplication of rhythms and sounds. These skills are carried over into the parallel phrasing and symmetrical, balanced constructions of rapping, signifying, boasts, threats and dozens. Sophistication of language and idea in these latter forms comes during the adolescent, junior high school years, approximately age eleven to sixteen, which is also the age of sexual discovery. That sophistication of language is later incorporated into the abrasive dialogues and sustained narrative flow of the mature toasts, beginning with the high school years. *Jokes,* like the other forms, would begin in rudimentary forms in the early years and follow the same developmental arc.

The *ideal progression* would arrange the forms into a synthetic drama of dynamic movement (prologue and exposition, complication and development, climax, resolution) whereby each form would lead, logically and inexorably, into the next, with increasing intensity. Thus, any given occasion (a casual gathering in the playground, barber shop, street corner or corner bar, or a social evening, a stage presentation, etc.) might open with the uncomplicated verses and clever parodies of *children's rhymes* (prologue and exposition), then build up into the exhibition of verbal artistry and the emotional engagement of *rapping, signifying, boasts, threats* and *dozens* (complication and development). Initially self-centered and self-directed, the ego-tripping of rapping and signifying easily spills over into the self-praise of boasts, which comes with its dialectical complement—the denigration of others: for the accomplished and assured self stands best in relief against nonentities ("I'm the main man, but *you* ain't shit!"). The implied or expressed hostility of boasts intensifies into a fiery exchange of dozens and threats, bringing the occasion to its climax. From this point, the dramatic resolution would have to be either a violent physical confrontation between the contending parties (a true catastrophe), or an adroit and timely deflection of aggression into the urbane recitation of *toasts*.

The telling of toasts throws a magic net of mellowness, ease and community over the gathering, skillfully weaving for their entertainment and admiration the shorter and earlier forms—children's rhymes, rapping, signifying, boasts, threats and dozens—into a spectacular tapestry of immense color and drama. The toast replaces the sharp, witty, aggressive repartee of the dozens and threats with a leisurely and friendly exhibition of narrative memory, descriptive detail, and prosodic virtuosity, and the raucous catalysts and provocateurs who constitute the dozens audience are replaced with a quiescent, attentive audience whose mature taste is for a tale well told.

From the healthy resolution of toast telling, the occasion may then modulate into an epilogue of prose *tales* and *jokes*—shorter forms, less demanding than toasts, in which the lesser skilled might play key roles. Toasts are, in one sense, a specialized brand of the broader genres of tales and jokes. Tales and jokes, like the other shorter forms, may be viewed as rehearsals for toasts, the most elaborate of the modern oral forms. However, one may excel in the shorter forms but never develop the skill for toasts, whereas a good toast teller would almost invariably be a master of the shorter forms.

CHILDREN'S RHYMES AND GAME SONGS

We might begin our consideration of children's rhymes and game songs by taking account of the work of two couples, one British, the other Anglo-American, whose ground-breaking studies, each on their side of the Atlantic, have in the past three decades helped define the genre of children's folklore, or childlore, illuminating its surprisingly rich and lengthy history as well as the contemporary contexts of its flowering.

Childlore is unique in that it is almost entirely child generated and child transmitted. As Iona and Peter Opie and Mary and Herbert Knapp have stated, childlore constitutes a separate, autonomous universe, parallel to and independent of adult folklore, duplicating elements of adult folklore such as jokes, riddles, sex lore, praises and abuses, superstitions, and games, but operating quite beyond the control and sometimes even the awareness of adults. The Opies open their study of British children, *The Lore and Language of School-children* (1959), in these words: "The scraps of lore which children learn from each other are at once more real, more immediately serviceable, and more vastly entertaining to them than anything which they learn from grown-ups" (Opie and Opie 1). The point is accentuated in the subtitle of the Knapps' *One Potato Two Potato ...: The Secret Education of American Children* (1976). Childlore, they argue, is an instrument of self-education: "in the unsupervised nooks and crannies of their lives ... children learn what no one can teach them" (Knapp and Knapp 9).

The main literary vehicle of this "secret education," the signature form of childlore, is the rhymed verse (variously termed *school rhymes, children's rhymes, game songs*). These rhymes are distinct from conventional nursery rhymes. Nursery rhymes are verses composed by adults, written down and transmitted in written form over the decades or centuries, and used in written form by adults for the amusement and education of children. Children's rhymes, on the other hand, are verses composed by children, to be recited or sung, sometimes to accompany a specific game or activity such as hop-scotch, jump rope, ball bouncing, running and chasing games, or even the process of choosing sides to play a game. The distinguishing features of these rhymes are their *orality* and *exclusivity:* they are composed by children for children, are exclusively used by children, and are disseminated among children orally. "While a nursery rhyme passes from a mother or other adult to the small child on her knee, the school rhyme circulates simply from child to child, usually outside the home, and beyond the influence of the family circle" (Opie and Opie 1).

Children's rhymes may be contemporary creations, or they may be decades or even centuries old, but they are transmitted from child to child down the generations. Even if they get written down at some point by ethnographers or folklorists, the children who use them are often unaware of that fact and may not necessarily consult the written text.

However, the case for separateness and autonomy of childlore is very nearly overstated by the Opies and Knapps. Children do indeed learn much of their lore from one another, but they also learn a great deal of it from adults. Just as they learn by playing at being adults—playing house, playing doctor, trying on their parents' (oversized) clothes and shoes—so do they *sound on* adult lore (as they heard or misheard it) to create their own. Between children and adults an inexorable dialectic is at work—in lore as in life. Children's verses are chock-full of imitations and parodies both of adult lore and adult life. These include conscious parodies of written texts—of well-known adult-generated poems, prayers, religious songs, popular songs, and nursery rhymes. Again, the texts parodied may be of recent vintage, or they may be very old, but as long as they are accessible to children they become grist for the creative mills of the playground.

In childlore, as seen in our text, the one ingredient that is conspicuously missing from the children's attitude to things adult—conspicuous only in that adults might foolishly have expected it—is a sense of humility or smallness. Quite the contrary, the children's defiant self-assurance is almost palpable; their irreverence fairly explodes in your face. They maintain a critical, even mocking regard for the adult social world, its history and politics and manners.

These observations are as applicable to Anglo-American or British as to African-American childlore. For one thing, there is considerable overlap between children's verses from these three cultures, thanks to a relentless cross-cultural traffic that in our time has attained digital speed. However, our concern is not with sources or paths of transmission, nor with borrowings especially as between European and African elements. Rather, we shall treat these verses *as given,* as played and replayed and *culturally stamped* by African-American children, particularly in the urban North.

Now, to our text. A study of two variants of the same verse will underline one of the basic technical characteristics of children's verses:

See My Heart	**See My Pinky**
See my heart	See my pinky
Gee, you're smart	See my thumb
See my thumb	See my fist
Gee, you're dumb	You better run

In "See My Heart" the rhyme is fortuitous, expedient, leading nowhere, dissociated from rational meaning. By contrast, "See My Pinky" is a purposeful progression, tightly packed as in a riddle, building up to a climax, issuing in a sharp surprise.

How can two brief verses on the same frame differ so widely? "See My Heart" is marked by over-anxiety and lack of assurance; the *rhyme* is the thing—the speaker must get to the rhyme at all costs, before it slips away and the verse flops. Having achieved the first couplet, then, the neophyte rhymester congratulates himself and goes on to show off his new talents. Unsurprisingly, his second couplet is as unaccomplished as the first. Except for their harmonious sounds, the words make no connected sense. (However, it is possible to read the poem, out of context, as a plea for fellow-feeling that sees beyond the physical and external.)

It is in "See My Pinky" that we find the beginnings of sophistication in the manipulation of words. Here, it is the idea, the *sense* and not the *sound,* that is dominant. And that sense includes an appreciation both of *grammar* and of *drama*—or, if you like, of *the grammar of drama,* that is, the rhetorical ordering of images, in this case on an escalating scale (pinky, thumb, fist), ending in an explosion of meaning.

The ideal, of course, is always to marry the sound to the sense. But in the heat of improvisation, while thinking on his or her feet, with a performance grid and some keywords but no physical text to work with, the oral artist (blues singer, jazz singer, bard) sometimes reaches for the sense to wrap with the sound but is unable to find or seize it before the beat rolls in, and, to beat the beat, will hang to the sound alone.

But when all is said and done, the truth is that children's verses (and adults' too) are as comfortable and fulfilled in the one mode of verbal engineering as in the other. Nonsense can make great music—in song as in rhyme. Scat singing, of course, is the ultimate in great non-sense music—from Louis Armstrong to Betty Carter. (When Ella Fitzgerald couldn't remember the words, she reached for scat—and an old style was revalidated!)

In the kingdom of African-American oral poetry, rhyme is all-powerful. It is the founder and finisher, the center and the frame. Enthroned on a driving rhythm, its engine stoked by humor, rhyme sweeps everything before it, yoking together the incongruous with stunning effects, justifying every illogicality, conjuring beauty from rubbish, including the rubbish of poetic formulas, repetitive patterns, stock phrases, cliches and commonplaces.

Rhymes are invented, learned, altered, passed on, their mnemonic core intact, their trunk the base from which will bloom a thousand fresh florets of sound. Children's game songs are full of rhymes, some old, some new, some borrowed, some blue: *Oh yeah, baby, scooby doo, turn around, shake it, shake it, shake it, to the front, to the back, to the side-side-side. I said it, I meant it, I'm here to represent it. Don't like it, don't take it. Here's my collar, I dare you to shake it.* And in the 1960s came a new sound of *africanité: Ungawa, Black Power!*

The children's rhymes in our collection range in theme from the simple wish for an ice cream cone to the mature wish for a man; from nonsensical rhymes to weighty social comment about drug overdose and infanticide. The horror of a mother wrapping her baby in toilet paper and throwing it down the elevator is worked into the rhyme matter-of-factly, unremarked, as though such things happen every day. But such *sangfroid* is characteristic of folklore generally.

Similarly unremarked are the vulgar and explicitly sexual matters. It is a huge leap from the early innocence of many of the verses to such over-experience, but the stretch is true to life. All these are rhymes from the lives and mouths of black children, reflecting the joy and love and violence and vulgarity that are a part of life, and of their lives.

Part I, Children's Rhymes and Game Songs, opens with what is, broadly speaking, a prelude and general rehearsal of themes. In that first section, The

World as We See It, the voices are both male and female, mostly pre-adolescent. Their child's society has its own code, its sense of propriety. Children who fall below the norm (as in "Cry, Baby," "Kindergarten Baby," "Tattle Tale") get teased or censured. Parents are treated with a mixture of love and dread reminiscent of fairytales (see "Grandma," "I Hate Bosco," "Father Shot the Kangaroo"). The children are given to innocent pleasures, celebrating their favorite foods—chicken, peanut butter, watermelon, beans.

In the choral chant "Sardines and Pork and Beans," we witness in early form the process of squeezing art from adversity. The drama is most poignant in the third version, subtitled "The Welfare Song." Canned food, poor fare that keeps one alive even if eaten with the bitterleaf of humiliation, is worth its song after all. "Sardines" might be called a child's version of the blues. The laughter is in every line but the tears are suppressed.

Equally hard and unsentimental are the children's visits to other scenes of their concern. They are sharply aware of economic inequities ("It Ain't Gonna Rain No More") and the havoc wreaked by drugs ("Stop"), even if they cannot yet connect the two. These children may be limited in their historical knowledge, but even so, there is no mistaking their (dis)regard for received history. Abe Lincoln and John Brown are treated as disembodied abstractions. The "continental soldier" is used merely to supply cadence and rhyme. And George Washington's youthful probity is dismissed as the myth it is. What seems true to history in a deep and disturbing way is the surreal, virtually accidental image of a hardy, heartless, enduring Jim Crow, a figure of racist violence and repression that refuses to die:

> Old Jim Crow come riding by
> Said old man your heart's going to die
> Said if he die I'll bury his skin
> If he lives I'll ride him again.

Racial self-awareness is further glimpsed in the parody of "Silent Night" and the stereotypings of "Sambo," "Nigger," and "Nappy." "Now I Lay Me Down to Sleep" is probably the most parodied prayer in America. Each variant reflects the child's concerns—anxiety over school work, dread of violence, junk food and its possible consequences, and the as yet distant temptation of gambling whose double-edge is surely though vicariously felt through the fortunes of its adult beneficiaries and victims.

Juvenile reaction to consumer culture ranges from ambivalence ("McDonald's is our kind of place") to resistance (cigarettes are an evil-tasting "fifty-cent waste") to open revolt ("I Want My Money Back").

Assertiveness, resistance and pluck are the hallmarks of the second section, Marching Songs and Threats. These are aggressive, boasting rhymes that confront the world, particularly the white world. Black children in the simple act of walking down the street can turn the walk into a dance, the loose talk into a military chant, a chant that reinforces the feeling of power and joy and togetherness. Here the volume of chanting voices and stamping feet depends on numbers for strength:

> We're gonna F-I-G-H-T
> We're gonna Fight-Fight.

The 1960s is an era of black consciousness and black power, striving to redress the balance, denigrating white and celebrating black. And the children have tasted the heady wine. The tables are turned on self-hate:

> Black is beautiful
> Brown is hip
> White ain't nothing but
> A piece of shit!

The chants are gang-like, defiant of the forces that seek to reduce and confine. They are songs of self-definition and self-assertion, of youth straining to find its voice, its place, and sometimes arriving at superbly smooth, balanced lines, assured rhythm and faultless rhyme:

> I'm little, but I'm loud
> I'm poor, but I'm proud
> I'm a little piece of leather
> But I'm well put together.

The Marching Songs and Threats constitute a child's version of the more mature Boasts and Threats. Here is an outrageous outpouring of energy, but no one could mistake these for sounds of warfare, whether of gang or of race. It is all aggressive bluster, more postured than real, like raucous cheerleading at a football game:

> We are the kids don't take no stuff!
> Take off your shoes and smell your feet.

The joke is on the rowdy chorus, and they intend it to be. The spirit of laughter is triumphant.

Approximately a third of Part I is devoted to games of the street, the school-yard and the playground: circle games, jump rope, hand clap, run and chase games, ball-bouncing games—the games and songs of celebration that make childhood such a joy to remember.

In the notes she wrote for this section, Ellease Southerland (novelist Ebele Oseye) recalled the rhyme, rhythm and imagination of the games of her New York childhood: "At the mere mention of some games that African-American children play—'Cookie Jar,' 'Miss Mary Mack,' 'Pizza, Pizza, Daddy-O,' or 'A Sailor Went to Sea,'—a fast smile breaks on the faces of many mature women who will remember and begin to chant the rhymes. For these are the games and rhymes that transformed the lonesome afternoons in city streets, giving life to the dead gray concrete. The ringing vibrancy of black voices chanting was the best part of a summer's day. Even long after all the children had been called in to supper, there was a feeling of summer peace, or autumn quiet as the year progressed. . . .

"There was no money for fancy bicycles or other expensive toys. But there were other resources: The bare, empty street. Soda tops. Ice cream sticks. A rope. Sometimes a rubber ball. And, most importantly, there was the rhyme. The rhyme was the power. With the rhyme, the black imagination and the street, all that was missing was the people. And throughout the summer afternoons, sometimes starting mid-morning, from late spring into fall, before the cold of winter set in, the commonest sound was one child calling another, one house to the next, one foot on the stoop, hollering up to the third floor, sometimes running into the old buildings, but always calling: 'Can you come out? Can you come out to play?' And whenever the answer was No there was quiet disappointment. Players were needed. One person because she had a reputation as a great rope jumper. Another could turn double dutch with style. Another had such a loud voice, knew so many rhymes. The children needed each other. . . ."

Indispensable indeed to the lives of children are other children—and the rhyme. Rhyme, rhythm, imagination: expressing each other, fulfilling each other, driving each other.

Games might be regarded as beginning with choosing sides or choosing first, but of course this is not always the case in reality. Choosing is something of a ritual, a game within a game, setting the ground rules, bringing in a sense of ceremony and of adult-type order that would govern the games. Competition is mild: children's games are for fun, not for the winning of prizes. And there is a solidarity of children: today's opponents will be tomorrow's teammates.

Of all children's games, jump rope is surely the most visible and readily identifiable, if not also the most popular. Its rhymes encompass a broad range of subjects, but since it is a game played mostly by young girls, the themes are often of love, kissing, marriage, sometimes jealousy, sometimes future hope. Jump rope games involve fancy footwork, rivaling the most sophisticated of dance steps for intricacy and rhythm. Often the player is asked to go through the motions of simple dramas while jumping: to march upstairs, to stoop, turn around. Then the jump rope becomes a stage, a kitchen, a mountain, a street.

The young Steppers of today are most closely identified with the dances of Southern Africa, particularly the Pata-Pata and the Boot Dance made famous by Miriam Makeba, the Ipi-Tombi, "Sarafina" and the *a capella* singers of Lady Smith Black Mambazo. But Steppers owe just as heavy a debt to the humble jump rope of the city streets!

The Hand Clap section includes the famous "Cookie Jar" game-drama in which each player acts out an arrogant part when her number is called and she is accused of stealing the cookie ("Who, me stole a cookie from the cookie jar?"). This, like most ring games, follows the familiar pan-African call-and-response pattern. Here the accused plays leader and the accusers chorus.

Undergirding the drama is a simple and solid rhythm of hand clapping, which gets louder and more compelling as players are added and the circle gets bigger and bigger. The rhythm attains a double sound as each player first claps her hands, then turns each hand outward to clap with her two neighbors, so that the entire circle comes momentarily in touch.

Hand clap games require a minimum of two players. The pleasure is in the heavy rhythms of hand and voice, and the sound changes from sharp hand claps to clear clicks of fingers snapped, to soft slaps of thighs or breasts. And the intricate routines of hands turned up, down, and crossed are done to rhythmic chanting.

Woven into the game songs, as in other children's verses, are parodies of nursery rhymes, of contemporary radio and television commercials, and of old ballads. We witness the awakening of sexual interest, still coy and controlled:

> First comes love
> Then comes marriage
> Then comes the lady
> With the baby carriage.

Winos and dope addicts are satirized. Other denizens of the street—pimps and prostitutes, street toughs and preachers—will feature in the maturer dozens, signifyings, toasts and jokes.

The games in our collection are overwhelmingly female, but the closing two sections of Part I, Wine Rhymes and Vulgar Rhymes, are dominated by males, older teens who relish their emerging masculinity, their transition from adolescence to adulthood. They are discovering liquor and sex, and celebrating them in exaggerated poses. Thunderbird, Tiger Rose, Gypsy Rose, Bacardi, Newberry, Haig & Haig, J & B, Bourbon Supreme: they know all the brands even if they haven't tried them all. The familiar stereotypes are here: "us colored folks" drink the most, cop the most, dance the most.

The vulgar rhymes are heavy with sex and scatology. The four-line "Food Chant," packed with dynamite, is as disgusting as they come. "Listen My Children" plays with the tale of Paul Revere. Variants of "Stranded" will be found on bathroom walls across the nation. "Your Ma," "Your Mama Don't Wear No Draws," "Kiss My Ass!" and "A Gal from Kansas City" anticipate the dozens. "Bang Bang Lulu" is a replay of Mighty Sparrow's popular Caribbean calypso. And running like a refrain through the section is the seducing rap: "your mother did the same," even if she is "surprised to see her belly rise." This is the "birds and bees," urban style. There is no moralizing or guilt.

The celebration of the newfound wonders of the body reaches a crescendo in "The Titty Shout." "The Titty Shout" is an anthem of sexual arrival, a stupendous chorale of untrammeled male joy. Fascinated from infancy by the female breast, these young men finally know why, and they take turns proclaiming it: the titty is round, is hard, is soft, full of soul:

The more the ounces, Oh! yeah!
The more it bounces, Oh! yeah!
And when you squeeze
It wants to please.

The titty is big, is bad, makes you happy, never sad. Back then it filled you up; now it makes you feel divine. This is their graduation song, their valedictory to childhood. It is their "Hallelujah Chorus," their "Ode to Joy," their "Love Supreme." Their self-education complete, they are certified in one final catechism of question/answer/choral chant. It is a sacred ritual, attended with the profound, irreverent humor of black Christianity. The young men kneel before that prominent symbol of female power, as generations of their fathers have done. There is a naturalness and innocence about it all, an acceptance of themselves as sexual creatures. The Wizard King of Hawthorne's "Young Goodman Brown" might just as well be addressing *this* generation about to be inducted into adulthood: "Welcome, my children, to the communion of your race. Ye have found thus young your nature and your destiny." He meant the human race. This time it's globally *black*.

Of all the children's rhymes, it is in the game songs that inter-cultural overlap seems greatest. Several of the games in our collection are recorded, with variations, by the Opies and Knapps.

It is interesting to observe how exquisitely Langston Hughes captured the contemporary youth-spirit in his "Children's Rhymes" (1951), fitting out this naive and humble form for serious engagement in the political consciousness battles of the day:

> By what sends
> the white kids
> I ain't sent:
> I know I can't
> be President. . . .
>
> What don't bug
> them white kids
> sure bugs me:
> We knows everybody
> ain't free! . . .
>
> What's written down
> for white folks
> ain't for us a-tall:
> "Liberty And Justice—
> Huh—For All."
> (*Collected Poems* 390)

THE VERBAL CONTINUUM:
RAPPING, SIGNIFYING, BOASTS,
THREATS AND DOZENS

The terms *rapping, signifying, boasts, threats* and *dozens* pose problems of definition. First of all, there is considerable regional variation in terminology, and these rhetorical forms are known by different names in different places. For instance, the dozens is known in some regions as *sounding* and in others as *signifying*, while in still other regions the term *sounding* is reserved for direct insults to a person, *signifying* for indirect insults, and *dozens* for insults targeted at family members (Kochman, *Rappin'* 257–258; Mitchell-Kernan 316–317). Such overlapping in usage is hardly surprising, given the dynamic and fluid nature of oral culture. These forms exist in a state of true symbiosis: they are so organically related, borrow so much from one another, and shade so readily one into another that they are difficult to slice apart for purposes of definition and demonstration. More often than not, they are to be found in their "pure" states in one-liners; a passage of any length will almost certainly spill over into another genre.

To put it differently, the foundation upon which the key modern forms of African-American orature are built is *rapping* (to be distinguished from rap music). All that clever handling of language, whatever it may involve and whatever genre or rhetorical form it might ultimately be said to be in service of, is rapping. No one can be much good at boasts, threats, signifying, dozens or toasts unless he is able to rap. One might get away with one-liners for a while, but without skill at rapping, a more extended passage, including the lengthy toast, may only be learned and stiffly repeated by rote, with no improvisational latitude. Rapping provides both the basic grammar of these other genres and the skill and material for their advanced and complex formations. Rapping is that sophisticated throwing together of words, that imaginative image making, those hyperbolic metaphors, allusions, rhymes, puns, balanced lines and parallel constructions, wit and raucous humor, all orchestrated to produce passages of great intensity and beauty, as in the following excerpts from H. Rap Brown's "Sweet Peeter Jeeter" and Dan Burley's "A Harlem Jive Spiel":

> Man, you must don't know who I am.
> I'm sweet peeter jeeter the womb beater
> The baby maker the cradle shaker the deerslayer the buckbinder
>   the women finder
> Known from the Gold Coast to the rocky shores of Maine
> Rap is my name and love is my game . . .
> I'm the man who walked the water and tied the whale's tail in a
>   knot
> Taught the little fishes how to swim

Crossed the burning sands and shook the devil's hand . . .
Yes, I'm hemp the demp the women's pimp
Women fight for my delight
I'm a bad motherfucker. Rap the rip-saw the devil's brother 'n law
I roam the world I'm known to wander and this .45 is where I get
    my thunder . . .
I might not be the best in the world, but I'm in the top two and
    my brother's getting old.

                              (Rap Brown 27–29)

Looka here, Babes, I'm too busy to spiel too long to any one hen.
But I wanna put it down for you once and for all I'm too hipped for
any small beg acts, and I ain't never in the mood to be so crude as
to drop my gold on a chick that's bold. I'm a CI. I ain't no GI, so
get on the right track and stay till I get back cause I'm a hustler,
a rustler, the solid hipster they all boost, and the King of the Rob-
ber's Roost. . . . I'm really BAD, Babes. I'm rough and I'm tough.
I've climbed the Rocky Mountains, fought the grizzly bear; I've
trailed the wild panther to his hidden lair. I've crossed the great
Sahara Desert, Babes, I've swum the Rio Grande; I fought with
Pancho Villa and his bloodthirsty band. (Burley 284)

Rapping (rap, jive, talking shit, talking trash), then, insofar as it may be
isolated from the other forms, is basically a *monologue,* lively in style, color-
ful in language, rich in images, intended to persuade or give information, or
to exhibit oratorical skills before an approving audience, whether the audience
is limited to the person or persons being addressed or includes some sidelin-
ers. As Thomas Kochman puts it, rapping is "a performance [rather] than a ver-
bal exchange," and "projects the personality, physical appearance, and style of
the performer" (Kochman, *Rappin* 245). Thus, one raps to friends to inform
and impress them; to a woman to seduce her; to a naive, gullible person (a
"lame") to con him out of his money; to a parent, teacher, police officer, or other
authority figure to escape punishment when caught doing wrong; to gangsters
or hoodlums to escape their violence; and so on. The self-defensive rap ("shuck-
ing and jiving" and "copping a plea") is well illustrated in the monkey's words
to the lion:

The monkey looked up with tears in his eyes
And said, "Please, please, Mr. Lion, I want to apologize."

The lion said, "Oh no, motherfucker
I'm going to stop you from this signifying jive."

The monkey started crying and tried to cop a plea
"Please, Mr. Lion, you're hurting poor me."

All this wasn't getting the monkey anywhere, so he said:

"Mr. Lion, if you let my nuts up out of this sand
I'll get up and fight you like a natural man."

The lion jumped up and squared off for a nice clean fight
That's when that monkey jumped damn near out of sight.
("The Signifying Monkey" #3)

A few moments earlier, Monkey had rapped aggressively to Lion, taunting and threatening him from the safety of his tree perch:

"King of the jungle! Now, ain't you a bitch!
All swelled up like you got a seven-year itch

When you came by here yesterday the jungle rung
Now you come back with your asshole hung

Shut up, you motherfucker, you better not roar
Or I'll come down there and kick your ass some more."
("The Signifying Monkey" #6)

This aggressive rap, sometimes referred to as *sounding,* which operates by direct insult, is to be contrasted with the sly indirection of *signifying.* Signifying, when it insults, does so by *innuendo* and *suggestion,* with put-downs so cleverly phrased they sound (to the uninitiated) like praise, or at least as neutral/harmless. Such *indirection* has come to be accepted as the key element distinguishing signifying from the other forms. As Claudia Mitchell-Kernan puts it,

> One of the defining characteristics of signifying is its indirect
> intent or metaphorical reference. . . . Indirection means here that
> the correct semantic (referential) interpretation or signification of
> the utterance cannot be arrived at by a consideration of the dic-
> tionary meaning of the lexical items involved and the syntactic
> rules for their combination alone. . . . Meaning conveyed is not
> apparent meaning. . . . The apparent significance of the message
> differs from its real significance. The apparent meaning of the
> sentence "signifies" its actual meaning. (Mitchell-Kernan 326)

But indirection is not all; as Geneva Smitherman has shown, signifying is a virtual dictionary of modes and figures:

> Signification has the following characteristics: indirection, circum-
> locution; metaphorical-imagistic (but images rooted in the every-
> day, real world); humorous, ironic; rhythmic fluency and sound;
> teachy but not preachy; directed at person or persons usually pres-
> ent in the situational context (siggers do not talk behind yo back);

punning, play on words; introduction of the semantically or logically unexpected. (Smitherman 121)

The Signifying Monkey earned his name from his preeminence as a "man of words," a master of irony, circumlocution, innuendo and indirect insult:

> This cat was known by all as the Signifying Monkey, or so
> they say
> For he could talk more shit than anyone, in a most implicat-
> ing way.
>> ("The Signifying and Pool-Shooting Monkey")

We see him at work in his initial encounter with Lion when, pretending concern for Lion's family honor, he insults Lion indirectly by repeating the insults supposedly spoken by some third party:

> Deep down in the jungle where nobody goes
> Lived the signifyingest monkey the world ever knowed
>
> He told the lion one bright hot sunny day
> "There's a big burly motherfucker a-down the way
>
> Now you know, Mr. Lion, he couldn't possibly be your friend
> 'Cause he talked about the shape your dear family is in
>
> He said your mother is a whore and your father is a punk
> Your sister's got the pox and, motherfucker, you eat cock."
>> ("The Signifying Monkey" #3)

Monkey's tale-bearing is specifically intended to incite, and he succeeds only because Lion is naive and gullible, unsuspecting of ill will.

But signifying is not always this malicious, nor does it ordinarily by itself lead to such disastrous results. It would have to be aided by the other forms, as in the second confrontation ("King of the jungle! Now, ain't you a bitch!") where it is mixed with direct insult and propelled by a powerful rap. Much of the time, signifying by itself is mildly exploratory, tentative, playful, diplomatic, euphemistic and double edged, and as often *self-directed* as *other-directed*. It is a magic wand that can heal as much as wound, depending on how it is used. When other-directed, signifying permits a latitude that dozens, boasts and threats do not, namely, the option of saying things to make the other person feel either good or bad. "If you had just destroyed someone or if they were down already," says H. Rap Brown, "signifying could help them over." When self-directed, signifying serves as a vehicle for expressing one's own feelings and creating humor by poking fun at oneself. The following example from Brown's *Die Nigger Die!* demonstrates the tremendous flexibility of the form:

> Man, I can't win for losing
> If it wasn't for bad luck, I wouldn't have no luck at all

I been having buzzard luck
Can't kill nothing and won't nothing die
I'm living on the welfare and things is stormy
They borrowing their shit from the Salvation Army
But things bound to get better 'cause they can't get no worse
I'm just like the blind man, standing by a broken window
I don't feel no pain
But it's your world
You the man I pay rent to
If I had your hands I'd give 'way both my arms
'Cause I could do without them
I read the books you write
You set the pace in the race I run
Why, you always in good form
You got more foam than Alka Seltzer.

(Rap Brown 29–30)

Here the performer indulges in mild self-pity or mock self-pity (can't win for losing), pokes gentle fun at himself (Salvation Army; blind man who can't feel a broken window pane/pain, who can't write but only reads the books others write), and jousts with his buddy, alternately inflating his buddy's ego with playfully hyperbolic praise (it's your world, you the main man, the pace-setter, etc.) and just as playfully and slyly deflating it (if I had your hands/claws so ugly I'd cut off my arms just to be rid of 'em, you bloated, foamy old seltzer).

A similar flexibility and gentle, self-deprecating humor are observable in the following passage from our text, which is rap, signifying, tall tale and joke all in one:

My mother never told me a story in my life. Every time she
said something about she goin' to whip me, she did. My people
on my father's side, they all of them is in big business. My
uncle and my aunt, they had a iron and steel business. My
uncle went out and stole all night and my aunt stayed home
and ironed. Yes, they was great people. I had another uncle.
He was a great dancer. Last time I seen him, he was dancing
on the end of a rope.

("My Family")

Signifying, then, is a species of rapping, distinguishable from the other sub-species primarily by its indirection, and ranging from the harmless and gentle, as between friends, to the malicious and deadly, as between antagonists such as the Monkey and the Lion.

Boasts and *threats* complement each other: even in their separate, unalloyed forms, each usually implies the other. Like rapping, signifying and dozens, each is consciously hyperbolic. In its pure form, the boast is relatively innocuous and neutral, in contrast to the aggressive intensity it takes on when coupled with a threat. Like H. Rap Brown's "Sweet Peeter Jeeter," quoted earlier, the following are pieces of hyperbolic ego-tripping (boasts) with little or no cutting edge:

> I'm a love man
> Yes, that's me, darling
> Too slick to be tricked
> Too cool to be fooled
> Too old to be cold
> A slice of life twice as nice.
>
> ("I'm a Lover")

> The first bitch said, "Whore, my pussy is big as the Chesapeake Bay,"
> She said, "It holds two gallons loaded down with hay."
>
> The second bitch said, "Whore, my cunt is big as the sea,"
> She said, "Bitch, the whole Titanic could have sunk in me."
>
> The last bitch said, "Whore, my cunt is big as the moon,"
> She said, "Bitch, I fuck in January and come in June."
>
> ("Three Wine-Ole Bitches")

> My name is Joe Taylor
> My dick is a whaler
> My nuts weigh forty-four pounds
> If you know a fat lady
> That wants a big baby
> Just tell her Joe Taylor's in town.
>
> ("Joe Taylor")

The sole concern of these boasts, Brown's included, is the assertion of the performer's personal charm, beauty, wit, intelligence, sexual prowess, physical toughness and general superiority to others. They are *boast-raps* (rather than *boast-threats*), and if they are delivered in a contest situation at all, it is (for the moment at least) a friendly rather than a fierce contest. But when coupled with a proper threat, the character of the boast changes dramatically; its playful signifying and punning become subordinated to the sharpness and immediacy of the threat:

> I'm a bad little diddy-bop don't take no sass
> Mess with me and I'll kick your ass.

Threats are of immediate bodily harm, of disfiguration and dismemberment; they embody a vision of metamorphosis from the beautiful to the grotesque. The Ugly Dozens might be said to describe a person on whom such threats have been carried out (unless a natural grotesque).

Threats could come in the middle of a dozens exchange, in the middle of a basketball game, or in any other situation in which a confrontation is possible.

Like the dozens, boast-threats usually involve an active audience and, like the dozens, usually take two forms: (a) as a formalized warning before a fight, conveying the intensity of anger and defining the limits to which the opponent may go before physical violence erupts (in which case an audience is not necessary); and (b) as entertainment, in which case an audience is indispensable, and the whole process is applied theater. The dynamics of performance will be considered in further detail a little later.

Stylistically speaking, boasts and threats are at their most sophisticated when first yoked together as boast-threats, then stoked and hammered down to quintessential one-liners in which the one fuses with and disappears in the other. But in the majority of cases, close scrutiny will reveal the weld-lines, as in the following:

Boast:	Man, I don't play. I quit school because they had recess.
[*Implied Threat:*	If I could go that far for a little thing like that, you know what I'll do if you go soundin' on me.]
Threat:	You would rather stand on your dick and whistle through your asshole than fuck with me.
[*Implied Boast:*	I'm some bad, tough, mean motherfucker.]

However, in a few cases the elliptical economy of concealment and fusion is entirely triumphant, and the resulting line is a new creature altogether— neither boast nor threat except by implication:

I'm hitting hard, moving fast, breaking jaw and kicking ass.

[*Implied Boast:*	I'm the baddest-assed motherfucker in town.]
[*Implied Threat:*	Mess with me and I'll kick your ass and break your jaw.]

The verbal game of trading abuse has been known for generations as the *dozens,* but few black youth of the second half of the twentieth century or the beginning of the twenty-first have known it by that name. Their term, depending on their locality, has been *signifying, sounding, screaming, ranking, hiking, woofing (wolfing), capping, joning (joaning), lugging, snapping*—and the list is not exhaustive. Almost as varied are the theories of the origin of the primal term, *dozens;* however, our concern is with the distinguishing features of the form, and on that, happily, there is little or no disagreement.

Dozens is distinguishable from rapping, signifying, boasts and threats in that those focus on the antagonist, whereas dozens broadens the attention to his family. *The game, whatever its form, turns into dozens once it touches upon family.* The female relatives, especially the mother, are singled out for particular abuse. The dozens is basically a male game. Female players constitute a large exception, but not enough to nullify the rule. Older sisters given charge of younger siblings are forced to become street-smart and, less for "game" than for self-defense, can become as sharp at rapping, signifying, boasts, threats and dozens as any male. More generally, women use the dozens to defend themselves from games that men play, games ranging from tickling to life-threatening. Mastering the art becomes a training in verbal protection, a martial arts of the mind. But then, some women too are simply "game"; they are as much in love with repartee, with thrust and parry, and will play the dozens for the sheer fun. H. Rap Brown, who ought to know, has testified that in his experience "some of the best Dozens players were girls" (Rap Brown 27). Even an early stranger-scholar like John Dollard discovered as much back in 1939:

> Girls in this town are said to play the Dozens as well as boys. The informant says that "fourteen and fifteen year old middle-class girls take an active part in the Dozens as they take part with the boys at the meetings of their various class clubs." (Dollard 287)

One of our contributors, a young woman, reports: "I remember as a child playing dozens in the street, telling dirty jokes at pajama parties, watching my best friend's big brother and his friends go off to another room to tell stories. The best of the tales are told in men's locker rooms, at poker games, at bars, places where women are generally not accepted." Over the years the scholarship came so close to seeing the dozens as an exclusively male activity that the historic participation of women has had to be asserted and reasserted. But all the same, the general rule holds.

Brown calls the dozens "a mean game because what you try to do is totally destroy somebody else with words. . . . The real aim of the Dozens was to get a dude so mad that he'd cry or get mad enough to fight" (Rap Brown 26, 27). Again, Brown ought to know. But then, the conscious aim of the youthful players is but a fraction of the story, the tip of the proverbial iceberg. As we have seen, there are larger cultural forces propelling the blindfolded battle royal that is the dozens.

Early commentators on the dozens glimpsed some of these forces. John Dollard, who in 1939 gave the dozens its first full treatment in North America, called it "a valve for aggression in a depressed group," a mechanism for channeling inwards and neutralizing black aggression against whites, whose racism and economic repression are responsible for the "high level of frustration" among blacks (Dollard 291). In 1953 Samuel J. Sperling restated and expanded Dollard:

> This teasing game promotes the toughening of emotional sensi-tivity, and the inhibiting of impulses toward physical aggression. Frustrated outgroup aggression is safely channeled into the in-group. In this way the formalized game of "The Dozens" has social value to a group subjected to suppression, discrimination and humiliation. (Sperling 470)

A decade later (1963), Roger D. Abrahams gave this "social value" a point-edly Freudian sexual cast by insisting that it operates "in a totally male environment in which the necessity to prove one's masculinity (and to reject the feminine principle) recurs constantly" (Abrahams 54). He saw the dozens as "an expression of boys in transition to manhood [who] enunciate their growing sense of masculine power and sexual differentiation" by indulging in verbal obscenities "forbidden in the matrifocal home." But, in addition, he saw it as a device by which the "nascent man" will develop verbal weapons of offense and defense in the "contest world" in which he must live (Abrahams 32, 54, 55).

But if the sexual dozens are the most dramatic, they are certainly not the only type: dozens about ugliness and poverty occur about as frequently as do dozens about sex—though, admittedly, Mother is still the favorite target. In any case, it was not until Grier and Cobbs (quoted earlier) joined the conversation in 1971 that the dozens came to be seen in the round. Their analysis represents less a rejection of Dollard, Sperling or Abrahams than a broadening and deepening of them. Theirs, too, is applied Freud, but more subtle and nuanced. They see the dozens as an overwhelmingly healthy activity. To them, too, the dozens is a type of puberty ritual, a process designed to rescue boys from "the stifling aspect of the maternal bond" (Grier and Cobbs, *Jesus* 5). It is also a channeling of aggression inwards, with the specific aim of training the child to withstand verbal and psychological abuse without flinching—an ability he desperately needs as a black child growing up in a historically murderous racial environment:

> In the deepest sense, the essence of the dozens lies not in the insults but in the response of the victim. To take umbrage is considered an infantile response. Maturity and sophistication bring the capability to suffer the vile talk with aplomb at least, and, hopefully, with grace and wit. (Grier and Cobbs, *Jesus* 5)

Grier and Cobbs reject any suggestion that the dozens is "dysfunctional." In a society historically hostile to black males, but one that also holds the balance of power, "the warrior posture [is] suicidal" (Grier and Cobbs, *Jesus* 10). One must learn to fight with wit and not with fist. The dozens teaches forbearance, self-control and the development and deployment of mental weaponry. One of our contributors put it this way: "Violence is a dangerous way for a black man to relieve his frustration. This verbal exercise [dozens] is relatively free from penalty in the white world. . . . In a white world where you are physically powerless, if you aren't verbally and mentally strong, you ain't shit." In place of pathology, Grier and Cobbs see "healthy youngsters" developing "grace and balance" under the "vicious pressure" of the dozens. Instead of shamefaced apology, they proudly proclaim the dozens as "a highly evolved instrument of survival [that] has persisted because it meets a group need, accomplishes certain work, and does it all in a universal language" (Grier and Cobbs, *Jesus* 6, 9).

In short, Grier and Cobbs chased away the clouds that had hung over the dozens for three decades. They inaugurated a new criticism that views the dozens as a positive learning experience for those black youngsters who do (as some do not) happen to grow up in this "street culture."

Among the central functions of the dozens, then, is social behavior control: channeled aggression, ritualized release of violence within rigidly defined boundaries, following understood and accepted conventions. But its conventions notwithstanding, the dozens is, like rapping, signifying, boasts and threats, always ambiguous and double edged. Always, it could be used either to amuse or abuse; depending on context and intention, it amuses by abusing, or abuses without amusing.

Take for instance an adult gathering of childhood friends in a relaxed social setting. Everyone is sitting around, signifying and rapping and generally having a good time. Then someone makes a particularly stinging remark, and the person attacked simply says "Joe," and everyone bursts out laughing. "Joe" is a corruption of "Yo'," which is short for "Your mother," a standard opener for a dozens exchange. What the respondent has done is dip into the vast storehouse of culture and tradition of which everyone present is a participant, and from it bring back memories of the days when they played the dozens seriously, *unlike now*. Using the familiar dozens retort shows how close he is to his friends, for only among close friends is the dozens played *as a game*. And by thus calling upon the shared experiences of childhood and youth, he has drawn the group together and strengthened their bond.

An altogether different situation might be one in which a group of people—friends, acquaintances, near-strangers and strangers—are gambling. Even if they were all friends, the competitive activity would make real adversaries of them. Their contest is grim, not gamely, neutralizing or negating the friendly side of friendship. As often is the case on such occasions, an argument breaks out, and after some name calling, one angry person shouts the standard opener, "Your mother!" He has said in effect, "Look, punk, I'm ready to fight!" It is an open challenge understood by everyone present.

In the one case the dozens retort, together with the further exchange that was likely to follow, was used to amuse, and in the other to abuse. The dozens is therefore dual in form and function: it could be used as an unequivocal expression of anger and provocation, and thereby serve as prelude to a seriously hostile encounter; or it could serve as entertainment—as a means of introducing light humor in a gathering of friends, or passing the time on a mundane, boring, routine job (dishwasher, cook, laborer, chain gang, etc.), in which case it parallels the singing of work songs. When used to entertain, the dozens is the equivalent of a joke well told, an exhibition staged before an approving audience by contestant-performers gifted with high imagination and verbal virtuosity.

The commonest settings for a dozens performance are pool halls, gyms, playgrounds, schoolyards, shop classes, stoops, street corners, barber shops, bars, house parties, the army, navy, air force, jails—indeed, anywhere that males usually gather. Usually two contestants will trade abuses until one submits to the superior skill of the other, or until feelings run so high as to cause a fight, or until interest shifts elsewhere. The drama involves three major personae: the two contestants, whom we may call *protagonist* and *antagonist,* and the *audience* that incites them each against the other. The audience may be one person, or a crowd. A lengthy session may not necessarily be played out by the same two contestants. For instance, the protagonist, especially if he is having the worst of it, may warn the audience: "If you laugh, you're in!" Accordingly, he may direct a barb at someone in the audience who has annoyed him with his comments or laughter or whom he considers an easier target. That person may then get drawn into the contest and may replace the antagonist.

The audience is always vital: the most vicious player is often the audience. The opening jibe of "Joe!" or "Your mother!" may routinely be ignored by those used to it; but if a listener shouts "Sound!" "Hike!" "Rank!" etc., one feels honor-bound to respond, and the contest is on. Or, less likely, one could still bow out with "I don't play that shit!" or some such line.

The game starts slowly, then builds in intensity and can get quite personal (instead of staying fictional). Just because a game of rapping, signifying, boasts, threats or dozens starts out as entertainment doesn't mean it will stay that way. Whether the exchange continues as entertainment or degenerates into physical violence quite often depends on the audience. The drama is staged for their appreciation, and they are, in their responses, the final arbiters of excellence. At a good score they will break into laughter, or shout their admiration: "Oooooo!!!" "Sound!!!" "Hike!!!" "Rank!!!" It is the crowd's comments, their derisive or approving laughter, that most readily turns the game into a fight. The crowd could channel the contest toward one goal or the other; or they could see-saw it, pushing it first in one direction, then in the other. To that extent the players are unfree, and unless one player simply bows out, a crowd that is determined to see a fight will manipulate them until it gets one.

A fight may break out if the contest, for whatever reason, deviates from ritual to reality. For instance, a contestant may state what his antagonist and the audience know to be a fact, an accurate description of the state of affairs in the antagonist's family (e.g., that "your pap's in jail and your mother's around corner shouting pussy for sale"), in contrast to the obviously fictitious descriptions and accusations that are standard currency (e.g., "your mother is so ugly when she cries tears run down her back"). The antagonist may retort with a charge equally personal and true, in which case the exchange may switch from fun to fact, from amusement to abusement. The exchange may get redirected into the kingdom of fiction, either by the players themselves or by the audience; but if it is left to travel the track of the real for any length of time, it may indeed lead to a fight.

The easy mutation of one form into another—with the ever-present possibility of violence—serves to underline the fact that rapping, signifying, boasts, threats and dozens are not separate, autonomous and finished forms but a single complex and evolving set, a dynamic process that is constantly moving and changing, whose course is not predetermined, whose action is not tied to a single given script. The script is open, replete with options provided by a vast repertory of alternative lines, props and gestures (non-verbal gestures every bit as potent as words in their ability to devastate or to soothe). And the contours of the unfolding plot are heavily influenced by the reactions of the audience. In short, this is the livest of live theaters, and because it deals so brutally with matters so sensitive and personal, it is always a gamble, a tightrope walk or snake-handling act whose outcome is always in doubt: the wrong word or gesture from protagonist, antagonist or audience, or even the mere presence of the wrong person in the audience, could easily turn a happy pastime into a tragedy.

The major themes of the dozens include (a) poverty, (b) physical ugliness, (c) stupidity, (d) promiscuity. These themes all come together in those dozens that describe in a general way "the condition your dear family is in," to borrow the Signifying Monkey's phrase. The poverty dozens stress the rats and roaches with which ghetto dwellings are overrun, and the ragged clothing and evil-tasting welfare food. The ugly dozens probe every nook and cranny of the human anatomy, and look upon blackness of skin and nappiness of hair with that old self-contempt that the black pride of the 1960s reduced but did not entirely eliminate. Sex roles are conventional and stereotyped: the father is the breadwinner, the mother fragile and pure, and deviation from these ideals, as in effeminacy or impecuniousness in the male, or mannishness or promiscuity in the female, is ridiculed. The influence of the media is felt, for instance, in the references to King Kong, Phantom of the Opera, and Preparation-H. Awareness of current events, coded in references to Vietnam, for example, is minimal.

Dozens range in intensity from very light, as in the simple retort "Yo' ma," to heavy: "Your mother looks like her face caught on fire and someone tried to put it out with an ice pick" (or a chain, brick, pipe, etc.). Intensity depends to a large degree upon dramatics and timing: a juvenile line, delivered with theatrics and conviction by an adult, will make an impact; at the same time, however blandly delivered, the simple, innocent question, "How come your father don't live with you?" will be especially painful because understated.

Nowhere is hyperbole more consistently and effectively employed than in the dozens. Especially notable are the lines built on the formula: if B was A you'd be Z (the furthest thing from A):

Your mama is so black if *snow* was *black* she'd be a walking *blizzard*.

If *brains* was *sight* you'd be *Ray Charles*.

If *brains* was *light* you'd be *midnight*.

If *brains* was *heat* you'd *freeze* to death.

If *ugliness* was *holiness* you'd be *Jesus Christ*.

The order is varied somewhat in the last example, but the formula holds.

Narrative Form

The *toast* is at the apex of the modern tradition of African-American oral poetry. It is an expansive form powered by the same pervasive energies of rapping, and employing the same rhetorical strategies as the shorter or more fragmentary forms (children's rhymes, signifying, boasts, threats, dozens, proverbs and jokes) that it incorporates and utilizes where necessary. At its most extended, the toast's only rival in comprehensiveness and brilliance is the folk sermon which, because so open-ended in text and unlimited in subject matter, is itself extensible to epic lengths.

The toast is, by common consent, a narrative poem, sometimes long, sometimes short; but clearly, it is the longer narratives that form the core of the canon. By far the best known of all toasts are "The Signifying Monkey," "Stagger Lee" and "The Titanic" (which, of course, like all others, exist in innumerable versions). These constitute a sort of holy trinity, attended by such other action pieces as "Dolemite," "Honky-Tonk Bud," "The Fall," "The Great MacDaddy," "Doriella DuFontaine," "Death Row," "Mexicana Rose," and the sensational fornication contest between Pete Revere and Sadie the Whore or Lulu the Schoolteacher. For prosodic form, many toasts come in rhymed couplets, with lines varying greatly in length and number of stresses, but almost as many are cast in traditional ballad quatrains of alternating four- and three-stress lines rhyming *abcb*.

Again, theories abound as to the origin of the term. The African-American toast is obliquely related to the conventional European "drinking toast," a festival of limericks and sundry bawdy verses among "jolly good fellows." It is also related to the more sober European convention of the toast as a speech in praise of bride and groom or of colleague or friend before drinking to their health and future success. In the hands of the maladroit, this latter convention is notorious for its tendency to produce pompous, platitudinous, iterative and boringly long prose or verse. In the hands of a master, however, it can be entertaining, jovial, witty, even profound.

The African-American toast is a jazzy riff on both conventions, paralleling the relationship of spirituals and gospel to Protestant hymns. The shorter forms require a gift of wit and a mastery of rhythm and rhyme. But the longer narratives demand something of the depth of memory and imagination, and the metrical prowess exercised, admittedly on a vaster landscape, by the bards and *griots* of oral epics in Africa and the world over. Such longer narratives are the work of masters, and provide a dramatic enactment of an engaging story intended to entertain and school the audience and win their admiration. The toast-master is self-chosen. He has paid his dues. He has honed his histrionic and rhetorical skills by prolonged study, working his way up through the preparatory, fragmentary forms. And he knows he must perform well or be hooted off the stage by an exacting and intolerant audience.

Some toasts also share affinities with Anglo-American balladry. Some are parodies, imitations or re-workings of songs from the other side. Some originating on this side have crossed and re-crossed the line, picking up story elements along the way. In addition, whether or not in ballad stanza, some toasts have had a double life as songs, with a documentable musical history.

Given these interrelationships, it should come as no surprise that the toast, too, poses problems of definition. Some scholars have refused to make a distinction between ballads and toasts, more often treating toasts as a species of ballad. For example, Langston Hughes and Arna Bontemps, who first anthologized "The Signifying Monkey," "Stagger Lee" and "Titanic" in *The Book of Negro Folklore* (1958), grouped them (and "Bad Man") under "Ballads," along with "John Henry," "Frankie Baker," "Betty and Dupree" and four other poems conventionally regarded as ballads (Hughes and Bontemps 345–370). Curiously enough, the editors of the more recent *Norton Anthology of African American Literature* (1997) did exactly the same, grouping the three canonical toasts under "Ballads," along with "John Henry," "Frankie and Johnny," "Poor Lazarus," "Wild Negro Bill" and "Railroad Bill" (Gates and McKay 41–52).

Such muddyings-up of the generic lines would seem to demand that at least two definitional boundaries be drawn, separating the toast from the ballad on the one side, and, on the other, from the short narratives and epigrammatic micro-verses whose closest kin is the limerick.

First, the ballad. Many of the best known toasts, including "The Signifying Monkey," "Stagger Lee," "Titanic," "Mexicana Rose," and "Kitty Barrett," are in rhymed couplets, which may give the impression that this is the standard prosodic unit of the toast. But a galaxy of toasts of equal accomplishment, including "Honky-Tonk Bud," "Konky Mohair," "The Fall," "The Free Snorter," "Eddie LeDoux" and "Doriella DuFontaine," are in ballad stanza. Some toasts, including "Stagger Lee," exist in both forms. The difference between the toast and the ballad is therefore not one strictly of prosodic form. The difference is partially one of style.

There are, broadly speaking, two classes of ballads: those intended for singing, and those for reading. (These correspond roughly to the "folk" and the "literary" ballad.) Ballads intended to be sung are usually marked by a sing-song metric regularity and faultless rhyme, with excess syllables elided or contracted, and the diction simplified. The plot is shorn of distracting detail, leaving it lean, with only the barest essentials of the story, supported sometimes with repetitions and refrains. The musical mode confers other freedoms, most notably freedom from logical narrative sequencing. The plot in a song ballad is usually non-linear: it moves in spirals, zigzags or loops, creating those gaps or jumps in story line for which ballads are notorious. Ballads intended only for reading or recitation are richer in details, with sequential continuity in plot, complex constructions, multisyllabic or even "learned" diction, and a more relaxed, less dedicatedly exact rhythm or rhyme. Syllabic equality and faultless rhyme are not essential. The verse tends to be more ragged and harsh, less regular, less rounded at the edges, less smooth. Repetitions and refrains are rare. And whereas the singing voice, melodic and mellow, is tuned to a distant, sometimes invisible audience, the voice of a recitation ballad is clearly a speaking voice, speaking to an active listener or listeners in close proximity.

These differences are illustrated in the following excerpts from "John Henry," a song ballad, and "Doriella DuFontaine," a reading-recitation poem in ballad stanza.

> John Henry went down de railroad
> Wid a twelve-poun' hammer by his side
> He walked down de track but he didn' come back
> 'Cause he laid down his hammer an' he died
> 'Cause he laid down his hammer an' he died
>
> John Henry hammered in de mountains
> De mountains wuz so high
> De las' words I heard de pore boy say:
> "Gimme a cool drink o' watah fo' I die
> "Gimme a cool drink o' watah fo' I die!"
>
> John Henry had a little baby
> Hel' him in de palm of his han'
> De las' words I heard de pore boy say:
> "Son, yo're gonna be a steel-drivin' man
> "Son, yo're gonna be a steel-drivin' man!"
>
> (Brewer 202)

> Now, when I got to the pad it was some kind of bad
> And was filled with a real boss scent
> On the floor was a three-inch carpet imported from the market
> Somewhere in the Orient
>
> Now the stereo was wailing, but, fellows, I was failing
> I just couldn't rap to this deb
> I wasn't too bold until she broke out some soul
> Some dynamite Panama Red
>
> Now with coke on her thumb she massaged my gums
> And gave me some wine to sip
> You should have heard her purr when I grabbed hold of her
> And massaged her gums with my lips.
>
> ("Doriella DuFontaine")

Except for parodies, the musical mode also places controls on vulgarity of language and extravagance of image, especially given the context of performance and the prospective national audience should a commercial recording opportunity arise. In the musical mode, "subdued" is the word. A bull like Stagger Lee, running so wild and free in the toasts, is trimmed and tamed and virtually caged in the song ballad:

> It was early, early one mornin'
> When I heard my bulldog bark
> Stagolee and Billy Lyons
> Was squabblin' in the dark
>
> Stagolee told Billy Lyons
> "What you think of that?
> You win all my money, Billy
> Now you spit in my Stetson hat." . . .
>
> Billy Lyons told Stagolee
> "Please don't take my life
> I've got three little helpless chillun
> And one poor, pitiful wife."
>
> "Don't care nothin' about your chillun
> And nothin' about your wife
> You done mistreated me, Billy
> And I'm bound to take your life."
>   (Henderson 103)

Imagine Stagger Lee saying he's been "mistreated"! Such self-pity would be shockingly out of place in a proper toast. Far more typical is the following:

> Well, I waded through six inches of shit and ten inches of mud,
> And came upon a place called The Bucket of Blood
>
> I told the bartender, "Give me sumpin' to eat."
> He gave me a muddy glass of water and a tough piece of meat
>
> I said, "Look, son-of-a-bitch, you know who I am?"
> He said, "Frankly, I don't give a damn."
>
> I said, "Well, motherfucker, you better wake up and see
> I'm that mean son-of-a-bitch they call Stackalee."
>
> He said, "Yeah, I've heard of you from down the way
> But I meet you motherfuckers most every day."
>
> Well, that's all he said
> 'Cause he lay behind the bar with six holes in his head.
>   ("Stackalee" #5)

Regardless of form, then, the critical difference between a toast and a ballad is in the style and spirit of the telling. In ballads the exploits of badmen, bad women, pimps, whores, and hustlers are presented from a preeminently human-interest angle, in language that is modest and subdued. The protagonists are pictured as ordinary men and women who may overreach, suffer remorse or stand stiff-necked and pay the price. But in toasts these figures are transformed into monsters, freaks and grotesques. They grow larger than life. The language they speak becomes violent, and the language of the telling, vulgar. Their extravagant adventures are played to the gallery with melodramatic excess, with much fantasy and little reality. In short, the toast might be said to be a further remove from life than the ballad; their two worlds, so close, are yet so distinct.

And yet, notwithstanding such exaggeration, the audience of the toast recognize these figures as people like themselves, as a composite of people they encounter in everyday life. They know them by circumstantial details: by the way they dress, the way they "walk that walk and talk that talk," the places they go and the things they do—in short, by their style. Both reciter and audience identify with the hero to some extent. For good or ill, the hero plays a role in personality formation: one watches Stagger Lee, for instance, to learn how a bad dude operates, then becomes one by imitating him. The creative process comes full circle: first, art copies life (Stagger Lee modeled on real-life bad dudes), then life copies art.

And now, the shorter narratives. We have included three four-line vignettes of "Stagger Lee," and a sixteen-line fragment of "Titanic," but only because they serve as prelude to the full narrative. Otherwise there seems little justification for grouping extra-short narratives together with narratives of 60 to 100 lines or more and calling them all "toasts." (Wepman, Newman and Binderman's *The Life* seems to hold the record for length: seven of its thirty-four toasts run 140 to 324 lines.) Bruce Jackson's fine collection of toasts, *Get Your Ass in the Water and Swim Like Me,* contains 150 pieces, including, surprisingly, twenty-eight "short verses and drinking toasts." Some of these, it must be said, are little more than epigrams and cute parodies:

> Hickory wood is the best of wood,
> crackin' does the women good,
> make them open their eyes and stretch their thighs,
> give their ass exercise.
>
> (Jackson 231)

> Well here's to the fool that writes upon the shithouse walls,
> may he roll his shit in little balls.
> And he that reads those words of wit,
> should eat those little balls of shit.
>
> (Jackson 229)

Short poems of this sort, much like those grouped under "Children's Rhymes," "Rapping" or "Miscellaneous" in our collection, might better be called potshots, snaps, snapshots, or graffiti—at least until the critical terminology is refined and more appropriate designations are invented for them. But they cannot be called toasts in the same breath as the great moving-picture narratives of "Titanic," "Dolemite" or "The Signifying Monkey."

Length is, like narrative style and language, a major consideration in determining what is or is not a toast. Coherent or summative fragments of the essential story line of a major narrative (like the fragments of "Stagger Lee" and "Titanic" cited above) represent a special case and may belong with the genre, but unrelated short poems, even when they "tell a story," as well as fragments from the detachable peripheries of major narratives, all deserve a different classification.

To test this proposal, let us examine some of the short narrative poems grouped under "Rapping, Signifying, Boasts and Threats" in our collection. "Dime," for example, is an enumeration of classically impossible tasks that an old friend, now down and out, must perform in order to earn pitifully small alms. The specific tasks vary with the version. When embedded in a longer narrative, as in the misogynic invective of "The Letter" (Labov 337), or the pimp's complaint in "Sweet Lovin' Rose" (Jackson 118–119) and "Prison Walls" (Dance, *Shuckin' and Jivin'* 238–239), "Dime" would be subsumed in the generic identity of its host. But when standing by itself, as in our text, or as in Wepman's "One Thin Dime" (Wepman 150–151) or Abrahams's "A Hard-Luck Story" (Abrahams 158–160), "Dime" is best classified as a magnificent piece of rapping, or else a joke in verse.

It should be noted, however, that the first of Abrahams's three versions differs somewhat from the rest: it sports claws made of threats, and teeth sharpened with invective. The generic identity of that particular version should probably be determined by its dominant mode, which is invective.

But whatever the case, "Dime," isolated and standing by itself in whatever version or style, cannot, as these scholars would have it, properly be classified as a toast. Consider the many passages of signifying, boasts, threats, dozens, anecdotes, tall tales, jokes, epitaphs and aphorisms embedded, say, in "The Signifying Monkey," "Stagger Lee," "The Titanic" or "Dolemite." Once extracted from the body of the toast, isolated and standing alone, such pieces would not by themselves be classifiable as toasts. If we accept that the toast is a comprehensive, epical form that incorporates virtually all other forms, then it stands to reason that none of those other forms *by itself* could be a toast.

So then, if a powerhouse like "Dime" does not qualify as a toast, such modest proto-narratives as "Ninety-Four Whores," "Twenty Women," "When I Die," "Three Wine-Ole Bitches," "I'm a Lover" and "My Legend Has Come to Pass," each more rap and boast than anything else, have even less of a chance.

Another of our poems, "On the Corner," raises the classificatory question from a somewhat different angle. The piece is pure invective; and as it turns out, the prevailing critical practice has been to treat invective as a subspecies of toast. But perhaps it is time to reconsider.

Like the toast, the *invective* is a comprehensive, epical form that needs the powerful accessories of rapping, signifying, boasts, threats and dozens to do its work. It differs from the toast in that its goal is not to tell a story or enact a drama but *to abuse, intimidate, break down and grind an opponent into the dust*. Invective is the opposite of panegyric: it is not a poem of praise but of dispraise, not a song of approbation but of scorn. Like boasts, threats and dozens (its closest kin in the oral family), invective is an utterance marked by violence and passion. But whereas those forms are short and sharp, coming in staccato outbursts, invective is an *extended* outpouring of rage, a tongue-lashing, brutal and cutting in the extreme, which goes on and on and on, threatening not to end until its object is pulverized and annihilated totally.

The existence in the literature of lengthy invectives of great virulence and rhetorical power should justify the recognition of invective as a separate genre. That genre would include "On the Corner" as well as some pieces presently classed as toasts in various collections: "Pimping Sam" in *Shuckin' and Jivin'* (Dance); "Pimping Sam," "Wicked Nell," "The Pimp" and "Hustlin' Dan" in *Get Your Ass in the Water* (Jackson); "Pimping Sam," "The Letter" and "Answer to the Letter" in *The Life* (Wepman); and, as noted above, Version #1 of "A Hard-Luck Story" in *Deep Down in the Jungle* (Abrahams). When the invective is brief and embedded in a longer form, as in the six concluding lines of "The Big Man" (Abrahams 160–162), it would be subsumed in the generic identity of its host (in this case, a toast). Such re-classification would free up and trim the too amorphous genre of *toast,* reserving the term more strictly for the classic extended narratives.

But all this would leave still unsettled the question of *length*. How extended is *extended*? How long is long enough to make a toast? We can take comfort in the fact that when it comes to length in prose fiction, oral or written, the critical vocabulary is just as tentative and uncertain; nevertheless, distinctions, partly of function and partly of length, continue to be made between such forms as *anecdote, fable, exemplum, sketch, short story, novella* and *novel.* Always, a certain amount of overlap is unavoidable. By the same token, it should be possible to sort the shorter oral verses into *equivalent forms* determined partly by function and partly by length, ranging from those that might take two to five minutes to recite, to those that, like the toast, might require ten to twenty minutes or more.

"Make a Joyful Noise" and "Jonah and the Whale" (in our collection) represent a special case of toasts that because of their subject matter might more readily be placed with "Preacher Tales and Parodies." "Joyful Noise" is in irregular rhymed couplets with chunks of unrhymed lines thrown in. "Jonah" was recited in what would be transcribable into either rhythmic prose or verse, and we have deliberately rendered it in the jazzily experimental free verse of the idiosyncratic 1960s and 1970s.

Prosodic Framework

Much as in jazz, the toast is constructed within a prosodic frame built for improvisation, one that plays off freedom against constraint, innovation against convention, and the experimental against the established. The result is a mix that is at once old and new, predictable and fresh.

One element of the mix is rhyme, that powerful driving mechanism. Another is the treasury of well-made phrases, figures, aphorisms and proverbs that the poet may work into his lines, appending the proper rhymes:

a hell of a day / *a hell of a way*

the lion popped his tail *like a .44*

Shine takes off, making waves *like a motorboat*
lion takes off *like a motorboat* / *PT boat* / *late freight train*

it's gonna be *you and me* / *you or me*

They *fought all night* and they *fought all day*
And *I still don't know how* the lion got *away*

They *fought for* thirty *days* and they *fought for* thirty *nights*
And *I still don't see how* the lion *got out of that* fuckin' *fight*

the lion was on the monkey *like stink on shit* / *like a German on a Jew*

Like a streak of lightning, a bolt of blue heat / *white heat*
The lion was on the monkey *with all four feet*

Lion comes through the jungle *more dead than alive* /
looking like *a pile of dirty laundry* /
looking like a cat with *the seven-year itch*

She killed poor Pete, *the dirty bitch*
But she shall die of *the seven-year-itch*

You *just let me get my nuts* / *balls* / *head* / *chest out of the sand*
I'll fight your ass *like a natural man.*

The entire tradition of African-American oral poetry is rich in what conventional standard English would consider half-rhymes or off-rhymes. Many of these are generated by difference in pronunciation (as in *chin* / *again*), including the dropping of end letters and sounds such as *d* and *s* (as in *king* / *wings; down* / *ground; man* / *sand; should* / *woods*). There are also non-rhymes, words with only the remotest resemblance in sound but which the oral poet in his urgent need presses into service: *sticks* / *bitch; knot* / *drop.* Internal rhymes are a staple of the narratives in ballad quatrains, creating uncanny echoes between, say, "Doriella DuFontaine" or "The Free Snorter" and a poem like Edgar Allan Poe's "The Raven." Nowhere is African-American oral literature closer to Anglo-American written literature.

Opening stanzas are sometimes irregular, while the poet struggles to remember his lines, but once he hits his pace it's smooth sailing—until he encounters turbulence, at which point he might throw in a one-liner, a triplet, or a couplet that doesn't rhyme.

Hero Figures

Ever since Roger Abrahams's analysis in *Deep Down in the Jungle* (1963), it has come to be regarded as more or less canonical that the toast has two basic hero types: one is the bully or badman, hard, tough, physically strong, dedicated to dominance through violence (Stagger Lee; Dolemite; Boothill McCoy; Black Jack Tucker), and the other is the trickster, flexible but cunning, fleet of foot and smooth of tongue, seeking mastery by brain rather than brawn (Signifying Monkey) (Abrahams 62). Of course there are other hero types, though they could also be read as variants or sub-types of the basic two. These include the badman-trickster, a combination of the prime types (Shine); the hustler or pimp (the narrator-protagonists of "Doriella DuFontaine," "Mexicana Rose" and "The Fall"); the stud or sexual athlete (Pete Revere); the prostitute (Doriella DuFontaine; Mexicana Rose); the junkie or dope fiend (Honky-Tonk Bud; the Free Snorter; Dumbo the Junkie); the freak (members of "Freaks' Ball"; Marie, Voodoo Queen and other transvestites); the crime buster or narco-squad hero (Kitty Barrett; the cop who busted Honky-Tonk Bud); the loser, or hustler past his prime (Konky Mohair).

As embodiments of fragments of African-American sensibility, both badman and trickster are existential nay-sayers, with their roots deep in slave life and lore, saying no to domination and exploitation, yes to freedom and self-mastery. The badman is, as we have seen, a descendant of the hard, tough slave rebel or "bad nigger" who would rather die than bend, and the trickster a type of the wily slave John of the John and Ole Massa story cycles, and of Brer Rabbit.

The main limitation of Abrahams's analysis stems from his Freudian/Jungian commitments. Just as earlier he slipped and called the dozens "regressive" (Abrahams 51), he now calls the trickster "childlike," "amoral," "a perpetual child," and the badman "a perpetual adolescent":

> Indeed, in almost every sense the trickster *is* a child. He has no perceptible set of values except those dictated by the demands of his bodily needs. One could not say that he is immoral; rather he is amoral, because he exists in the stage before morality has been inculcated in his being. . . . As such, the trickster may reflect the real childlike state of a severely stunted ego. (Abrahams 63, 65; his emphasis)

> Where the trickster is a perpetual child, the badman is a perpetual adolescent. . . . He is consciously and sincerely immoral. (Abrahams 65–66)

Such name calling could have been brushed aside as the thorns that come with the rose (Abrahams did such an otherwise fine job), were it not so deeply reminiscent of the racist anthropologies of the past that have wreaked such havoc on the black image and self-image. It did not go down well with black scholars at all. But a quarter century passed before there was a thoroughgoing and authoritative demolishment of its thesis.[3] In 1989 came *From Trickster to Badman: The Black Folk Hero in Slavery and Freedom,* and with that huge broom John W. Roberts swept away a generation of folklore scholarship that was often ethnocentric and condescending as well as honestly limited in its outsider's knowledge of a beleaguered culture.

We have already noted two limitations of Roberts's analysis, namely his unnecessary and failed attempt to de-link the "badman" of late nineteenth/early twentieth-century ballads and heroic narratives from the "bad nigger" of slave days, and his blindness to the African sources of their praise names. But these are minor failings. Roberts's great achievement is his detailed study of the rationale of these folk hero types (trickster, badman and their multiple mutations), of the historical circumstances that gave them birth and justified them, and of the positive values they embodied—values that have been forwarded to successive generations and that continue vibrant and relevant in their ever-changing forms up to the present day.

Roberts begins his discourse with the explanation and warning that

> the embodiment of the exploits of a particular figure in folk heroic literature is not designed to provide a model of adaptive behavior in a literal sense. Rather, folk heroic literature offers a conception of attributes and actions that a group perceives as the most advantageous for maintaining and protecting its identity in the face of a threat to values guiding action. (Roberts 6)

Specifically, Roberts argues that the trickster hero was born in circumstances of material scarcity. In Africa, it was a "natural" scarcity—from insufficient or excessive rainfall, failed crops, famine. "There was famine in the land of the animals . . ." was a typical story opening. And in such conditions the trickster, adept at bargaining, wheedling, stealing and concealing food for himself, his family, clan or village, is a hero. A primordial example is the semi-divine trickster Anansi, who by his wit and cunning "manages to obtain from the all-powerful Sky God his food, thoughts, and stories" and bestows them on mankind (Roberts 29).

In America, conditions of scarcity continued, this time an artificial scarcity enforced by the slavemaster. Enslaved Africans produced enough food and material goods to enable them to live in comfort, but the slavemaster swallowed it all, leaving the producers with crumbs, scraps, guts, rags and shacks, with no choice but to steal and lie and trick and cheat just to survive. In those circumstances the African story tradition of the *righteous trickster* survived and flourished, with appropriate environmental modifications.

The trickster, then, is an authentic African-American culture hero. He is anything but childish, childlike, regressive, immoral or amoral. Quite the contrary, he is the acme of maturity, sophistication and resourcefulness, scaling obstacles, beating murderous odds, keeping the peace, finding a way to make a way out of no way. The trickster is the very embodiment of *morality,* of what is highest and best in humankind—what Robert Hayden called "the deep immortal human wish, / the timeless will"—the will to justice, freedom, fairness (Hayden 70). For what the trickster does, says Roberts, is to highlight the imbalance, redress the balance, balance the equation, level the playing field:

> The trickster tales offered a model of behavior for equalizing conditions between masters and slaves by breaking the rules of the system that gave the slavemasters a clear economic, political, and social advantage. It, in essence, functioned as an outlaw tradition within the value system of slavery. (Roberts 185)

In other words, *trickery is outlawry by other means.* And trickster heroes, animal or human, mirror living reality not only in slavery but in modern America: it surely took tremendous self-discipline and all a trickster's resources of mind and body to live through the South from 1877 to 1977.

Needless to say, what Roberts says of the trickster also holds for the badman. He too comes from a long line of resisters. But, as noted earlier, Roberts makes a distinction between the badman of late-nineteenth / early twentieth-century ballads who struck a personal blow against oppressive white power, and the latter-day badman of the toasts whose exploits are black-on-black and malign. The badman hero has received a bad press because conclusions about him were drawn almost entirely from the *toasts,* which might explain why he is routinely described as "asocial, self-centered, and futile" (Levine 420); "sociopathic," a "rebel without focus [waging] an undirected rebellion against an unspecified opponent," and "dangerous to his community" (Jackson 31, 33); or, as Abrahams called him, "consciously and sincerely immoral."

Roberts argues that such conclusions emphasizing "the destructive and unproductive nature" of badman heroes, especially in their relation to their community, amount to a distortion of the record. A proper perspective requires that the entire rebel tradition be taken into account. When the "bad niggers" of slave days and the badmen of the ballads are taken into proper account, it becomes clear that the badmen of the toasts are a minority, an exception, and their anti-black actions an aberration. In the main tradition their battle has never been against their own community (and, Roberts might have added, the danger to their community has, as we have noted, always been marginal except perhaps in reprisals following a slave revolt or such other large-scale assault). Their battle has been overwhelmingly against law that is unjust and an order that oppresses. Roberts emphasizes the point:

> While white Americans have had every reason to view the law as supportive of their interests and rights ... African-Americans have had very few reasons to view the law as anything other than antagonistic to their interests. (Roberts 182)

All in all, then, the badman hero is not so very unlike the "noble robber," "gentleman killer" and "social bandit" of Anglo-American and European outlaw legends. His crimes, too, are "selective, aimed against those with economic or political power" (Levine 415). In other words, black banditry actually belongs with the brand of banditry that the scholars normally approve—unless their "ethnocentrism" gets in the way (Roberts 175).

Roberts calls his approach "afrocentric," that is, one that looks at the subject matter (and the world) through pan-African eyes, rather than "eurocentric," through pan-European eyes. And from that perspective he concludes that the terms "trickster" and "badman" are not "value judgments" as such (certainly not pejoratives), but rather "descriptions" of "models of behavior" that people of African descent in America have historically needed and lived by (Roberts 221).

In effect, Roberts did for toasts what Grier and Cobbs did for the dozens. And he brought to folklore scholarship what Langston Hughes, Amiri Baraka, Maulana Karenga and the other theorists of a "black aesthetic" brought to literary scholarship.

The Canonical Toasts

And now, a brief look at the three best known toasts.

The Signifying Monkey

"The Signifying Monkey" is by far the most popular and best known of all toasts, and for good reason: its plot is the most exciting, its characters the most complicated and interesting. The story is usually set in the jungle, sometimes explicitly in Africa. (On the flip side, the adventure of the Pool-Shooting Monkey, involving the same Monkey and his sometime cousin Baboon, always takes place in the "concrete jungle," the city where bars and pool halls reign. It may open in the jungle but quickly shifts to the city.)

Monkey is a wisecracker, mouthy and loud, the quintessential trickster. He loves to set two people against each other by carrying tales. Physically weak, he survives by his brains. Lion is a bully, a brute (there's one in every neighborhood). He is pompous, conceited, square, easily led, a "lame." Elephant is cool, stately. His human analogues are the husky country types (truck drivers, farmers) who do hard physical labor, live simply, don't bother anybody, and don't play or mess around.

For the Lion, seeking status as he does in physical strength, the Elephant is a mountain that must be climbed. Elephant is the archetype of the test or ordeal that the hero must accomplish in order to prove himself worthy. The true hero usually does, but Lion is a cheap braggart, an aggressive predator.

His title of King of the Beasts seems conferred on him by lesser animals mostly out of fear. The title is relative: Lion himself is aware there are stronger animals (Buffalo, Rhino, Hippo, but most notably Elephant) more worthy of the title. He is therefore extremely insecure, sensitive to real or imagined insults, eager to prove his legitimacy by force.

Monkey is an instigator, a catalyst, a generator of drama, an agent of justice. In this respect he is, as Henry Louis Gates recognized, not unlike the Yoruba deity Eshu, the spirit of mischief, the original practical joker whose signature is "uncertainty or indeterminacy" (Gates 32). Mischief making, destabilization, the creation of tension and uncertainty, is his *metier;* to him, peace and quiet seem unnatural. He is bored when "nothin's happenin'," and he undertakes to shake things up:

> Now there hadn't been any shit in the jungle for quite a bit
> So the monkey decided he'd start some shit.

But insofar as he is malign, his malignity may not be entirely motiveless. For one thing he thinks Lion's pompous carryings-on are in bad form, that his bloated ego needs deflating. And in some versions (including our Version #5) he complains that Lion's roaring disturbs his sex life and his sleep.

For Monkey, pulling tricks is a compensatory mechanism. He needs the excitement both to counter a dull day and to make himself the center of attention. Why should all the attention go to the bigger, stronger animals—"with [their] grrrr shit"? Monkey's trickery helps him establish his identity as one of the Big Boys, as a major player and a force to be reckoned with in the Animal Kingdom. He wants recognition even if it means disapproval. Like Machiavelli's Prince, he would rather be feared than loved; a weaker animal would survive better in the jungle that way.

The Elephant in a sense exists outside the jungle hierarchy, beyond the obsession of the smaller animals for status. He has no ambition to be titled King, though perhaps he is the real king (the natural king as against the socially defined king). Elephant is aloof, indifferent, like a natural phenomenon, an abstract force. In mythological terms, he too is an agent of the gods, his assignment being, among other things, to teach conceited overreachers like Lion the limits of their humanity—or their beasthood.

Version #8, "The Signifying and Pool-Shooting Monkey," is perhaps the most self-consciously "artistic," the most delicately nuanced in our collection. For one thing it is twice as long as the others, weaving into a single unbroken fabric the signifying and pool-shooting adventures that are normally kept separate. In the other, "straight" versions the Monkey is in a slapdash hurry, rolling out his words rapidly and without subtlety, as if afraid the Lion might slip his noose. In this version, however, Monkey's innuendos are so carefully calibrated, his tone so patronizing and sarcastic that any fool could see he is "puttin' on a show." He is self-assured, cool and deliberate, taking his time. He knows his man and how to get to him. He is a master psychologist:

Most folks think you'd do something about it, except you're afraid
The elephant will scatter your ass like paper in a New York parade

Pardon me, Brother Lion, I do understand your fear
And if I didn't sympathize with you I wouldn't be here

Just let all the jungle talk, and don't let it bother your head
'Cause if you fight the elephant it's your ass that will be kicked,
    and this we dread.

Monkey is an artist of the cruel. He works on Lion's emotions, molding him
like putty, watching his reactions and relishing his dastardly work:

The lion stood up, his pupils as keen as a pin
It gave the Signifying Monkey such a good feeling to see the bull-
    shit was sinking in.

We are reminded of two of literature's greatest villains—Shakespeare's Iago
("Work on, my medicine, work!"), and Poe's Montresor, casually bantering with
his friend as he buries him alive in "The Cask of Amontillado."
    The Elephant is unusually reflective in this version. He utters just four
lines, and the first two, which speak volumes about his personality, must count
among the most beautiful lines in all literature:

The elephant said, "I don't know what the game is, and I wish
    you'd go away
I'd just like to lie here in the sun, it's such a beautiful day."

But the Lion persists:

The lion says, "You don't get off that easy, hot shot
Time I mop your ass across this jungle floor you'll only be a big
    greasy spot."

And Elephant finds he must make war to win peace:

The elephant says, "I see I won't get any peace, and this I regret
Till I slap you on your ass so you can knock off the threat."

The Lion, normally seen only from the outside, lets us into his mind in a
flash of interior monologue:

The lion thought, "Why did I let that monkey talk me into this jive?
Lord knows I'm lucky to get out of this shit alive."

And just in case the reader should miss the point, Monkey articulates the
moral of this drama when in his final taunt he scolds the Lion: "Yeah, you
running around believing everything I say. . . ." But teaching wisdom is
hardly the Monkey's goal. As Mary and Herbert Knapp so aptly stated it,
"The trickster is . . . an adventurer and showman with unabashed pride in

his work. If his tricks serve to educate, so be it, but their main purpose is to celebrate—himself" (Knapp 100). The Monkey is a narcissist.

The story ends with the narrator inserting himself in the action not just in signature as the teller (a common gesture in the oral tradition) but as a participant:

> I jumped up into that coconut tree and tied his tail in a knot
> He swore by God and three other responsible people he
> never would drop.

Stagger Lee

So much has already been said in this essay about Stagger Lee (variously spelled Stagolee, Stackolee, Stackalee, Stack-o-Lee, Stacker Lee, etc.) that just a few more words should suffice. Stagger Lee is the exemplary badman of the toasts. His actions are raw and unpremeditated, his reactions unmediated by reflection or guile. He is a creature of reflex, full of destructive rage. He has "a tombstone disposition and a graveyard mind" and "doesn't mind dying." He casts a cold eye on life, on death.

Like some badman ballads, "Stagger Lee" has affinities with the Wild West tradition where gunplay and hyper-masculinity are the rule. Versions #7 and #8, involving the figures of Billy the Kid, Geronimo, and Frank and Jesse James, are obviously closest to that tradition. Another such toast in our collection is "Black Jack Tucker," whose cast and setting are almost entirely from the Wild West.

Apparently in an attempt to "explain" Stagger Lee, some versions suggest that he was "born in a whorehouse, raised in a cave," or that his wife threw him out because, she said, "your love's grown cold." Others have constructed for him a mythic childhood of abuse: at one day old his father "kicked his ass till his blood ran cold," and next day snatched away his milk and replaced it with hard liquor. But these explanations fall short. We really don't know why Stagger Lee is the way he is, anymore than we know why the Monkey is a trickster or the Lion a brute. We accept their personalities as given, universal human types. Folklore is all too silent on causation: it is given as being in the nature of things, for instance, that co-wives are jealous, stepmothers are cruel, godmothers are protective, and love and hate happen at first sight. Rarely is there an attempt to explain sympathy—or antipathy. Things are as they are. Stagger Lee is as he is.

It is curious, though, that with all his hyper-sensitivity, and the violence with which he responds to insult, Stagger Lee never seems to resist arrest. Before the police he is unnaturally tame, confronting handcuffs with an icy resignation. The badmen of the ballads (and those of the Wild West sagas) would have started a gun battle. But with Stagger Lee, only in those versions where one of his henchmen invades the courtroom is there a violent confrontation.

Otherwise Stagger Lee sits calmly through his trial and accepts his long sentence with a mocking retort:

> He said, "Shit, Judge, [ninety-nine years] ain't no time
> I got a brother in Sing-Sing doing one-ninety-nine."

When hanged, he doesn't struggle either. It is only when he gets to hell that his old bad self seems to wake up, and he tackles the devil, bests him, and takes over. A man so bad needs a kingdom, a place where he is boss—and that place is hell!

The Titanic

Historically, the Titanic sank on April 14–15, 1912. For the rest of the century, a period of eighty-eight years, history had it that there was no black passenger or crew on the ship. Undocumented history had it that Jack Johnson, the heavyweight boxing champion, was rejected as a passenger because of his race, and the great bluesman Huddie Ledbetter (Leadbelly) celebrated the irony of it in a song. However, for most of those years, black folklore had it that there *was* a lone black man on that ship, a stoker or cook named Shine (another name for "nigger"). Then, suddenly, as the century closes down, a historian digging through the records discovers that there was indeed one black man on that ship—nay, *a whole black family:* a Haitian named Joseph Phillippe Lemercier Laroche (age 25), who was returning home with his pregnant French wife Juliette (22) and two daughters Simonne (3) and Louise (1) after his engineering studies in France. They traveled second class. When the iceberg struck, Laroche safely stowed his family on a lifeboat, but himself went down with the ship. His son Joseph was born in December of that year (see Z. Hughes 148–154; Geller 94–98). So much for history.

The author of the Titanic toast is unknown, as is the date of composition. The ship sank in April, but the toast almost always places it in May, which seems easier to rhyme:

> The 4th/8th/10th of May was a hell of a day /
> It was a hell of a day in the merry month of May
> When the great Titanic was sailing away.

"The Titanic" is a playlet in three scenes, framed with a brief prologue and epilogue. The contest is between the lone black man and, first, the Captain, the great authority figure that commands the ship; then, the cream of white society (sundry millionaires and their ladies) that own it; and, finally, the great ocean itself, with the great swimming beasts that inhabit it. It is an unequal contest all the way, but Shine triumphs each time and is the only one that lives to tell the tale (historically, of the 2,224 souls on board, 711 survived while 1,513 went down with the ship. The figures vary somewhat, depending on the source).

The Captain's arrogance is almost palpable: the builders called their ship "unsinkable," and, for his part, he's got 99 pumps / 49 pumps / 48 pumps to pump the water out. But then comes the moment of truth, with the Captain's daughter as gauge: she comes running distraught, her intimate garments all in the wrong places, struggling to hold things in place (if only she had four hands!), fighting a losing battle against indecent exposure:

> with her drawers in her hand / around her ankle, bra around
>   her neck /
> with her titties in her hand and her kotex around her neck /
> hands on her pussy, drawers around her neck

Those who thought Shine had misread the signs see the Captain's daughter and realize this is no joke. It is comical—but only as disaster and death can be comical. One by one the others plead for help. They have only fear—and money. From back in slave days, they have been used to standing helpless, wringing their hands, while the *servus validus,* the stereotypically strong black male (and female), did all the serving—and saving:

> Shine, Shine, save poor me
> Give you more [*what?*] than you ever did see.

Well might they know how deprived Shine has been all his life, and how his greed must want it all now. An offer they are convinced he couldn't possibly refuse. The men offer money and status, the women jewels and sex. Miserable little chips in the vast kingdom of Oceanus. And Shine's sassy reply: These things are good in their time and place; but on the ocean, man, if you can't swim, that's your ass. Of course the Captain can swim, else he wouldn't be captain. But this promises to be no ordinary swim and he knows it—sort of.

When, as occasionally, the offer includes a patronizing reference to his race ("Give you more ... than any black man see"), Shine lashes back with scorn:

> You know my color and you guessed my race /
> You hate my color and you despise my face
> Jump your ass in this water and give these sharks a race.

The sharks, whales, dolphins and porpoises are a race of swimmers. They don't care what race you are; you must win their race (in their element, on their terms), or lose your race. The pun is just as sharp even if unintended.

The swimmers want a race. And they are game, are willing to tease and play with Shine, give him a sporting chance. But if he tires or slackens, as they are sure he will, he's theirs.

Shine's reply is pure bluff, the tough guy's bad-mouthing and sass. It's a confidence game. He sounds confident, but he's scared as hell. Except he mustn't show it; the code forbids it! At least half of his tremendous effort is driven by pure terror. Shine is running (rather, swimming) for dear life; and as the Igbo would say, *oso ndu anaghi agwu ike* (a person running for his life doesn't get tired). And so Shine outswims the swimmingest creatures on earth. The feat is even more astounding than running faster than a bullet, something we see often enough in tall tales and hyperbolic boasts.

Shine gets to shore before the sea creatures and also before the wireless. Neither nature nor technology could bend his body or soul or will. His business accomplished, pleasure follows: the news finds him living it up at some nightspot.

A number of independent tales, jokes and rhymes have found themselves, as sometimes happens, sucked into the orbit of the Shine and Titanic Cycle, creating additional episodes in our Versions #5, #7 and #9. These include the Fornication Contest, the Dick Contest, Beating the Devil at His Own Game (three versions are in our Joke section) and the Harrowing of Hell (wherein the Devil and his family get it so bad they beg for mercy!). Versions #6, #7 and #8 are amalgams of verse and prose, while #9 is wholly in prose. In #6 and #8 the incidents are "true" but the ship is not the Titanic.

Shine is a remarkable hero, combining the trickster's brains with the badman's brawn. He is both mouthy and mean. In Version #2 he says to the captain's daughter:

> Now I know you're pregnant, about to have *my* kid
> But you better hit the water like old Shine did.

The next request—to save someone else's child—is therefore doubly ironic. And his answer underlines a simple truth:

> Shine looked at the boy with a tear in his eye
> "I'm sorry, little fellow, but every motherfucker is born to die."

The emotion may be genuine but the "tear" smells of crocodile, like a studied theatrical act. His stark declarative on natural law undercuts the "tear." The juxtaposition creates humor—the painful humor of the blues. Of course the request is absurdity itself: Shine would be lucky to save his own black ass.

This version is very rare indeed. And it tells us, in case we had any doubts, that the ice is not only in the iceberg, it's in Shine's heart too.

In Version #8 we see more of the Stagger Lee in Shine. He has steadily declined offers of sex—until he meets up with a black woman floating on a board splintered from the sinking ship. He answers her call for help, clambers onto the board, takes his sexual pay-off in advance, jumps back in the water and leaves her to drown!

Admittedly, this version of the story is also rare. Nonetheless, it provides a hilarious comment on Abrahams's conclusion that "It is also clear throughout that [Shine's] triumph is achieved in the name of his race" (Abrahams 81). Bah! The man had no race pride! . . . But of course that is not what Abrahams meant at all.

But, seriously, there is some validity in reading Shine as a representative African-American figure. However, his rejection of offers of money and sex and status is temporary, as dictated by the occasion; he is not "renouncing" them, nor is he thereby "reborn" into a saint nor "transformed" into a messiah—as we see him back on shore immersed in those same pleasures. Rather, the rejection is a demonstration of the steadfastness, singlemindedness and strength that black men and women must command in order to override the barriers placed in their path by America. To thrive, they must continuously perform the metaphorical equivalent of Shine's impossible feat. There is no alternative. And it is in this vein that Larry Neal viewed Shine as a mythical archetype of the "survival-motion" of the black person in the United States (see Neal, "Shine" 638–656).

THE PREACHER MAN

If paradox is the life of humor and humor the life of the oral tradition, then the African-American preacher occupies a unique place in that he embodies so many of the contradictions of that tradition. The preacher is a figure of intense paradox. He purveys a European Christianity in whose name the People were bought and sold, brutalized and murdered. He is involved in africanizing and domesticating that faith, refurbishing it and rendering it usable by its victims. His sermons are of imagined joys and real pains. He paints glowing pictures of heaven while giving his congregation hell. His language is at once puritan and vulgar, archaic and hip. And even as he dips a new convert in the waters of baptism, all the while preaching eternal life, the congregation stands on edge, knowing the real possibility of sudden death as the initiate leaps from the water, struggling for air ("I believe . . . I believe you're trying to drown my ass!"). The preacher calls for mortification of the flesh, with his own rampant lust firing his jeremiad. He calls on his flock to behold the pie in the sky while knowing full well their burning need is for pork in the pan. He can preach the virtues of poverty, then pass the collection plate. He is both trustee and trickster, at once revered and reviled, a figure both of utmost innocence and calculated wickedness.

The preacher is not a dope peddler or a pimp. But then, he does not need to be: he has a stable of responsible men and women who bring him a portion of their hard-earned income, enabling him to live in style with a fine house, fancy car, fashionable clothes (they would be embarrassed to see him otherwise). In exchange he assuages their pain with comforting myths, visions of future reward for present suffering—what Karl Marx perhaps unkindly called "the opium of the people," more powerful than any narcotic.

The preacher is indeed an illusionist, a magician. His wand is his eloquence. He is a master of words, a philosopher, raconteur, poet. But he is also a psychiatrist, confessor, consoler, peace maker, healer. If he didn't exist, he would surely need to be invented. Indeed, no society has ever found it possible to live without him: he is the African community elder, priest and medicine man bundled into one. At his best he is a Malcolm X—an opener of minds, a reconstructor of consciousnesses and of selves. Or a Martin Luther King—a doer of the word, an actualizer of the dream here on earth. At worst he is . . . a seducer to no end, a hustler out for himself.

The preacher, then, is an inhabitant of the crossroads, that passionate intersection at which all the powerful gales whipping through the community meet and tangle. He is God's lightning rod, bringing down the too-great-power and running it safely down into earth. But he is also a conductor of the people-generated electricity, a carrier of their messages of demand to the powers of earth and the principalities of heaven.

A figure of such centrality will necessarily be the butt of many jokes. Hot air (talk) is his stock in trade, and his balloon, so visible, so colorful, so vulnerable, continuously invites pricking. Wherever the preacher goes, parody, burlesque and laughter quickly follow. His holier than thou posture is a mask that pleads to be torn off, exposing the none too pretty, all too human face. His preachments are in sharp contrast with his well-known failings. The whole community knows him—stereotypically as gluttonous, concupiscent and vain, a sinner in the first degree. As critic Nigel Thomas puts it, "the preacher of folklore is lecherous, greedy, alcohol-loving, power-hungry, boastful, ostentatious, cunning, lazy, unprincipled, and occasionally militant" (Thomas 45). In the folklore, the chickens run and hide when they see the preacher coming to visit. In real life, Richard Wright relates how once in his childhood the preacher came to dinner. Because the boy wasn't permitted to eat until he finished his soup, which he couldn't, he was forced to sit there and watch as the preacher greedily consumed most of the chicken. When he protested, he was ordered to bed without dinner for his "bad manners" (Wright, *Black Boy* 33–34). In our story "G.Y.B.A.P.C." the preacher is the man who has found a way to shirk work, regardless whether he is truly "called," that is, endowed with eloquence and the spirit, or just a charlatan.

These reservations notwithstanding, the preacher endears himself to his congregation especially through his skills as a performer. He is an actor, lead singer, sound artist, dancer, poet. He delivers as much value as any other artist born and bred in the tradition. He was interactive long before the term was invented, exchanging energies with the congregation in an unbroken stream of pan-African call-and-response:

PREACHER:	Anybody here . . .
CONGREGATION:	Know my Jesus?
PREACHER:	Anybody here . . .
CONGREGATION:	Know my Jesus?
PREACHER:	Anybody here . . . [*tone changes*]
CONGREGATION:	Know my Jesus?
ALL:	Anybody here know my Lord?

PREACHER:	He healed the sick . . .
CONGREGATION:	Yes, yes!
PREACHER:	He raised the dead . . .
CONGREGATION:	Oh, yes!
PREACHER:	He's a wonderful savior . . .
CONGREGATION:	Yes, he is!
ALL:	Does anybody know my Lord?

Such an exchange could have come from any African village, whatever the occasion: Yes! It is true! *Ese! Ye-uwaa!* That's right! *Ezi okwu ka-obu!* Tell it! *Namu!* The preacher can gauge the power of his delivery by the volume of response. When he has really set the church on fire, when he has brought joy to their souls, the church will become a bedlam of voices, calling out different things, "speaking in tongues": *Have thine own way, Jesus! Save us, Lord! Help us, Lord! It's alright! Have a little talk with Jesus!* The energy of sound tangling with sound, including sounds of the street: *Teach hard! Fix it! Do it!*

The response may not be so controlled. Someone may simply holler. Another may jump up, shout, and break into a dance. The dance in the church, so subtle in the movements of the swaying choir, and so frenzied in the whirling of the "possessed" ("I Want to Testify"), finds its moderate center in the movements of the preacher at the climax of his sermon. He may shout, tremble and wiggle. He may simply point a foot and hop a little, as though the spirit has grabbed him and won't let go. Or he may jump up and down, take small running steps across the rostrum, reverse in a burst of energy and run in the opposite direction, not unlike a Reggae Rastaman on stage, or James Brown executing steps while hollering into the microphone, or Chinua Achebe's High Priest Ezeulu as he reenacts communal history and legend and does a sacred dance at the Festival of the New Pumpkin Leaves:

> The *ogene* sounded again. The Ikolo began to salute the Chief Priest. The women waved their leaves from side to side across their faces, muttering prayers to Ulu, the god that kills and saves. . . . [Ezeulu] ran forward, halted abruptly and faced the Ikolo. "Speak on," he said to it, "Ezeulu hears what you say." Then he stooped and danced three or four steps and rose again." (Achebe, *Arrow of God* 390)

Meanwhile (back in America) the congregation has kept up their chorus, some swaying in their seats, each one saving in the memory comic moments and motions that will enrich the treasury of jokes on the Preacher Man.

The preacher is a superb sound artist. He can holler, while holding the side of his head. Or he may have a special moan, a moan so low it pulls him to his knees. His moan can modulate from low-soft to suddenly harsh and loud. He might break a loud, rolling sermon with sudden whispers. Or he might preach a paragraph of biblical thees and thous, then skip to the language of the streets, as when our artist reenacts the story of Jonah in the belly of the whale:

Can't go out the front & afraid to go out the back
And he fell on his knees on this great blubbery rug
And the prettiest sound came from Jonah: [*moaning*]
"Loooooooord! . . . Looooooooord!
Can you dig me in this here fish?"

The preacher is a fine poet, as the numerous transcripts of his sermons extant in the literature attest. His cosmic imagery is at once biblical and contemporary. When he says, "Satan's hell hounds are on my track. My soul is in a slippery condition, my feet are almost in hell," it is the hounds of the patterollers trailing the fugitive slave through the swamps; it is the dogs of the lynching mob, and the fires of the South licking at the hanging man's feet, preparing to immolate him. When the preacher is not creating new images, he is giving new life to old ones. If he is going to speak on the Feeding of the Five Thousand, for instance, the congregation can anticipate a lively sermon that might concentrate on the little boy who gave his simple lunch to Jesus, and through this small act became part of a big miracle.

The preacher makes generous use of the technique of repetition. When it is humdrum or inept, repetition will put the congregation to sleep; but when done with poetry and passion it will keep them wide awake and clapping. The preacher may make a simple statement: "Sometimes all we need is a little talk with Jesus." And the congregation responds: "Go on and talk to him." Repeat: "I said we need to talk, we need to talk, we need to talk, talk, to have a little talk, with Jesus." And the members will answer. If this repetition should approach the sound of music, he can half-sing and preach on that one word, "talk," until the clapping and answering builds to a crescendo. It is the energy generated by such repetition, which when put on paper may appear naive and pointless, that fires the oral tradition.

The combined power of these talents—singer, shouter, dancer, poet—captures the black imagination and permits the preacher to believe in his own seriousness while at the same time undercutting that seriousness as effectively as only the best actor-comic can. And when it comes to acting out the concept of God as THE VOICE, a concept that has brought more tears of laughter to street stories and jokes about God, the preacher shows himself as the most talented of actors. In the pulpit, which is a stage, he is standing in for God. He becomes THE VOICE, becomes God.

THE VOICE is at the pivot of Judeo-Christianity and Islam. It is THE VOICE that says to Adam: "Who told you that you were naked?" It is THE VOICE that tells Noah to build an ark, that speaks to Moses from the Burning Bush, that commands Jonah to go and preach to the Ninevites. And while THE VOICE is invisible and abstract, it nevertheless has a well-defined character. It is thunderous, heavy, and walking. Holds space. It is commanding and regal in its ponderous pacing. And it is always, always DEEP! *Basso profundo*. A thing so grand and so sacred cannot escape the humor of the streets.

The law of humor is that the higher and more serious the object, event or idea, the deeper the humor it evokes. And the preacher, his church and his Bible with their high seriousness are bound to inspire some low laughter. Whether playful or bitter and cutting, it is laughter that is universal among African-American households, that touches all black lives. It is not confined to the young and disrespectful: much of what might at first seem irreverent or sacrilegious is, quite often, simply funny.

This humor is relentless in shoving fantasy aside in favor of reality. It humanizes and familiarizes, calling Saint James "Jim" or "Jim Dandy," and Jesus Christ "J.C." or "my man J.C." It is a humor that exhibits the preacher not as a son of God but as a son of man. The preacher who condemns heavy drinking is given as a heavy drinker ("Fresh Air"). The man who preaches against sexual incontinence is himself caught in the act ("Make a Joyful Noise!"). Our "Mock Sermon" shows him in his element, at his hyperbolic and comical best. "Jonah and the Whale" is a toast-sermon as he might have delivered it "off-line," at a social gathering, among friends, in mufti, incognito.

It could be said that the strength of the preacher, the very real power he exercises over the lives and imagination of the folk, is most clearly demonstrated when the humor aimed at him, sometimes playfully, sometimes not playfully at all, must rely so heavily on those forms and skills which, in their peculiar combination, are uniquely those of the preacher himself. And if it is the profane and the real side of the religious life that is more frequently affirmed by the oral tradition, this is only a natural response to the gripping sacred sermons of the Preacher Man.

JOKES

As we saw at the beginning of this essay, race is at the nuclear center of African-American humor. "Nuclear" is an apt metaphor, for race as we know it (as racism, or the ideology of white supremacy) is the most explosive and poisonous idea of the past five hundred years. It is an idea fraught with incalculable consequences. It is as deadly as it is hilarious in the powers it assigns and those it denies. In life the racial line, which holds itself as inviolate, is crossed and re-crossed daily, though not always without consequences. In folklore it is rarely crossed without laughter. Race has an almost infinite capacity for generating both comedy and tragedy, laughter and tears, and laughter-with-tears.

Race-generated humor is *expository:* it draws out the hidden contradictions for mockery, the absurdities for cathartic laughter. For instance, the "logic" of segregated facilities (one drinking fountain for whites, another for blacks) could issue (why not?) in differential speed limits (35 for whites, 90 for blacks, especially since the aim is to get blacks out of town as rapidly as possible), or differential traffic signals (green for whites, red for blacks)—and the danger of this "happy idea" becomes clear to all. The quality of mercy is strained when a man who rushes to catch a woman stumbling from a train suddenly realizes he is black and she is white and that, to put it lightly, their close encounter would likely be misunderstood. He stops midstream, leaving her to fall and break her neck.

The South is topsy-turveyland: "suicide" is twenty-three bullets in the back, and "Southern hospitality" is hostility for blacks, immunity for whites. Even the "good Nigras" are in revolt: called to advertise the South on television, they instead yell "Help!"

But it is in the inter-ethnic humor that the white supremacist philosophy is most profoundly mocked. With Black Man, White Man, Chinese Man and Jew Man, a representative Gang of Four from the multicultural dispensation, the hard racial lines disappear. The Four enjoy each other's company, "in defiance of the Jim Crow laws." They are "together" Brothers and don't even seem to know it. They go everywhere together and do everything together: they walk the streets together, visit the whorehouse together, go to court together, go to jail together, get out of jail together, go to hell together, go to heaven together. The jokes about them are gems of unconscious racial harmony, a benign parody of the world as it might have been before racism was invented. The racial stereotypes are here, of course, sometimes straight, sometimes tweaked: White Man is bland, undistinguished by any extremes; Jew Man is sharp and clever; Chinese Man is small of stature but sensible and prudent.

Black Man, naturally the butt and hero of his own jokes, is the *mostest* in every way, good and bad. He is the strongest, boldest, stinkiest and cleverest, the best lover and the best liar. With his "nigger jive" he confuses the jailer and defeats the devil, gets himself out of jail and out of hell. Only he can assign the devil a task too great for his vast powers. His companions (White, Jew, Chinese) live in a relatively rational world, so they propose extraordinary but eminently sensible tasks, which the devil easily accomplishes. But Black Man's historical circumstances have in many ways been unnatural, surreal and absurd, and he has learned to navigate life with the supra-rational mechanism of language and metaphor driven by an over-fertile imagination. It is deep from the abyss of the illogical and unnatural that he formulates the task he poses for the devil— a task with all the mystery and simplicity of a riddle or pun, one that turns on the tiniest pin-head of fact and fancy. And the devil, over-matched, out-flanked, played out (poor devil!), falls flat.

You can count on Black Man to overdo everything, to produce a triumphant twist and deliver a winning punch line. His comic dare is overwhelming. In heaven he gives Saint Peter the Afro handshake, greets Saint Paul with the Black Power fist, and demands, "Where's my man J.C.?"

Manipulation of language is of course how jokes are made. The Englishman's language, which carries a sense of his unflappable, understated national character, is the source of numerous jokes when it clashes head-on with the brash and overstated American language and personality, resulting in awkward misunderstandings. But it is an even further remove from African-American

English, and the contrast is simply delightful in "Englishman, Black Man." "The Nigger Announcer" is a register of language difference possibly marking the arrival of Ebonics in the national media. In "Bowels" we are treated to a grave parable of the colonial encounter. The Native American is in an untenable position, which his adoption of the language of his colonizers does nothing to improve. Given the imbalance of military power, it was only a matter of time before he would lose control of his land and join the Trail of Tears westward. The historical fact that African Americans fought on the side of Native Americans but also, more decisively, on the side of their dispossessors ("You Want the Indians to Hate Us?") prepares us for the cruel jabs of these jokes. African-American humor can be just as pitiless to fellow victims as Anglo-American humor.

"Reno's Comin'!" is a type of the tale of the innocent who doesn't know what fear is—until he experiences it in "absolute" terms. And "Who Is the King of the Jungle?" is a fragment of the larger cycle to which "The Signifying Monkey" also belongs. Here the focus is on a self-starting, arrogant Lion who doesn't know when to stop. If only he had read "The Perils of Insistence" in the *Thousand and One [Arabian] Nights,* he surely would not have so risked his health for an answer he didn't need (see Mathers 505–508).

"Lucky Strike" is a cigarette brand-name joke built on double entendres. It parallels jokes on names of various consumer items, including wines, beers, insurance companies and racehorses. Such jokes are widely circulated in typescript in offices, factories and other workplaces in the larger society—establishments that Alan Dundes and Carl Pagter have dubbed the "Paperwork Empire" (see Dundes and Pagter 200–205; Abrahams 255). "Books and Authors," so neatly packaged, may well have originated in the same Empire.

The jokes collected in "Riddles" are gems of distilled folk wit, as powerful as the best of proverbs and axioms, taut, exact in observation and concise in language. They too may well have their genesis, in part at least, in the Paperwork Empire.

JOKES ON CHILDREN

The only thing that saves these jokes from charges of child abuse is that they are jokes *told on* children to other adults, not jokes *told to* children or *played on* children. In that sense they are the opposite of childlore: they view children from the large end of the telescope and indulge in secret laughter at their expense. If children should encounter these jokes, they would not understand them; if they do understand, then they are probably old enough to take the hard knocks the jokes deliver.

A possible exception is "Close Your Legs!" in which a disreputable adult addresses a child in words amounting to abuse. But the joke is also on the mother who would send a child on such an errand. Child abuse is also implicit in "Coming and Going," "Felt," and "I Was Walking Through the Park." These represent the corruption of innocents, the acts of sexual assault visited on children daily in actual life, which is no laughing matter.

The dominant mode is the double entendre. Language, at once so transparent and so opaque, stands between the child (and the adult fool) and reality: the child misunderstands both the word spoken and the act committed. The humor of "rectum my ass" and "I don't want none of that shit" is, first, in the disjuncture between this crude explosion and the well-behaved environment in which it takes place. Then there is the child's forthrightness (or childishness, which in an adult would be self-righteousness or pigheadedness), which could not possibly countenance any other mode of articulating, of asserting or denying. And finally, there is the misapprehension of the words spoken, the inverted malapropism that cannot square-match the word to the object, that does not recognize "rectum" except as an attempt at censorship (which it partly is), or that, in the alternate version, views "wreck'd 'um" as a synonym of too light weight for "damn near killed him."

If the purblind messenger (the best kind for jokes) understood the message in "Check Her Reaction," he might have exercised a number of options: revise the message; withhold it; query the action ("What do you mean this is the last check I'm gonna get?"); or query the reaction ("What do you mean I'm not his son?"). Exercising an option would transform him into an active agent (manipulator) and the joke into fireworks of multitudinously unfolding shapes and colors. But the same could be said of virtually any joke: an option exercised gives birth to new dimensions (or variants), and whatever version of the joke we find is a result of the actions and inactions of its principals. "Check Her Reaction" is, ultimately, a variant of the well-known joke in which the mother says to her unhappy son: "You can go right ahead and marry her. She *is* your father's daughter, but then, you're *not* your father's son!"

"Grits and Wonder" could as well be titled "Grin and Bear It"—the stuff of the blues. The one pointed political joke, anchored on current affairs, is "What's Wrong, Seymour?" wherein Arthur Jensen and his white supremacist crew are derided.

One of the central sources of jokes on children is of course the child's discovery of sex—the child's surprise, bewilderment and apprehension at what he or she overheard, found traces of, or possibly observed of the parents' or other adults' lovemaking, and his or her uncertainty as to what exactly was taking place. Several of the jokes in our collection dance around the issue—until "How to Kill an Eel in One Easy Lesson" throws the covers off. According to G. Legman, the high priest of sexual humor, this joke has been in circulation in printed form "since at least the 1920's" (Legman 1: 59–60). This may explain the incongruity of the closing line, "Mother fainted": for, since in our version the mother herself arranged this lesson in sex education, there is no reason for her to faint at the clinically graphic account of what was learned. What then might have remained a puzzle requires but a simple inference: "Mother fainted" is a carryover from earlier versions in which the mother is unaware of her daughter's activities or her son's spying. Incongruities in folklore often result from such mismatches of version, such incomplete revisions or adaptations as the story travels from mouth to ear to mouth.

AND THE BEAT GOES ON ...

In this study, as elsewhere in the literature, the emphasis has been on the youthfulness of the participants in the verbal games of modern African-American orature. But of course in this as in other sports, players and spectators are apt to remain fascinated right into adulthood. They continue as observers, and whenever the opportunity arises they indulge their nostalgia as participants. In particular, the attitudes and perspectives developed from verbal play in childhood become an essential part of the adult personality, and the rhetorical skills acquired from playful sparring are kept in active reserve, modified, adapted and deployed as occasion demands in the adult "real world." We have already noted how, for instance, an adult gathering of old friends might casually slip into the dozens for recreation. Individually, those same former players might wield the dozens as a gladiator's sword in confrontations in the public arena—in the office, on the motorways, in the ball park, even on television. Not fists, not guns, but the dozens remains for them the choice weapon of offense and defense.

These rhetorical skills also prepared the youth for a variety of adult careers, including (a) the negative career of pimp and hustler, combining physical strength, verbal virtuosity and style (sharp dresser, extravagant exhibitionist), and (b) the positive careers of comedian (Redd Foxx, Dick Gregory, Richard Pryor); of orator, preacher, activist and political leader (Martin Luther King, Malcolm X, Jesse Jackson, Eldridge Cleaver, Stokely Carmichael, H. Rap Brown, Louis Farrakhan, Maulana Karenga, Muhammad Ali); and of poet, playwright, novelist, essayist (Amiri Baraka, Larry Neal, A. B. Spellman, Ishmael Reed, Ed Bullins, Askia Muhammad Toure, Haki Madhubuti, Sonia Sanchez, Nikki Giovanni, Gil Scott-Heron, Lightnin' Rod, The Last Poets).

The legendary boxer Muhammad Ali ("the man who was Cassius Clay") is unique in that he achieved dual fame as a pugilist of mouth and fist. He earned his tag of "Louisville Lip" as H. *Rap* Brown earned his—by word of mouth. Ali would regale the press corps with his rhymes, predicting the round in which his opponent would fall ("They all must fall / In the round I call") and celebrating his greatness: "Some say the greatest was Sugar Ray / But they have not seen Cassius Clay." His fight with Joe Frazier, staged in the Philippines, he called "the thrilla in Manila," and his fight with George Foreman in Zaire "a rumble in the jungle." As they prepared to enter the ring, he would browbeat his opponent with a barrage of boasts, threats and dozens: "This preacher will be your teacher." He would counsel the audience, "Before you bet your money /

Remember what happened to the Sonny"—the formidable Sonny (Liston) who twice suffered a "total eclipse" at his fists.

In the ring, Ali would, in his own words, "float like a butterfly, sting like a bee." He would dance back and forth, pummeling his opponent's head (always and only the head!) and floating out of reach. "Come on, come on," he would sometimes beckon, and assume his famous "rope-a-dope" posture, standing still and shielding his head while his opponent battered his midriff as best he could; then Ali would spring back and unleash a bombardment on the hapless opponent's head. "Who on earth thought when they came to the fight / That they would witness the launching of a human satellite?"

Ali's most ambitious composition, a poem of self-praise, opens with a flourish reminiscent of the great toasts of tradition: "It all started twenty years past / The greatest of them all was born at last / The very first words from his Louisville lips / 'I'm pretty as a picture, and there's no one I can't whip' ..." (Wiggins 57–59).

Ali was indeed the greatest of them all. But when he retired from the ring, then returned, retired and returned again, he lost to "rust" and "athletic old age" the spring in his feet and the hammer in his fists. It was his younger opponents, who meanwhile had thoroughly imbibed his technique, who now floated like a butterfly and stung—at the head! But in the long years when he was king of the ring, Muhammad Ali scored two victories for every fight: a verbal-psychological victory, clearing the way for the physical victory. His style of verbal warfare will leave its mark on the rap music yet to be born. Its echoes are also heard in the banter ("hot-dogging," "talking trash") of today's professional basketball players.

Throughout the twentieth century, a significant number of musicians and entertainers also thrilled their audiences with dozens, toasts and jokes incorporated in their repertory. As Lawrence Levine points out in his impressive study, *Black Culture and Black Consciousness* (1977), the dozens featured in folk songs and blues starting back in 1891—usually in the raw in backwoods juke joints and some nightclubs, but cleaned up and chaste for most commercial recordings. The artists included Little Hat Jones, Speckled Red, Tampa Red, Leroy Carr, Ben Curry, Victoria Spivey, Kokomo Arnold, George Noble, and Leadbelly (Levine 352–354). Entertainer Rudy Ray Moore built a nightclub and recording career on the raw dozens, "off-color" jokes, and unexpurgated toasts, while comedian Richard Pryor brought them into R-rated Hollywood movies. Other entertainers, such as Oscar Brown Jr., recorded cleaned up versions of "The Signifying Monkey" and other oral pieces.

Literary artists have also borrowed significantly from the modern oral forms. The great title poem of Margaret Walker's *For My People* carries the thunder and lightning of the folk sermon, while the narrative poems are modeled some on the ballad, some on toasts. Zora Neale Hurston's novels *Jonah's Gourd Vine* (1934) and *Their Eyes Were Watching God* (1937) display outstanding examples of rapping, signifying, dozens and sermons. So, in its own way, does Ellison's novel *Invisible Man* (1952). But of all African-American writers, it was Langston Hughes who most completely integrated into his work the oral tradition, ancient and modern. We have already seen how Hughes adapted Children's Rhymes ("Liberty And Justice— / Huh—For All") in his *Montage of a Dream Deferred* (1951). In his Tales of Simple, Hughes frequently has that lovable Man of the People rapping, signifying, boasting and joking, "unraveling his pedigree":

> These feet have stood on every rock from the Rock of Ages to 135th and Lenox. These feet have supported everything from a cotton bale to a hongry woman. These feet have walked ten thousand miles working for white folks and another ten thousand keeping up with colored. These feet have stood at altars, crap tables, free lunches, bars, graves, kitchen doors, betting windows, hospital clinics, WPA desks, social security railings, and in all kinds of lines from soup lines to the draft. If I just had four feet, I could have stood in more places longer.... (*Best of Simple* 2–3)

> In my time, I have been cut, stabbed, run over, hit by a car, tromped by a horse, robbed, fooled, deceived, double-crossed, dealt seconds, and mighty near blackmailed—but I am still here! I have been laid off, fired and not rehired, Jim Crowed, segregated, insulted, eliminated, locked in, locked out, left holding the bag, and denied relief. I have been caught in the rain, caught in jails, caught short with my rent, and caught with the wrong woman— but I am still here! ... (*Simple's Uncle Sam* 2–3)

These hyperbolic catalogues of achievements and woes, with their felicitous word play and bluesy humor that cuts both ways, jabbing at the self and jabbing at the Other, are clipped from the same cloth as Dan Burley's "Harlem Jive Spiel" and H. Rap Brown's "Sweet Peeter Jeeter."

Hughes modeled a long narrative poem, "Death in Harlem," on the high jive style of the toast, assisted by the ecstatic call and response of the folk sermon.

> At the big piano a little dark girl
> Was playin jazz for a midnight world.
>> Whip it, Miss Lucy!
>> Aw, pick that rag! ...

> Everybody's happy. It's a spendin crowd—
> Big time sports and girls who know
> Dixie's ain't no place for a gang that's slow.
>> Rock it, Arabella,
>> Babe, you sho can go!

It's a tale of love rivalry in a Harlem nightclub: "brown and bold" Bessie, Arabella Johnson and the Texas Kid. "The crudest melodrama," as Jean Toomer would say. Arabella leaves the Kid to go to the powder room—and comes back to find Bessie sitting in her place. "It was just as if somebody / Kicked her in the face." She pulls out her gun—

> [And] Bessie took a bullet to her
> Heart and died. . . .
> Take me,
> Jesus, take me
> Home today!

Arabella is nabbed and dragged to jail—

> But the Texas Kid,
> With lovin in his head,
> Picked up another woman and
> Went to bed.
>
> *(Collected Poems* 179–183)

The story is detailed but terse, the pace is brisk, as in the classic folk manner. Like "The Signifying Monkey" or "Stagger Lee," "Death in Harlem" is a tale of blood and laughter, a tragedy told as a joke.

Langston Hughes practiced *restraint,* sometimes of subject matter but always of language—a distinction that his detractors usually missed, or dismissed. The entire modern oral tradition is reflected in his poetry, prose fiction, and drama—*except* in one respect: he scrupulously avoided the vulgar and obscene language which, as we have seen, is endemic to that tradition. That Hughes was able to walk such a tightrope and yet produce works of first quality so unequivocally redolent of the folk, must be adjudged an element of his greatness as a poet. A writer so daring—and skillful—that he could construct an entire book, *Ask Your Mama* (1961), with the dozens for title and refrain, thumbing his nose at white power, white racists, and white liberals—but without uttering a vulgar word! To white neighbors who ring his bell and ask if he would recommend a maid, Hughes's black suburbanite replies: "Yes, your mama." To the creditor who threatens legal action, the debtor, "Once [his] brother's keeper / Now not even keeper to [his] child," retorts, "Tell your ma." And to the question, "Did I vote for Nixon? / I said, Voted for your mama" (*Collected Poems* 501, 511, 516). And so on. On two occasions Hughes approaches the suggestiveness of the popular dozens, but stops short:

> And they asked me right at Christmas
> If my blackness, would it rub off?
> I said, Ask your mama. . . .
>
> They asked me at the PTA
> Is it true that Negroes—?
> I said, Ask your mama.
>
> *(Collected Poems* 480, 509)

Hughes lifted the dozens out of the schoolyards, pool halls, barbershops and street corners of the black community, and deposited it on the Washington Mall, revealing something of its potential uses in the verbal battles on the floor of the Congress and the corporate boardroom. But even his provocative title is still a half-step from the war cry of Julius Lester's *Look Out, Whitey! Black Power's Gon' Get Your Mama* (1968), and a full step short of Amiri Baraka's *Up against the wall, motherfucker!*

No, Hughes's famous restraint was anathema to the generation that succeeded to his legacy. That generation embraced all of his matter and manner *except* for his linguistic restraint. It was a new day. The younger generation came to maturity in the active resistance of the civil rights movement of Martin Luther King and the radical nationalism of Malcolm X and the Nation of Islam. In Hughes's day the NAACP fought the cause in the courts, winning victory after victory through four decades of quiet litigation, but Martin Luther King carried the fight to the streets and, via television, into virtually every American home. The great pan-African nationalist of Hughes's day, Marcus Garvey, was easily silenced through jail and deportation, and his huge grassroots organization broke apart and dissipated. Malcolm too was silenced—but not before his voice and face had been registered and disseminated worldwide on audio and video tape, and his mind engraved in the consciousness of the younger generation.

In short, the genie was out of the bottle and would not go back in. The furious eloquence, sassy irreverence and vulgar vocabulary of contemporary rapping, signifying, boasts, threats and dozens were precisely what the violent 1960s seemed to demand, and the new generation of literary artists, especially the poets, embraced it all. Into the language, spirit and style of these oral forms they poured all their militant rage—rage at whites who had so outrageously used and confused blacks; rage at blacks that they had let themselves be so outrageously used and confused. They exhorted black people to change, to stop jiving and get serious, to come together, to act instead of dream, to get rid of liquor and narcotics and other habits of self-destruction, to love themselves, to understand the nature of America, the nature of the world, the nature of power. They urged a new orientation and new values—new ethics, new theology, new aesthetics. Adopting the Nation of Islam's slogan "We are an African People," they preached a pan-African worldview that affirmed the Homeland, highlighted its historical achievements as the mother of civilizations, and sought to rediscover and embrace its entire heritage in the Americas. Their method was closest to that of the preacher who seeks through excoriation and exhortation to reclaim his erring flock to the paths of righteousness, salvation, decency and progress.

This was the momentous Black Arts Movement, which Larry Neal, one of its architects, described as "the aesthetic and spiritual sister of the Black Power concept" (Neal, "Black Arts" 257). At its center was poetry, and then theatre, music and the visual arts. These were the *communal arts,* briefer and cheaper to produce and disseminate than prose fiction, and produced in sufficient quantity and quality to serve as sounding boards for the definition of a new Black Aesthetic.

Among the definitive texts of the new poetry were Baraka's "Black Art," "Black People!," "A Poem for Black Hearts," "A School of Prayer," "All in the Street" and "It's Nation Time"; Sonia Sanchez's "Blk/Rhetoric," "221-1424," "A Poem for My Father," "A / Coltrane / Poem" and "We a BaddDDD People"; Gil Scott-Heron's "The Revolution Will Not Be Televised"; David Nelson's "Die Nigga!!!"; The Last Poets' "New York, New York," "When the Revolution Comes" and "Niggers Are Scared of Revolution"; Nikki Giovanni's "The True Import of Present Dialogue," "Of Liberation," "The Great Pax Whitie," "Ego Tripping" and "Poem for Aretha"; and Haki Madhubuti's "Don't Cry, Scream," "Re-act for Action," "Malcolm Spoke / who listened?" and "A Poem to Complement Other Poems." To these should be added *Hustlers Convention* (1973), a 1048-line "jive epic" (ballad-toast) by Lightnin' Rod (Jalal Uridin), a member of The Last Poets.

Taking their cue from Langston Hughes's decades-old practice of reading poems to the accompaniment of jazz and blues, the new poets added music—a lone drum, an orchestra of drums, a chorus of two or three voices, a full gospel choir, a rhythm and blues band, a traditional or avant-garde jazz orchestra. The performance followed the traditional pattern of call and response: the leader recites at rapid-fire pace, the chorus dance, sing, chant, echo, shout, mock and exhort. The words can be heard and understood; but heard or not, the words soon become less important than the harmony of voices and music and the intense electricity of the performance as a whole. The result was a new kind of theater, a new style of poetry-reading fusing black preaching, black oratory, and black music, and a new species of poetry that at its extreme might look amorphous, nonsensical or incoherent on the printed page but that in performance would explode in glory like fireworks. In this "performance poetry" the poem ceases to be only "literature" for the reading eye and becomes "orature," something delivered by the mouth (oral) to the ear (aural) and for the eye (a spectacle or pageant). The poem takes on the identity of a drama script, an opera libretto, or a music score that must be performed to be realized, seen to be appreciated, heard to be enjoyed.

Amiri Baraka, with added advantage as a playwright, is the absolute master of the new poetry—in print and in performance. His phonodisc anthology *It's Nation Time* (1972) is a classic of the genre, as is The Last Poets' *The Last Poets* (1970), Gil Scott-Heron's *The Revolution Will Not Be Televised* (1971) and Nikki Giovanni's *Truth Is On Its Way* (1971). The two long poems sampled below will have to be heard on these recordings for the full force of their beauty and power to be felt:

Niggers are scared of revolution
But niggers shouldn't be scared of revolution
Because revolution is nothing but change
And all niggers do is change
Niggers come in from work and change into pimping clothes

And hit the street to make some quick change
Niggers change their hair from black to red to blond
And hope like hell their looks will change . . .

Niggers are players / Niggers are players, are players
Niggers play / football / baseball / and basketball
While the white man
Is cutting off their balls . . .
But when you say let's go take our liberation
Niggers reply—I was just playin'. . . .

Niggers are lovers are lovers are lovers
Niggers loved to hear Malcolm rap
But they didn't love Malcolm
Niggers love everything but themselves
But I'm a lover too / Yes I'm a lover too
I love niggers / I love niggers / I love niggers
Because niggers are me
And I should only love that which is me
I love to see niggers go through changes / love to see niggers act
Love to see niggers make them plays / and shoot the shit
But there is one thing about niggers I do not love
Niggers are scared of revolution.

(The Last Poets)

Time to get
together
time to be one strong fast black energy space
            one pulsating positive magnetism, rising. . . .
all niggers negroes must change up
come together in unity unify
for nation time
it's nation time . . .

        Boom
        Booom
        BOOOM
        Dadadadadadadadadadad
        Boom
        Boom
        Boom
        Boom
        Dadadadadadadad
                Hey aheee (soft)
                Hey ahheee
                (loud). . . .

It's nation time, get up santa claus
   it's nation time, build it
      get up muffet dragger
         get up rastus for real to be rasta farari
         ras jua
           get up got here bow

It's Nation
Time!
(Baraka, *It's Nation Time* 21, 22, 24)

As a multimedia event, "performance poetry" attained a peak that no one could have predicted—in Ntozake Shange's *For Colored Girls Who Have Considered Suicide / When the Rainbow Is Enuff* (1975), a "choreopoem" (dance drama) that held Broadway enthralled for many months.

Starting with the death of Malcolm in 1965, the Black Power / Black Consciousness / Black Arts Movement, with Amiri Baraka as pathfinder and chief theoretician, set the artistic agenda for black America for the next ten to fifteen years. The reverberations of that Big Bang are still being felt today—in the pan-African world, in the Anglo-American world, in the entire English-speaking world. African-American music may be decades ahead in pervasiveness and global conquest; but in its own limited sphere, the "performance poetry" that was the signature of the Black Arts Movement is today in practice all over the English-speaking world—sometimes with musical accompaniment, sometimes without.

Curiously enough, a parallel development was taking place in African-American popular music. As poetry moved closer to music, a strand of rhythm and blues moved closer to poetry. The musical monologue or recitative has a long history, from field hollers and shouts to jazz scat-singing to talking blues wherein the bluesman punctuated his song with asides, jokes and wry observations, to the preacher gliding from speaking to chanting to singing and back again. But nothing prepared the listening public for Isaac Hayes's *Hot Buttered Soul* (1969), which featured a rendition of "By the Time I Get to Phoenix" comprising ten minutes of lightly accompanied monologue and eight minutes of song. Equally surprising, and pleasing, was "I Stand Accused," plus the numerous other "Ike's Raps" blended with the music in his successive discs: *The Isaac Hayes Movement; To Be Continued; Black Moses; Joy;* and the score for the motion picture *Shaft*. The enormous popularity of this smooth new music indeed blossomed into a movement, reaching new peaks in the following decade with the Chicago-based group the Chi-Lites, and with Barry White, a Hayes clone whose music and voice became virtually indistinguishable from his. But the greatest surprise of the movement was the coming of Millie Jackson, who broadened the straight-line monologue into a full-fledged rhythm and blues music drama, with supplementary dialogue and an answering chorus supporting the main actor-singer in her discs *Caught Up, Still Caught Up* and *Feeling Bitchy.*

These two major developments in the literary and musical culture of the 1960s and 1970s—the rise of "performance poetry" and the musical monologue and dialogue of the "Isaac Hayes Movement"—together provided the foundation, materials and techniques for the emergence of rap music in the late 1970s and early 1980s.

But it was a technological break that provided the bridge to the new art form, as well as a platform on which it would flourish. In other words, rap music was the result of a two-sided experiment, one involving oral poetry, the other involving electronic sound technology.

The technology came through experimentation with vinyl records and turntables by young record spinners or disc jockeys (DJs) at house parties, block parties, wedding receptions and other social gatherings mainly in the black and Hispanic communities of the South Bronx in New York. To keep the dance music going beyond the commercially provided three minutes (a limitation that for decades had been a source of irritation for good-timers, a major frustration for lovers), the DJ, armed with two turntables, a sound mixer and an earphone, would delicately synchronize (or "mix") the beat from two records so that as one ended the other took over. The song would change, of course, but when expertly done the transition would be seamless, and the dancer-lovers could groove on from song to song, longer than Isaac Hayes's eighteen minutes! (The arrival, later, of sophisticated digital multitrackers made the job of mixing simpler and more precise.) The DJ could also extract the beat from one song and keep the beat and the dance going indefinitely while he rapped into the mike. With time the music production function split in two, with one young man (the DJ) manipulating the machines, and another, dubbed MC (Master of Ceremonies), doing the rapping (see Morley xv; Perkins 5–8).

It is at the point of rapping into the mike that the poetic half of the experiment kicks in. The best rappers were young men who had passed through those stages of oral learning so richly illustrated in this anthology—from children's rhymes through rapping, signifying, boasts, threats and dozens to the able telling of jokes and toasts.

For years, black DJs in the radio stations had developed a pattern of bandying jokes on air, playfully boasting of their skills, embroidering the music and filling out the interludes with their rhymes and smooth talk, and generally creating a welcoming, homey atmosphere for their unseen listeners. To this milieu of fun and entertainment the DJs transferred the playful rivalries of their adolescence. The air became their playground, the broadcast studio their street corner, and the listening audience the (invisible) judges of their oral performances. DJs regularly tried to out-talk and out-boast each other. They rapped to women listeners and callers on live call-in programs almost as slickly as out on the street, only taking care to keep the language clean and the innuendos sufficiently subtle to escape reprimand from the FCC.

When radio DJs embroidered the music with rhythmic talk, they usually did so in the beginning and end bars. They would sometimes sing along for a while, or throw in a sentence or quick phrase in the middle. In short, they rapped *around* the music, not *through* it. However, starting in the mid-1970s, black DJs saw and were infected by the example of Isaac Hayes, and by the Chi-Lites, Barry White, and Millie Jackson. These artists actually *talked through the music,* delivering assorted messages of love and "sexual healing." The DJs also saw and heard the militant black poets delivering powerful political messages to musical accompaniment, in verses that echoed the street raps of their own experience. These artists, too, *talked right through the music.*

Talking (or rapping) through the music was something no radio DJ dared attempt on air. But out in the community, at house parties or outdoor parties on the street or playground, a receptive social environment coupled with a technological break (the beat extracted from the mixer and kept going indefinitely) provided an unprecedented opportunity for experimentation in rapping through the music. The DJ, now restyled the MC, threw everything he had into the blending of music and talk, following the example of Isaac Hayes and his followers on the one hand, and of Amiri Baraka and his followers on the other—and *rap music* was born. It comes as no surprise, then, that rap music, when it exploded on the scene, would incorporate this dual tradition.

The R&B tradition of the personal and private, of love lyrics and broken hearts and sexual rivalry, is captured, for instance, in Salt-N-Pepa's peppery boast "I'll Take Your Man": "I'll take your man right out the box . . . / If you get another lover, I'll take him too / All I have to do is say a rhyme or two" (Salt-N-Pepa 276–277). And the muscular black poetics of public statement, exhortation, political commentary and cultural nationalism is carried forward by such leading rappers as Public Enemy, Queen Latifah, Sister Souljah, Ice Cube, Ice T, Grandmaster Flash and the Furious Five, and Ed O.G. and the Bulldogs.

Public Enemy's "Fight the Power" is perhaps rap music's most famous restatement of the central message of the revolutionary 1960s: "We got to pump the stuff to make us tough . . . / To revolutionize, make a change, nothin' strange . . . / What we need is awareness, we can't get careless . . . / We got to fight the powers that be" (Public Enemy 258–259).

In "Be a Father to Your Child" Ed O.G. and the Bulldogs tackle head-on a community scandal of incalculable consequences, encapsulated, as we have seen, in the dozens question: *How come your father don't live with you?* This short line is surely the unkindest cut, the deepest dagger thrust in the entire African-American dozens literature. O.G. and Co. lecture their listeners, especially the young black males, on the community's long-festering sore of irresponsible fatherhood ("You see, I hate when a brother makes a child and then denies it"), abandoned children ("You could still be called daddy if the mother's not your wife . . . / How would you like it if your father was a stranger. . . ?"), and the disadvantages of growing up in a single-parent or no-parent household that have scarred an entire generation. They admonish their listeners: "It's never too late to correct your mistakes . . . / Be a father to your child" (Ed O.G. and the Bulldogs 106–107).

The rappers would go from heavy dependence on mixing, splicing and synthesizing other people's music (which the courts would rule as violations of copyright), to creating their own music with their own bands and original compositions.

In his brilliant introduction to *Droppin' Science,* a fine collection of critical essays on rap music and hip-hop culture, William Eric Perkins classifies the variant styles and themes of rap, from the fiery "political or message rap" to the macho posturings of "gangsta rap" to the sex-obsessed and foul-mouthed "booty rap." Male and female artists feature prominently in all the categories.

By Perkins's account, rap has a Grand Quartet of Founders: Afrika Bambaataa, Kool Herc, Grandmaster Flash and Grandmaster Caz (Morley lists DJ Hollywood in place of Grandmaster Caz). Perkins also highlights the probable influence of the "talking reggae" of U-Roy, Big Youth and others, brought in by Jamaican immigrant Kool Herc (Clive Campbell). He also insists that the relentless beat that forms the baseline of all rap music was borrowed from Afro-Latin popular music, which in its grand variety is invariably driven by a powerful, dominant beat (Perkins 6; Morley xxii).

Perkins divides *political or message rap* into three subsets: (a) the *neo-nationalist,* best exemplified by Brother D, Keith LeBlanc, and Public Enemy, which focuses on the black situation and public affairs in America; (b) the *Islamic,* represented by Lakim Shabazz, the Poor Righteous Teachers, Rakim, Pete Rock and C. L. Smooth, Brand Nubian, Two Kings in a Cypher, Star & Crescent, the Supreme Team, and Unique and 3 MCs, and guided by the philosophy and theology of the Nation of Islam, particularly the Five Percenter faction; and (c) the *Africa-centered,* best represented by XCLAN, whose African garb and Nile Valley afrocentrism are perhaps most closely reminiscent of the Black Arts Movement (Perkins 20–24).

Gangsta rap is a mostly West Coast affair, the original practitioners emerging from the real-life gangs of Los Angeles, Oakland, Compton and Long Beach. Exemplified by the defunct NWA (Niggas With Attitude), by Ice-T, Ice Cube and Dr. Dre (all survivors of NWA), and by the Houston-based Geto Boys, gangsta rap "celebrates hustling, street crime, women abuse, and the gun as social equalizer" (Perkins 19). But it also has its posse of "gangsta bitches" such as Yo-Yo, Boss, Leshaun, Hurricane Gloria, and Choice who, like their male counterparts, are "ready to slice, dice, cut, and shoot" (Perkins 33).

Rap music is full of misogynic lyrics, but perhaps it was Miami-based 2 Live Crew that first broke all records in woman bashing and sexual explicitness, earning the dubious distinction of founder of *booty rap.* This triggered a reaction, and the male gender soon met its nemesis: a number of female rappers, led by Hoez With Attitude (HWA), Bytches With Problems (BWP), and Little Kim, struck back with lyrics just as sexually explicit and violently degrading to males (Perkins 24–28). Perkins treats other female rappers in a vaguely *feminist* separate category, except for Queen Latifah, who seems to defy classification, and

Sister Souljah, who while towering above the rest would nevertheless belong in the political group (Perkins 28–35).

Throughout the twentieth century, virtually every new major form of African-American music gave birth to its Anglo-American counterpart, which in turn brought forth charlatans, mediocres, serious learners, and masters. Sometimes the music played virtually unchanged across the line, as with Big Band jazz; sometimes it metamorphosed into a major new form, as when rock and roll moved past Elvis Presley to evolve into the "rock" of the Beatles, the Rolling Stones, and the various "acid" and "funk" and "new age" groups. Meanwhile, on the black side, rock and roll had moved on to rhythm and blues or "soul"—which also had its white avatars, as in Tom Jones. This excursus is simply by way of saying that rap, too, has had its Anglo-American practitioners, some of them no longer in business: 3rd Bass, Vanilla Ice, Marky Mark, the Funky Bunch, the Young Black Teenagers, House of Pain, Blood of Abraham and, more recently, the prize-winning Eminem.

In conclusion, then, rap music represents the latest full flowering of the modern African-American oral tradition so richly represented in this collection. What is the next stage? No one knows. But there is a good chance that these forms—children's rhymes, rapping, signifying, boasts, threats, jokes, dozens and toasts—will be here, mutated perhaps but still recognizable, when the next millennium rolls around.

NOTES

1. Critic H. Nigel Thomas lists the following as "bad niggers": "John Henry, Black Moseses, the slave insurrectionists, Malcolm X, Adam Clayton Powell, even Martin Luther King and Jesse Jackson." *From Folklore to Fiction: A Study of Folk Heroes and Rituals in the Black American Novel* (New York: Greenwood, 1988), 56.

2. For an extended list of African elements in white American culture, see Melville J. Herskovits, "What Has Africa Given America?" (1935), in *The New World Negro,* ed. Frances S. Herskovits (Bloomington: Indiana UP, 1966), 168–174; and John Edward Philips, "The African Heritage of White America," in *Africanisms in American Culture,* ed. Joseph E. Holloway (Bloomington: Indiana University Press, 1991), 225–239.

3. For an early refutation of Abrahams's Freudian thesis, see Charles Keil, *Urban Blues* (Chicago: University of Chicago Press, 1966), 20–29.

WORKS CITED

Abrahams, Roger D. *Deep Down in the Jungle: Negro Narrative Folklore from the Streets of Philadelphia.* Chicago: Aldine, 1963. Revised ed. 1970.

Achebe, Chinua. *Arrow of God* (1964). *The African Trilogy.* London: Picador, 1988. 315–555.

————. *Girls at War.* London: Heinemann, 1972.

————. *A Man of the People.* New York: Anchor, 1966.

————. *No Longer at Ease.* New York: Fawcett, 1991.

————. *Things Fall Apart.* New York: Fawcett, 1959.

Asante, Molefi Kete. "African Elements in African-American English." *Africanisms,* ed. Holloway. 19–33.

Baraka, Amiri (LeRoi Jones). "Image." *In Our Terribleness* by Amiri Baraka and Fundi (Billy Abernathy). Indianapolis: Bobbs-Merrill, 1970. n.p.

————. *It's Nation Time.* Chicago: Third World Press, 1970.

Bett, Henry. *Nursery Rhymes and Tales: Their Origin and History.* London: Methuen, 1924.

Brearley, H. C. "Ba-ad Nigger." *Mother Wit,* ed. Dundes. 578–585.

Brewer, J. Mason (ed.). *American Negro Folklore.* New York: New York Times Book Co., 1968.

Brown, Claude. "The Language of Soul." *Mother Wit,* ed. Dundes. 230–237.

Brown, H. Rap. *Die Nigger Die!* New York: Dial, 1969.

Brown, Sterling A. *Southern Road* (1932). Boston: Beacon, 1974.

Burley, Dan. "A Harlem Jive Spiel." *Folklore,* ed. Brewer. 284.

Chesnutt, Charles Waddell. "Mars Jeems's Nightmare." *The Conjure Woman* (1899). Ann Arbor: University of Michigan Press, 1969. 64–102.

Dalby, David. "The African Element in American English." *Rappin' and Stylin' Out,* ed. Kochman. 170–186.

Dance, Daryl Cumber. *Long Gone: The Mecklenburg Six and the Theme of Escape in Black Folklore.* Knoxville: University of Tennessee Press, 1987.

————. *Shuckin' and Jivin': Folklore from Contemporary Black Americans.* Bloomington: Indiana University Press, 1978.

Davis, Ossie. "Our Shining Black Prince." Eulogy delivered at the funeral of Malcolm X. Faith Temple Church of God, February 27, 1965. <www.cmgww.com/historic/malcolm/eulogy.html>.

Dollard, John. "The Dozens: Dialectic of Insult." *The American Imago* 1 (1939): 3–25. Reprinted in *Mother Wit,* ed. Dundes. 277–294.

Dunbar, Paul Laurence. "Whistling Sam." *Complete Poems*. New York: Dodd, Mead, 1913. 156–158.

Dundes, Alan (ed.). *Mother Wit from the Laughing Barrel*. Englewood Cliffs, NJ: Prentice Hall, 1973.

Dundes, Alan, and Carl R. Pagter (eds.). *Urban Folklore from the Paperwork Empire*. Austin, TX: American Folklore Society, 1975.

Echewa, T. Obinkaram. *I Saw the Sky Catch Fire*. New York: Dutton, 1992.

Ed O.G. and the Bulldogs. "Be a Father to Your Child." *Rap*, ed. Stanley. 106–107.

Gates, Henry Louis, Jr. *The Signifying Monkey: A Theory of African-American Literary Criticism*. New York: Oxford University Press, 1988.

Gates, Henry Louis, Jr., and Nellie Y. McKay (eds.). *The Norton Anthology of African American Literature*. New York: Norton, 1997.

Geller, Judith B. *Titanic: Women and Children First*. New York: Norton, 1998.

Grier, William H., and Price M. Cobbs. *Black Rage*. New York: Bantam, 1968.

———. *The Jesus Bag*. New York: Bantam, 1971.

Harris, Joel Chandler. "The Wonderful Tar-Baby Story" (1880). *The Complete Tales of Uncle Remus*. Boston: Houghton Mifflin, 1955. 6–8.

Hayden, Robert. *Selected Poems*. New York: October House, 1966.

Henderson, Stephen. *Understanding the New Black Poetry: Black Speech and Black Music as Poetic References*. New York: William Morrow, 1973.

Herskovits, Melville J. Letter. *South Atlantic Quarterly*, 39 (1940): 350–351.

———. "What Has Africa Given America?" (1935). *The New World Negro*, ed. Frances S. Herskovits. Bloomington: Indiana University Press, 1966. 168–174.

Holloway, Joseph E. (ed.). *Africanisms in American Culture*. Bloomington: Indiana University Press, 1990.

Hughes, Langston. *The Best of Simple*. New York: Hill and Wang, 1961.

———. *The Collected Poems of Langston Hughes*. New York: Knopf, 1994.

———. *Simple's Uncle Sam*. New York: Hill and Wang, 1965.

Hughes, Langston, and Arna Bontemps (eds.). *The Book of Negro Folklore*. New York: Dodd, Mead, 1958.

Hughes, Zondra. "What Happened to the Only Black Family on the Titanic." *Ebony*, June 2000. 148–154.

Hurston, Zora Neale. *Their Eyes Were Watching God*. New York: Fawcett, 1969.

Jacobs, Harriet. *Incidents in the Life of a Slave Girl* (1861). *The Classic Slave Narratives*, ed. Henry Louis Gates, Jr. New York: Mentor, 1987. 333–515.

Jackson, Bruce. *"Get Your Ass in the Water and Swim Like Me": Narrative Poetry from Black Oral Tradition*. Cambridge, MA: Harvard University Press, 1974.

Johnson, James Weldon. *The Book of American Negro Poetry* (Revised Edition). New York: Harcourt, Brace, 1931.

Johnson, Samuel. "The Life of Cowley." *Rasselas, Poems, and Selected Prose*. New York: Holt, Rinehart, 1958. 469–472.

Kantrowitz, Nathan, and Joanne Kantrowitz. "Meet 'Mr. Franklin': An Example of Usage." *Mother Wit*, ed. Dundes. 348–352.

Keil, Charles. *Urban Blues*. Chicago: University of Chicago Press, 1966.

Kidd, Dudley. *Savage Childhood: A Study of Kafir Children.* London: Adam and Charles Black, 1906.

Knapp, Mary, and Herbert Knapp. *One Potato, Two Potato . . . : The Secret Education of American Children.* New York: Norton, 1976.

Kochman, Thomas (ed.). *Rappin' and Stylin' Out: Communication in Urban Black America.* Urbana: University of Illinois Press, 1972.

Labov, William, Paul Cohen, Clarence Robins, and John Lewis. "Toasts." *Mother Wit,* ed. Dundes. 329–347.

Last Poets, The. *The Last Poets* (disc). New York: Douglas Music Corporation, 1970.

Legman, G[ershon]. *Rationale of the Dirty Joke: An Analysis of Sexual Humor.* New York: Breaking Point, 1975. 2 vols. (Originally titled *No Laughing Matter: An Analysis of Sexual Humor.* Bloomington: Indiana University Press, 1968, 1975. 2 vols.)

Levine, Lawrence W. *Black Culture and Black Consciousness: Afro-American Folk Thought from Slavery to Freedom.* New York: Oxford University Press, 1977.

Lightnin' Rod. *Hustlers Convention.* New York: Harmony Books, 1973.

Madhubuti, Haki. *Tough Notes: A Healing Call for Creating Exceptional Black Men.* Chicago: Third World Press, Inc., 2003.

Marvin X. "The Black Bird." *New Plays from the Black Theatre,* ed. Ed Bullins. New York: Bantam, 1969. 109–118.

Mathers, Powys (trans.). *The Book of the Thousand Nights and One Night.* Vol. 4. New York: St. Martin's Press, 1972. 4 vols.

Mayer, Philip. "The Joking of 'Pals' in Gusii Age-Sets." *African Studies* 10 (1951): 27–41.

McPherson, James Alan. "Why I Like Country Music." *Elbow Room.* Boston: Little, Brown, 1977. 3–22.

Mitchell-Kernan, Claudia. "Signifying, Loud-Talking and Marking." *Rappin' and Stylin' Out,* ed. Kochman. 315–335.

Morley, Jefferson. "Rap Music as American History." *Rap,* ed. Stanley. xv–xxx.

Morrison, Toni. *Beloved.* New York: Plume, 1988.

Neal, Larry. "And Shine Swam On." *Black Fire: An Anthology of Afro-American Writing,* ed. Amiri Baraka and Larry Neal. New York: Morrow, 1968. 638–656.

———. "The Black Arts Movement." *The Black Aesthetic,* ed. Addison Gayle. New York: Anchor, 1972. 257–274.

Newsweek. "Saving Private Welch." May 29, 2000. 40–42.

Opie, Iona, and Peter Opie. *The Lore and Language of Schoolchildren.* London: Clarendon, 1959.

Page, Thomas Nelson. *In Ole Virginia.* Chapel Hill: University of North Carolina Press, 1969.

Perkins, William Eric. "The Rap Attack." *Droppin' Science: Critical Essays on Rap Music and Hip Hop Culture,* ed. William Eric Perkins. Philadelphia: Temple University Press, 1996. 1–45.

Philips, John Edward. "The African Heritage of White America." *Africanisms in American Culture,* ed. Holloway. 225–239.

Public Enemy. "Fight the Power." *Rap,* ed. Stanley. 258–259.

Roberts, John W. *From Trickster to Badman: The Black Folk Hero in Slavery and Freedom.* Philadelphia: University of Pennsylvania Press, 1989.

Russell, Irwin. *Poems.* New York: The Century Co., 1888.

Salt-N-Pepa. "I'll Take Your Man." *Rap,* ed. Stanley. 276–279.

Sanchez, Sonia. *I've Been a Woman: New and Selected Poems.* Sausalito, CA: Black Scholar, 1978.

———. *We a BaddDDD People.* Detroit: Broadside, 1970.

Sembene, Ousmane. *Guelwaar* (film). New York: New Yorker Films, 1992.

Shange, Ntozake. *For Colored Girls Who Have Considered Suicide / When the Rainbow Is Enuff.* New York: Scribner, 1975.

Simmons, Donald C. "Possible West African Sources for the American Negro 'Dozens'." *Journal of American Folklore,* 76 (1963): 339–340.

Smitherman, Geneva. *Talkin and Testifyin: The Language of Black America.* Boston: Houghton Mifflin, 1977.

Sperling, Samuel J. "On the Dynamics of Teasing." *Journal of the American Psychoanalytic Association,* 1 (1953): 470. Qted. in Abrahams, *Deep Down,* 53.

Stanley, Lawrence A. (ed.). *Rap: The Lyrics.* New York: Penguin. 1992.

Thomas, H. Nigel. *From Folklore to Fiction: A Study of Folk Heroes and Rituals in the Black American Novel.* New York: Greenwood, 1988.

Thompson, Stith. *Motif-Index of Folk Literature.* Bloomington: Indiana University Press, 1955–1958. 6 vols.

Watkins, Mel. *On the Real Side: Laughing, Lying, and Signifying—The Underground Tradition of African-American Humor That Transformed American Culture, from Slavery to Richard Pryor.* New York: Simon and Schuster, 1994.

Wepman, Dennis, Dennis B. Newman, and Murray B. Binderman. *The Life: The Lore and Folk Poetry of the Black Hustler.* Philadelphia: University of Pennsylvania Press, 1976.

Wiggins, William H., Jr. "'I Am the Greatest': The Folklore of Muhammad Ali." *Black Lines: A Journal of Black Studies,* 2.1 (Fall 1971): 56–68.

Wright, Richard. *Black Boy.* New York: Harper, 1945.

———. "Down by the Riverside." *Uncle Tom's Children.* New York: Harper and Row, 1965. 54–102.

CHILDREN'S RHYMES AND GAME SONGS

What's the word?
Thunderbird! ...

THE WORLD AS WE SEE IT

Oh Little Playmate

Oh little playmate
Come out and play with me
Underneath the apple tree
And bring your dollies three

Climb up my rainbow
Slide down my cellar door
And we'll be jolly friends
Forever more

Oh little playmate
I cannot play with you
My dolly has the flu
Boo hoohoo hoohoo hoo

Ain't got no rainbow
Ain't got no cellar door
But we'll be jolly friends
Forever more

Oh little devil
Come out and fight with me
And bring your fork-a-fee
Heehee heehee heehee

I'll scratch your eyes out
I'll make you bleed to death
And we'll be enemies
Forever more

Kissing in the Hall

Apples in the summer
Peaches in the fall
Don't let your mother
Catch you kissin' in the hall

I Saw You with Your Boyfriend

I saw you with your boyfriend
    How do you know?
Peeped through the peephole
    Nosey!
Wash the dishes
    Lazy!
Jump out the window
    Crazy!

I Wish I Had a Nickel

I wish I had a nickel
I wish I had a dime
I wish I had a boyfriend
To kiss him all the time

My mother gave me the nickel
My father gave me the dime
My sister gave me a boyfriend
To kiss him all the time

My mother took the nickel
My father took the dime
My sister took the boyfriend
And gave me Frankenstein

Oh You Can't Get to Heaven

Oh you can't get to heaven on Superman
    on Superman
    on Superman
Oh you can't get to heaven on Superman
'Cause the Lord up in heaven is a Batman fan
'Cause the Lord up in heaven is a Batman fan

Oh you can't get to heaven in Abeba's car
    in Abeba's car
    in Abeba's car
Oh you can't get to heaven in Abeba's car
'Cause Abeba's car stops at every bar
'Cause Abeba's car stops at every bar

Oh you can't get to heaven on Danny's lip
    on Danny's lip
    on Danny's lip
Oh you can't get to heaven on Danny's lip
'Cause Danny's lip goes flippety-flip
'Cause Danny's lip goes flippety-flip

[*The variations are endless*]

Miss Sue

Miss Sue, Miss Sue
Miss Sue from Alabama
Hey you! Scooby-doo
Now let me see you smoothing
Now let me see you smoothing

Your Mother's Got the Chicken Pox

Your mother's got the chicken pox
Your father's got the mumps
Your sister and your brother's
Got the black-eyed bump

Somebody's Calling My Name

Hey Cristel!
  Somebody's calling my name
Hey Cristel!
  Somebody's playing my game
You're wanted on the telephone
  If it ain't my honey tell him I ain't home
Well it is your honey, so get on the phone!

From City to City

From city to city
From country to country
You're sittin' on the table
Peeling a potato

Tic Tac

Tic tac tic tac   Tic tac tic tac
Walla-walla one   Walla-walla four

Tic tac tic tac   Tic tac tic tac
Walla-walla two   Walla-walla five

Tic tac tic tac   Tic tac tic tac
Walla-walla three   Walla-walla FREEZE!

I Received an Invitation

I received an invitation
    Ah chi-ka
From the Board of Education
    Ah chi-ka
From the people population
    Ah chi-ka
From the young generation
    Ah chi-ka

Said ooh, ah, ah chi-ka
Said ooh, ah, ah chi-ka

Just Plant a Watermelon

Just plant a watermelon
    Right over ma head
And let the juice [*slur-r-r-p*]
    Slip through

Just plant a watermelon
    Right over ma head
That's all I ask
    Of you

Now southern fried chicken
    Might taste mighty fine
But nothin' taste better
    Than a watermelon rine

Just plant a watermelon
    Right over ma head
And let the juice [*slur-r-rp*]
    Slip through

I Eat the Peanut Butter

I eat the peanut butter
I eat the bread
I drink my milk
And I don't pee to bed

Beans

Beans, beans, good for your heart
The more you eat, the more you fart
The more you fart, the better you feel
So eat those beans for every meal

Sardines and Pork and Beans

(a)

CHORUS: Sardines, hey! and pork and beans, hey!
                           Sardines

LEADER: Every morning by the river side

CHORUS: Sardines

I keep a can laying by my side
           Sardines

Every morning at the grocery store
           Sardines

People standing there a-begging for more
           Sardines

Every morning when I get out of bed
           Sardines

Sardines spinnin' around my head
               Sardines, hey! and pork and beans, hey!
               Sardines!

(b)

LEADER: Sardines on my plate
And I don't want no steak

CHORUS: Sardines, hey! and pork and beans

Sardines is my dish
And I don't want no fish
               Sardines, hey! and pork and beans

Sardines on the table
They tickle my navel
               Sardines, hey! and pork and beans

Sardines is my meal
In my blood I can feel
               Sardines, hey! and pork and beans

Sardines is my song
With sardines can't go wrong
               Sardines, hey! and pork and beans

Sardines is my might
For sardines I would fight
               Sardines, hey! and pork and beans

(continued on the next page)

(c)

THE WELFARE SONG

CHORUS: Sardines, hey! and pork and beans
LEADER: I can tell by your nose
             You wear those welfare clothes
                      Sardines, hey! and pork and beans
             I can tell by your feet
             You eat that welfare meat
                      Sardines, hey! and pork and beans
             I can tell by your eyes
             You eat those welfare pies
                      Sardines, hey! and pork and beans
             I can tell by your pants
             You get those welfare grants
                      Sardines, hey! and pork and beans
             I can tell by your bop
             You eat that welfare slop
                      Sardines, hey and pork and beans
             I can tell by your knees
             You eat that welfare cheese
                      Sardines, hey! and pork and beans

Now I Lay Me Down to Sleep

Now I lay me down to sleep
I pray the Lord my soul to keep
If I should die before I wake
That'll be one less test I'll have to take

Now I lay me down to slumber
I pray the Lord I hit the number
If I should die before I wake
Put all I own on 208

Now I lay me down to sleep
I pray the double lock will keep
May no brick through the window break
And no one rob me till I wake

Now I lay me down to sleep
A bag of peanuts [candy] at my feet
If I should die before I wake
You'll know I died of a bellyache

Winston Tastes Good

Winston tastes good like a cigarette should—
No filter, no taste, just a fifty-cent waste

I Want My Money Back

I want a piece of pie
The pie too sweet
I want a piece of meat
The meat too tough
I want to buy a bull
The bull too black
I want my money back

Old King Cole

Old King Cole
Was a merry old soul
Tried to get to heaven
On a telephone pole

One foot slipped
The other one fell
He didn't get to heaven
But he made it down to hell

Hi-Ho Silver

Hi-Ho Silver everywhere
Tonto lost his underwear
Tonto say me don't care
Lone Ranger buy me another pair

My Little Monkey

My little monkey
Sittin' in the country
Eatin' some gingerbread
Along came a choo-choo
Knocked him on his boo-boo
And now my monkey is dead

Silent Night

Silent night, holy night
All is calm, all is right
The niggas
Didn't come out tonight

Slap Me Five

Slap me five [*extend back of hand*]
On the black man side [*or:* on the nigger side]
Stick it in the hole [*with thumb and index finger make a circle*]
You are full of *soul*!

Sambo

Sambo, Sambo, where you been?   Sambo, Sambo, what you buy?
   To the store and back again   Piece of watermelon for 15 cents

Run, Nigger, Run

Run, nigger, run, de patterollers will ketch you
Run, nigger, run, it's almost day
Dat nigger run, dat nigger flew
Dat nigger tore his shirt in two

Nigger, Nigger

   Nigger, nigger never die
   Black face and shiny eye

Grandma

Grandma, Grandma, sick in bed
Called the doctor and the doctor said
Grandma, Grandma, you ain't sick
All you need is a hickory stick

I Hate Bosco

I hate Bosco   But I fooled my mother
It's no good for me   I poured some in her tea
My mother poured some in my milk   Now I don't have no mother
To try and poison me   To try and poison me

Old Abe Lincoln

Abraham Lincoln was King of the Jews
He wore long cotton draws and be-bop shoes

Old Abe Lincoln was a good old man
He washed his face in a frying pan

Old Abe Lincoln was a good old soul
He washed his face in a toilet bowl

Old Man Tucker

Old Man Tucker was a mighty man
He washed his face in a frying pan
Combed his hair with a wagon wheel
And died with a stick of toothpaste in his heel

John Brown's Baby

John Brown's baby had a cold upon his chest
John Brown's baby had a cold upon his chest
And they rubbed it with camphorated oil

John Brown's baby had a [cough] upon his chest
John Brown's baby had a [cough] upon his chest
And they rubbed it with camphorated oil

John Brown's baby had a [cough] upon his [touch chest]
John Brown's baby had a [cough] upon his [touch chest]
And they rubbed it with camphorated oil

John Brown's baby had a [cough] upon his [touch chest]
John Brown's baby had a [cough] upon his [touch chest]
And they [rub chest] with camphorated oil

Old Jim Crow

Old Jim Crow come riding by
Said old man your heart's going to die

Said if he die I'll bury his skin
If he lives I'll ride him again

The World as We See It

See My Heart

See my heart
Gee, you're smart
See my thumb
Gee, you're dumb

See My Pinky

See my pinky
See my thumb
See my fist
You better run

Father Shot the Kangaroo

My father killed the kangaroo
He gave me the miserable part to chew
Wasn't that a terrible thing to do
To give me the chew
Of the miserable part of the kangaroo

[Repeat stanza ten times, each time louder and louder]

Your Eyes May Water

Your eyes may water
Your teeth may grit
But none of my money
Will you get

A Monkey Found a Dime

Once upon a time
A monkey found a dime
The dime turned red
And the monkey fell dead

Look Up, Look Down

(a)

Look up, look down
Your draws hanging down

(b)

Look up, look down
I made you look
You dirty crook
You stole your mama's pocket book

I turned it in
I turned it out
I turned it into
Sauerkraut

Do Your Ears Hang Low?

Do your ears hang low?
Can you tie them in a knot?
Can you tie them in a bow?
Can you hang them on your shoulder
Like a continental soldier?
Do your ears hang low?

[Repeat three times slow, medium, fast]

McDonald's

McDonald's is our kind of place
They feed you rattlesnakes
Hamburgers up your nose
French fries between your toes
The next time that you go there
They'll steal your underwear
McDonald's is our kind of place

The Roaches and the Bedbugs

I woke up in the mornin'
I looked up on the wall
The roaches 'n the bedbugs
Was havin' a game of ball

The score was ten to nothin'
The roaches were ahead
The bedbugs hit a homerun
'N knocked me out of bed

Popeye the Sailor Man

I'm Popeye the sailor man
I live in a garbage can
I eat all the worms
'N spit out the germs
I'm Popeye the sailor man

I'm Popeye the sailor man
I live in a garbage can
I like to go swimming
With bowlegged women
I'm Popeye the sailor man

It Ain't Gonna Rain No More

CHORUS: It ain't gonna rain no more, no more
            It ain't gonna rain no more, no more
            How in the heck you gonna wash my neck
            If it ain't gonna rain no more?

A little boy sittin' on a railroad track
Pickin' buggers like mad
Rollin' 'em up in little balls
And throwin' 'em at his dad

CHORUS: It ain't gonna rain no more ...   [etc.]

A rich girl uses cold cream
A poor girl uses lard
My sister uses axle grease
And scrubs twice as hard

CHORUS: It ain't gonna rain ...   [etc.]

A rich man drives a Cadillac
A poor man drives a Ford
My old man comes around the corner
With four wheels and a board

CHORUS: It ain't gonna rain ...   [etc.]

A rich boy has a scooter
A poor boy has a skate
My brother comes down the street
With treewheels and a gate

CHORUS: It ain't gonna rain ...   [etc.]

A rich man sails a yacht
A poor man sails a boat
My grandpa swims around the dock
With four barrels that float

CHORUS: It ain't gonna rain ...   [etc.]

Cry, Baby

Cry, baby, cry
Stick your finger in your eye
See the water fly
Cry until you die

Cry, baby, cry
Stick your finger in your eye
Tell, tell
Ring the bell

Kindergarten Baby

Kindergarten baby
Stick your head in gravy

[*Also:* First grade baby . . .]

Red, Red

Red, red, pee the bed
Wipe it up with jelly and bread

Brown, brown, go downtown
With your britches hanging down

Green, green
Your father's got a baldie bean

Blue, blue
You belong in the zoo

[*Based on color worn at time of rhyme*]

Tattle Tale

Tell her
Smell her
Kick her
Down the cellar

Now She's Gone

Shirley was here, now she's gone
She left her name to carry on
To all those that know her, hello!
All those that don't can go to hell

Glory, Glory, Hallelujah

Glory, glory, hallelujah
The teacher hit me with a ruler
I popped her on the beanie
With a rotten tangerinie
And she never bothered me no more

April Fool

April fool, go to school
Tell the teacher she's a fool
If she hits you with the mop
Go downstairs and tell the cop
If the cop don't do his duty
Go downstairs and kick his booty

Booty Shine

Michael [*any playmate's name*] is a friend of mine
He will show me his behind
For a nickel or a dime
Fifty cents for overtime
Tararaboomdee-ay
Tararaboomdee-ay
It only cost a dime
To get your booty shine

Old Lady Had a Rooster

Old lady had a rooster
De rooster died
De ol' lady cried
Ma hens don't lay
Like dey use ta

Stop

S   is for sniffin'
T   is for takin' dope
O   is for overdose
P   is for please, please, call the cops

[*Sing to the tune of* "Stop, The Love You Save May Be Your Own"]

I Know Your Hair Is Nappy

I know your hair is nappy
But I refuse to lend you my comb
If you have to beg n' plead for my Dixie Peach
I don't mind 'cause you need it desperately

[*Sing to the tune of* "Ain't Too Proud to Beg"]

MARCHING SONGS AND THREATS

I'm Little but I'm Loud

I'm little, but I'm loud
I'm poor, but I'm proud
I'm a little piece of leather
But I'm well put together

I'm a Cool Cool Girl

I'm a cool cool girl
From a cool cool town
Takes a mighty big nigger
To knock me down

I Like Coffee

(a)

I like coffee
I like tea
I like the Jackson Five
And they like me

So step back, Osmond Brothers
You don't shine
I'll get the Jackson Five
To beat your behind

(b)

I like coffee
I like tea
I like a colored boy
And he likes me

Step back, white boy
'Cause you don't shine
I'll get a colored boy
To kick your behind

Soul Sister, Soul Brother

I'm cool, I'm calm
I'm Soul Sister Number Eight
Mess with me I'll bust your cakes

I'm cool, I'm calm
I'm Soul Brother Number Nine
Sock it to me one more time

Your Left, Your Left

Your left, your left
Your left right—
My back is aching
My belt is tight
My hips are swinging
From left to right

I Am Blind

I am blind
I can't see
If I knock you down
Don't blame it on me

Black Is Beautiful

Black is beautiful
Brown is hip
White ain't nothing but
A piece of shit!

Who Are the Pros?

Who are the pros?
The nigger-roes
Who are the freaks?
The Puerto Rics

Who Can Do the Freakin'?

Who can do the freakin'?
All the Puerto Ricans
Who can do the most?
Us black folks

Whitey Don't Excite Me

Whitey don't excite me
'Cause he has thirty-two teeth
And a shiny tongue
And his ass goes too
When the wagon come

White Cracker, White Cracker

White cracker, white cracker
You don't shine
Betcha five dollars
I can beat your behind

Take Off Your Shoes

Take off your shoes and stockings
And let your feet go bare
Because we are the girls
From Charleston, South Carolina
Touch us if you dare!
Now come on, shake it, shake it, shake it
Touch us if you dare!

Choo-Choo, Bang-Bang

Choo-choo, Bang-bang
Gots to get my boom-a-rang
Un-ga-wa, black power
Bartram is the best
Hit 'im in the chest

What you gonna do?
Dance the boo-ga-loo
C stands for Candy
D stand for Do
We're gonna F-I-G-H-T
We're gonna FI-GHT
We're gonna Fight-Fight

We Are the Rough

We are the rough
We are the tough
We are the kids don't take no stuff!
Take off your shoes and smell your feet
We are the kids from McIntosh Street

If You Don't Like It

If you don't like it, lump it
If you don't lump it, take it
Around the corner and dump it

Campers' Beans

Campers' beans and campers' gravy
Gee I wished I joined the navy
Left-o, right-o
Bring out the mop-o
Left-o, right-o, left

Sound off—one, two
Sound off—three, four
Bring it on down
One, two, three, four
One-a, two-op, three, four

The Soldier

There's a soldier in the grass
With a bullet up his ass
Pull it out, pull it out
If you wanna be a Scout

Marching Songs and Threats

Engine, Engine Number Nine

[Number of players: unlimited]

Engine, Engine Number Nine
Struttin' down Chicago line
If the train falls off the track
Do you want your money back?

Yes, — Y-E-S spells yes   *[or:]*

No, — N-O spells no

*[Played by one person touching each
person's foot as rhyme is sung. Person
with both feet out either first or last—
depending on rule established—
is "it."]*

Out Goes the Rat

Out goes the rat
Out goes the cat
Out goes the lady
With the see-saw hat
O-U-T spells out
And I mean out!

> *[or: My mama told me
>   To choose you.
>   Y-O-U spells you!]*

Odds, Evens

One, strike three . . . . shoot

*[One person chooses "odd," the other "even." Both simulta-
neously throw out one or two fingers on the word "shoot."
If the fingers add up to an odd number (3), the person who
chose "odd" is "it." If the fingers add up to an even number
(2 or 4), the person who chose "even" is "it."]*

My Mother and Your Mother

[*Each player places a foot in a ring. Touching each foot, one player recites:*]

My mother and your mother
Were hanging up clothes
My mother punched your mother
In the nose
What color blood came out of it?

Yellow
Y-e-l-l-o-w spells yellow
And you are out

[*The last player touched calls out a color. The color is then called out. The last player touched on the last letter of the word is "it."*]

Doggie, Doggie

[*Each player places a foot in a ring. One player calls, touching each shoe:*]

Doggie, doggie step right out

Ukie Dookie

Ukie dookie soda cracker
Does your father chew tobacco?
If your father chews tobacco
Ukie dookie soda cracker out you go

One Potato, Two Potato

One potato, two potato, three potato, four
Five potato, six potato, seven potato, more

[*Each person makes two fists, holds them vertically. As rhyme is chanted one member of the group touches each person's closed fist. Hand you land on last is out.*]

Criss-cross, Applesauce

Criss-cross, applesauce
Applesauce, applesauce
Now cross-criss, applesauce
Applesauce, now freeze

Rubba Dolly

My momma told me [*clap, clap*]
If I was goody [*clap, clap*]
That she would buy me [*clap, clap*]
A rubba dubba dolly [*clap, slap*]
But someone told her [*clap, clap*]
I kissed a soldier [*clap, clap*]
Now she won't buy me [*clap, clap*]
A rubba, dubba dolly [*clap, clap*]

Down, Down Baby

Down, down baby
Down by the roller coaster
Sweet, sweet baby
I'll never let you go
Shimmy, shimmy, co-co pop
Shimmy, shimmy pop
Shimmy, shimmy co-co pop
Shimmy, shimmy, pop

A Sailor Went to Sea, Sea, Sea

A sailor went to sea, sea, sea
To see what he could see, see, see
But all that he could see, see, see
Was the bottom of the sea, sea, sea   [*edge of hand over eyebrow, like a scout*]

A sailor went to chop, chop, chop
To see what he could chop, chop, chop
But all that he could chop, chop, chop
Was the bottom of the deep blue chop, chop, chop   [*chopping action*]

A sailor went to knee, knee, knee ... [*etc.*]   [*tapping of knee*]

A sailor went to Chi-i-na ... [*etc.*]   [*pull back corners of eyes to make them have an oriental look*]

A sailor went to ooh bah, shoo bah ... [*etc.*]   [*rotate hand near stomach*]

Cookie Jar

(a)

1 – 2 – 3 and a zing, zing, zing
Who stole the cookie from the cookie jar?

Number 1 stole the cookie from the cookie jar
Who, me stole a cookie from the cookie jar?
Yes, you stole a cookie from the cookie jar
Not I stole the cookie from the cookie jar

Then who stole the cookie from the cookie jar?

Number 2 stole the cookie from the cookie jar
Who, me stole the cookie from the cookie jar? . . . [etc.]

[Each child playing is assigned a number before the game begins and must remember her number, because you never know when it will be called.]

(b)
[short version]

Who stole the cookie from the cookie jar?
Number 1
Who me?
Yes you!
Not me
Then who?
Ah, Number 3!
Who me?
Yes you!
Not me!   [etc.]

I Won't Go to Macy's Anymore

I won't go to Macy's anymore, more, more
There's a big, fat policeman at the door, door, door
He'll take you by the collar and make you pay a dollar
So I won't go to Macy's anymore, more, more!

Miss Mary Mack

Miss Mary Mack, Mack, Mack
All dressed in black, black, black
With silver buttons, buttons, buttons
All down her back, back, back

She asked her mother, mother, mother
For fifty cents, cents, cents
To see the elephant, elephant, elephant
Jump over the fence, fence, fence

He jumped so high, high, high
He touched the sky, sky, sky
'N he never came back, back, back
Till the Fourth of July, ly, ly

Well, I like coffee, coffee, coffee
'N I like tea, tea, tea
'N I like the boys, boys, boys
'N the boys like me, me, me

Miss Mary stumbled, stumbled, stumbled
And bumped her head, head, head
On a piece of cornbread, bread, bread
Then dropped dead!

Have You Ever, Ever, Ever

Have you ever, ever, ever
In your whole darn life
Seen a farmer, farmer, farmer
Kiss his wife, wife, wife?

No, I've never, never, never
In my whole darn life
Seen a farmer, farmer, farmer
Kiss his wife, wife, wife

Have you ever, ever, ever
In your long-legged life
Met a long-legged man
With a short-legged wife?

Have you ever, ever, ever
In your bald-headed life
Met a bald-headed man
With a bald-headed wife?

Have you ever, ever, ever
In your long-legged life
Met a short-legged man
With a bald-headed wife?

My Boyfriend's Name Is Tony

My boyfriend's name is Tony
He comes from Abilone
With bells on his toes and pickles on his nose
And that's the way my story goes

One day while I was walking
I heard my boyfriend talking
To a pretty little girl with strawberry curls
And this is what he said to her:

    I L-O-V-E love you
    I K-I-S-S kiss you
    I L-O-V-E K-I-S-S
    Kiss you in the dark

My boyfriend gave me peaches
My boyfriend gave me pears
My boyfriend gave me fifteen cents
To kiss him on the stairs

I gave him back his peaches
I gave him back his pears
I gave him back his fifteen cents
And kicked him down the stairs

Eenie Meenie Gypso Leenie

Eenie, meenie, gypso leenie
Ooh ah oppoleeny
Oochy koochy coomarochy   [*or:* Liberace]
I loooo-ove you

Mister Bee's at the door
'N he sure look sick
Missus Bee's at the door
'N she sure look sick
The whole family's at the door
'N they all look sick

Take a peach, take a plum
Take a stick a' bubblegum
No mo' peach, no mo' plum
Just a stick a' bubblegum

Miss Lucy Had a Baby

Miss Lucy had a baby
His name was Tiny Tim
His mother put him in the tub
To teach him how to swim

He drank up all the water
He ate up all the soap
He tried to eat the bath tub
But it wouldn't go down his throat

His mother called the doctor
His mother called the nurse
His mother called the lady
With the alligator purse

In walked the doctor
In walked the nurse
In walked the lady
With the alligator purse

Teddy Bear

(a)

Teddy bear, Teddy bear
    Turn all aroun', aroun', aroun'
Teddy bear, Teddy bear
    Touch the groun', groun', groun'

Teddy bear, Teddy bear
    Go up the stairs, stairs, stairs
Teddy bear, Teddy bear
    Say your prayers, prayers, prayers

Teddy bear, Teddy bear
    Turn off the light, light, light
Teddy bear, Teddy bear
    Say good-nite, good-nite, good-nite

(b)

I went downtown to see Miss Brown
She gave me a nickel to buy a pickle
The pickle was sour, she gave me a flower
The flower was dead, she gave me some thread
The thread was black, she gave me a card
And on the card it said:

    Teddy bear, Teddy bear, turn all around
    Teddy bear, Teddy bear, touch the ground
    Teddy bear, Teddy bear, do the twist
    Teddy bear, do it like this

(c)

LADYBUG

My mother, your mother live across the way
216 East Broadway
Every night they have a fight
This is what they say:

    Ladybug, Ladybug, turn around
    Ladybug, Ladybug, touch the ground
    Ladybug, Ladybug, show your shoe
    Ladybug, Ladybug, please skidoo

Cinderella

Cinderella dressed in yella
Went downtown to see her fella

Cinderella dressed in yella
Went downtown to buy some mustard
On the way her girdle busted
Ay Ay Ay—was she disgusted

Cinderella dressed in yella
Went upstairs and kissed a fella
Made a mistake and kissed a snake
How many doctors did it take?

First Comes Love

First comes love
Then comes marriage
Then comes the lady
With the baby carriage
How many babies will she have?

Fire, Fire

Fire, fire, false alarm
I fell into a fireman's arms

How many kisses will I receive?
I'll close my eyes and I will see . . .
One, two, three, four, . . .   [etc.]

Does He Love Me?

Does he love me?
Oh yes, no, maybe so

Will we get married?
Oh yes, no, maybe so

Where will we live?
Oh house, church, garbage can

How will I wear my hair?
Oh, curls, knots, beebee shots

How many children will we have?
One, two, three, . . .   [etc.]

Strawberry Shortcake

Strawberry shortcake, cream on top
Tell me the name of your sweetheart . . .
A, B, C, D, . . . [etc.]

[Or: ice-cream soda, cream on top]

Gypsy

Gypsy, Gypsy, please tell me
What my husband's gonna be
Rich man, poor man, baker man, thief
Doctor, lawyer, Indian chief

[Repeat]

Hot Pepper

Mabel, Mabel, set the table
Don't forget the red . . . hot . . . pepper

[The rope turners turn the rope at an
incredibly fast speed at this point]

Old Man Daisy

Old man Daisy, you're driving me crazy
Up the ladder, down the ladder
One, two, three
Pepper, salt, vinegar hot

Be On Time

Be on time
Don't be late
Half-past eight
And the train won't wait

Be on time
Cheryl got a date
At half-past eight
If she's late
She'll lose her date

Do the Wicky Wacky

Do the wicky wacky
Where the boys chew tobaccy
And the girls go
Wicky wacky woo

[*Girls throw dresses up in the air
on "Wicky wacky woo"*]

Chitty Chitty Bang Bang

Chitty chitty bang bang
Sat on a fence
She tried to make a nickel
Out of fifteen cents
She missed
She missed
She missed like this   [*jump out*]

Vote, Vote, Vote

Vote, vote, vote for Donna
In comes Cookie at the door, door, door
She's the only one that can have a lot of fun
So we don't need Donna anymore

Vote, vote, vote for Cookie
In comes Gloria at the door, door, door
She's the only one that can have a lot of fun
So we don't need Cookie anymore   [*etc.*]

Anna Banana

Anna Banana played the piana
All she could play
Was the Star-Spangled Banner
Anna Banana played the piana
Anna Banana . . . Split!   [*jumping out on "Split"
and repeating rhyme*]

Sew, Sew, Sew Your Draws

Sew, sew, sew your draws
Hang 'em up for Santa Claus
If dey clean
Hang 'em up for Halloween

Stampede

Stampede	While you're there
Follow me	Wash your hair
To the bottom	And your dirty
Of the sea	Underwear

Taxi Cab, Taxi Cab

Taxi cab, taxi cab, over the hills to Mexico
Give a little kick, kick, kick
Give a little twist, twist, twist
Give a little split, split, split
Salute to the captain
Bow to the queen
And turn your back on the dirty submarine

Help, Murder, Police

Help!	Murder!	Police!
Help!	Murder!	Police!
Help!	Murder!	
Help!	Murder!	
Help!		
Help!		
Help!		
Help!	Murder!	Police! [*etc.*]

[*Each girl jumps three turns of the rope, then two, then one.
The result is a breathless racing, especially when it comes
to the single jump.*]

Hey Girl

Hey girl, how about a fight?
'Cause here comes Willie Mae
With the skirt on tight

She can wiggle
She can woggle
She can do the split
But I bet you five dollars
She can't do this

Lady on 1 foot, 1 foot, 1 foot
Lady on 2 foots, 2 foots, 2 foots

[*Continue up to 10 foots*]

Amos 'N Andy

Amos 'n Andy
Sugar 'n candy
All jump up I say now

Amos 'n Andy
Sugar 'n candy
All jump down I say now

Amos 'n Andy
Sugar 'n candy
All jump out

Up the Ladder

Up the ladder
Down the ladder
One by one   [*number of jumpers*]
Two by two
Three by three

[*Continue up to ten*]

All in Together, Girls

All, all, all in together, girls
How do you like the weather, girls?
January, February, March, . . .   [*etc.*]

[*Each girl jumps out on the
month of her birthday*]

George Washington

George Washington
Never told a lie
He ran around the cor-NERRR
    [*jumps out, runs around,
    jumps in*]
And stole a cherry pie

Up and Back

Up and back
And back and up 1
Up and back and back and up 2

[*Continue through 10*]

On the Mountain

On the mountain stands a lady
Who she is I do not know
All she wants is gold and silver
All she needs is a nice young man   [*or:* ice cream cone]
So jump in my _____   [*name a person waiting to jump*]
And jump out my _____   [*name person jumping*]

Down the Mississippi

Down the Mississippi River
The steamboats are pushing   [*on the word* pushing,
                                                  *one jumper is pushed out
                                                  by the person jumping in*]

Down in Mississippi
Near the bo-bo bush
Along came a lady
And gave me a push   [*one jumper jumps in,
                                  pushes the next out*]

Mother Dear's in the Kitchen

Mother dear's in the kitchen
Baking a pie
Watching all the children go by

Here comes one
Here comes two   [*goes on with the count until
                              all the kids playing are in*]

All these children in her kitchen
That's too many
I think it's time for them to scat

Out goes ten
Out goes nine   [*and so on until everyone is out of
                            the game; call numbers in order*]

I Lost My Handkerchief

I lost my handkerchief yesterday
I found my handkerchief today
    It was all full of rain water
        So I dashed it away
        Dish-my-dash   [*repeat*]

Fudge Olyolee

Fudge, fudge, fudge olyolee
I like fudge olyolee
Here come the teacher with a hickory stick
Wonder what I got in arithmetic?
One and one is two, olyolee
Two and two is four, olyolee . . .   [*etc.*]

BALL GAMES

Ball Bouncing

"A" my name is Aretha   [*give female name beginning with alphabet letter*]
My husband's name is Al   [*give male name beginning with same letter*]
We come from Alabama   [*give place beginning with same letter*]
And we sell apples   [*give item beginning with same letter*]   [*etc.*]

One Over One

One—over one
Put your right foot over one (one)
Two—over two
Put your right foot over two (two)
Three—over three
Put your right foot over three (three)   [*etc.*]

[*Player crosses leg over ball to equal
the number he is up to until he misses*]

Hello Bill

Hello Bill   [*cross leg over ball*]
Where ya' goin' Bill?   [*cross leg over ball*]
Uptown Bill?   [*cross leg over ball*]
What for Bill?   [*cross*]
To pay a doctor bill?   [*cross*]
How much Bill?   [*cross*]
A ten dollar bill?   [*cross*]

Bouncy Ball

Bouncy, bouncy bally   [*cross leg over ball*]
My sister's name is Paulie   [*cross leg over ball*]
I gave her a whack   [*cross*]
She whacked   [*cross*]   me back   [*cross*]
Bouncy, bouncy, bally   [*cross leg over ball*]

Oliver Twist

Oliver Twist could not do this
So what's the use of trying this?

He touched his heels, he touched his toes
He touched his back and over it goes!

Devil and the Pitchfork

[*Played by boys and girls under twelve. In this game, leader and angels are against the devil. Each angel is secretly given a color; when the devil comes knocking, if he calls an angel's color, then that angel must run.*]

DEVIL: Knock, knock.
LEADING ANGEL: Who's there?
Devil and the pitchfork
Flying through the air.
What do you want?
A chicken.
What color?
Red.

[*If no one has chosen the color red:*]

Wash your face in red.
Blue.
Wash your face in blue.
Purple.

[*There is much screaming and hollering as the angel who has chosen purple is chased about the yard. If the devil doesn't catch him, there is more hollering because he is "safe." If he is caught, he joins the devil and helps to catch the other chickens.*]

Ole Mother Witch

[Played by boys and girls under twelve. Group of children with one child selected as witch]

Ole mother witch are you ready at one o'clock?
  No, I'm jess wakin' up.
Ole mother witch are you ready at two o'clock?
  No, I'm jess climbin' outta my bed.
Ole mother witch are you ready at three o'clock?
  No, I'm jess goin' to de baffroom.
Ole mother witch are you ready at four o'clock?
  No, I'm jess brushin' my teeth.
Ole mother witch are you ready at five o'clock?
  No, I'm jess washin' my face.
Ole mother witch are you ready at six o'clock?
  No, I'm jess goin' to the kitchen to eat.
Ole mother witch are you ready at seven o'clock?
  No, I'm jess sippin' my tea.
Ole mother witch are you ready at eight o'clock?
  No, I'm jess puttin' on my shoes.
Ole mother witch are you ready at nine o'clock?
  No, I'm jess buttonin' my sweater.
Ole mother witch are you ready at ten o'clock?
  No, I'm jess lookin' for ma hat.
Ole mother witch are you ready at eleven o'clock?
  No, I'm jess collectin' my keys.
Ole mother witch are you ready at twelve o'clock?
  I got ma broom and here I come!

[Children all run to escape being caught by witch. Extremely improvisational; witch may give any answers she desires and can get her broom and catch whenever the mood strikes her.]

CIRCLE GAMES

Head and Shoulders

Head and shoulders, baby, one, two, three
Head and shoulders, baby, one, two, three
Head and shoulders, baby, one, two, three
Head and shoulders, head and shoulders
Head and shoulders, baby, one, two, three

Knee and ankle, baby, one, two, three
Knee and ankle, baby, one, two, three
Knee and ankle, baby, one, two, three
Knee and ankle, knee and ankle
Knee and ankle, baby, one, two, three   [*etc.*]

[*Variations:*   Close the door; Zip the zipper; Around the world;
Tie your shoe; Milk the cow; Hit your head, *etc.*]

That's all, baby, one, two, three
That's all, baby, one, two, three
That's all, baby, one, two, three
That's all, that's all
That's all, baby, one, two, three

Punchenella

Look who's here, Punchenella, Punchenella
Look who's here, Punchenella in a shoe

Oh what can you do, Punchenella, Punchenella?
What can you do, Punchenella in a shoe?

Oh we can do it too, Punchenella, Punchenella
We can do it too, Punchenella in a shoe

Oh who do you choose, Punchenella, Punchenella?
Who do you choose, Punchenella in a shoe?

[*At this point the whole song is repeated*]

[*This is a song game played and sung by very young children. They all circle around one child who is supposed to be Punchenella. When they sing "what can you do" she does a dance. When they sing "we can do it too" they imitate her dance. Then she closes her eyes and blindly points her finger at someone in the circle and the whole game is repeated with the new leader in the center.*]

Shake, Shake My Playmate

Shake, shake my playmate
    Come out and play with me
And bring your dolly three
    Climb down my apple tree

Climb down my rainbow
    Come through the cellar door
And we'll be jolly friends
    For ever more, one – two – three – four

My little playmate
    I cannot play with you
My dolly has the flu
    Boo hoo, boo hoo-hoo

I have no rainbow
    I have no cellar door
But we'll be jolly friends
    For ever more, one – two – three – four

I'm Going to Kentucky

I'm going to Kentucky
    I'm going to the fair
To see a senorita
    With flowers in her hair

Oh shake it senorita
    Shake it if you can
So all the boys around your block
    Can see your underwear

Oh rumble to the bottom
    Rumble to the top
And turn around, and turn around
    Until you make a stop

Dinah's Dead

(a)

Dinah's dead
   How did she die?
Oh she died like this
And she died like that

Oh she lived in a town in Tennessee
She wore short, short dresses up above her knees
She can shake that thing wherever she goes
Hands up tootsie, tootsie, tootsie, tootsie

(b)

Aunt Donna's dead
   Oh how did she die?
Oh she died like this
Oh she died like this

Aunt Donna's living
   Oh where's she living?
Oh she's living in the country, where the moon goes down
She gonna shimmy, shimmy, shimmy 'til the sun goes down

She never went to college, she never went to school
And when she came back she was an educated fool

To the front, to the back, to the side, side, side
To the front, to the back, to the side, side, side

The Green Apple Tree

[*Circle game. Everyone dances around in a circle.
When a player's name is called, the player faces outward.
Game is repeated until everyone's name has been called*]

All around the green apple tree
Where the roses so sweet
Miss Carrie, Miss Carrie
Your sweetheart is dead
He wrote you a letter
To turn back your head

Circle Games

133

Sally Waters
(Sally Walker)

Little Sally Waters
Sitting in a saucer
Weeping and a-crying
For someone to come

Rise Sally rise
Wipe your teary eyes
Put your hands on your hips
And let your backbone slip

Turn to the east, Sally
Turn to the west, Sally
Turn to the one that
You like the best

Yes Ma'am

Lil' boy, lil' boy
   Yes Ma'am
Did 'ja go to the store?
   Yes Ma'am
Did 'ja git those eggs?
   Yes Ma'am
Did 'ja give 'em to the cook?
   Yes Ma'am
Did he put 'em in da bread?
   Yes Ma'am
Was da bread good?
   Yes Ma'am
Well den, good ole eggs
[or: What good egg bread]

TOGETHER: I say chuck-a-luck-a chuck-a-luck . . .

Grandmama Hippie-Hoppa

Grandmama Hippie-Hoppa
Sent me to you

What for to do?

To beat *one* hammer
Just like I do [*pats foot once and the chorus follows.*
        Repeats and says "two," chorus
        following, etc.]

Let's Get the Rhythm

Let's get the rhythm with the feet 1-2-3   [*on count touch part*
of body named]
So we got the rhythm with the feet 1-2-3

So let's get the rhythm with the knees 1-2-3
So we got the rhythm with the knees 1-2-3

So let's get the rhythm with the hips 1-2-3
So we got the rhythm with the hips 1-2-3

So let's get the rhythm with the hands 1-2-3
So we got the rhythm with the hands 1-2-3

So let's get the rhythm with the head 1-2-3
So we got the rhythm with the head 1-2-3, 1-2-3

WINE RHYMES

What's the Word?

What's the word?
   Thunderbird
What's the price?
   30 twice
Where you cop?
   The liquor shop
Who drinks the most?
   All you colored folks

3 – 6 – 9

3 – 6 – 9
The goose drunk wine
The monkey chewed tobacco
On the streetcar line

The line broke
The monkey got choked
And they all went to heaven
But the sanctified folk

Hambone

Hambone, Hambone, where you been?
Down to the liquor store drinkin' some gin

Newberry Wine

Baby, you're just as fine as Newberry wine
Tonight I would surely like to take you to dine
And afterwards, we could go to the pines

Whiskey Song

Ahhh to the bush
Ahhh to the bush

I feel frisky
    To the bush
I want some whiskey
    To the bush
In my locker
    To the bush
That pint of vodka
    To the bush
In my sneaker
    A bag of reefers
Up my nose
    Some Gypsy Rose
It's on the roof
    One hundred proof

Ahhh to the bush
Ahhh to the bush

Went to a party
    Had some Bacardi
Who were the freakiest?
    Ahhh, the Puerto Ricans
Who danced the most?
    Us colored folks

Ahhh to the bush
Ahhh to the bush

It's on my knee
    Yeah, J & B
It's on my mind
    Yeah, that pint of wine
It's on my leg
    Yeah, that Haig & Haig

Ahhh to the bush
Ahhh to the bush

It's on my lip
    Yeah, a potato chip

Ahhh to the bush
Ahhh to the bush

Up on the Roof

(a)

Up on the roof
    Oh yeah
100 Proof
    Oh yeah

I'm feeling fine
    Oh yeah
I'm drinkin' wine
    Oh yeah

A fifth of vodka
    Oh yeah
Is in my locker
    Oh yeah

It's good and mean
    Oh yeah
Bourbon Supreme
    Oh yeah

It's thrilling me
    Oh yeah
That martini
    Oh yeah

I'm having fun
    Oh yeah
Drinking rum
    Oh yeah

It's up your nose
    Oh yeah
Some Tiger Rose
    Oh yeah

On your behind
    Oh yeah
Black Cherry wine
    Oh yeah

Pull up your dress
    Oh yeah
I'll do the res'
    Oh yeah

Just you and me
    Oh yeah
Down by the sea
    Oh yeah

Don't be ashame'
    Oh yeah
Your mom did the same
    Oh yeah

(b)

Up on the roof
    Oh yeah
100 proof
    Oh yeah

Down in the locker
    Oh yeah
A fifth of vodka
    Oh yeah

I got the spirit
    Oh yeah
It's in my hands
    Oh yeah

It's in my ears
    Oh yeah
I can't hear
    Oh yeah

It's in my sneaker
    Oh yeah
A little reefer
    Oh yeah

What's Your Name?

What's ya name?
    Mary Jane!
Whe're ya live?
    Down da lane!
What's ya number?
Cucumber!

What chu eat?
    Pig feet!
What chu drink?
    Sneaky Pete!

Wine Rhymes

Marcy Chaplins

Marcy Chaplins and a —
>High-Low

Chicall-Ma-laws and a —
>High-Low

Frankenstein —
>High-Low

A-drinka-my wine —
>High-Low

And all the Shaggies —
>High-Low

A-follow behind singing —
>High-Low

This Ole Heart of Mine

This ole heart of mine
Got me drinkin' wine

Got me sniffin' dope
Smokin' reefer too

I tried hard to stop
My mother called the cops

They came after me
I ran up the street

Takin' LSD
They came after me

I don't take no more
I can't say no more

Mary, Mary

Mary, Mary, I've been thinking
What the heck have you been drinking?
Is it whiskey, is it wine? . . .
Oh my God, it's turpentine!

You Missed Me

You missed me, you missed me
Your mother drinks whiskey

You missed, you missed
Your father swallowed my piss

Last Call

Last call
For alcohol!

Listen My Children

Listen, my children, and you shall hear
Of the midnight ride of diarrhea
Hasten, Jason, get the basin
Oops . . . plop! Get the mop!

Your Ma

Your ma, your pa
You're Orphan Annie
Your greasy granny
You're Frankenstein
With the black behind
You're Cleopatra
You titty snatcher

Stranded

Here I sit, brokenhearted
Tried to shit, but only farted

Here I sit in smelly vapor
Someone stole the toilet paper
The doorbell rings, I must not linger
Guess I'll have to use my finger

Here I sit in a hell of a caper
Some black motherfucker used all the toilet paper
Train is coming, cannot linger
Guess I'll have to use my finger

Stranded, stranded on the toilet bowl
What do you do when you're stranded
'N you don't have a roll
To prove you're a man
You must wipe with your hand

Stranded, stranded on the toilet bowl
What do you do when you're stranded
'N you don't have a roll . . .?

Fat and Skinny

Fat and Skinny had a race
Fat fell down and broke his face

Fat and Skinny layin' in the bed
Fat laid a fart and Skinny dropped dead

Fat and Skinny layin' in the ditch
Fat called Skinny a dirty son-of-a-bitch

Fuck the Duck

Fuck the duck that swam the lake
Who fucked his granny through a great mistake

A Gal from Kansas City

There's a gal from Kansas City
She's got meatballs for her titties
She's got scrambled eggs
Between her legs
That's the girl from Kansas City

Batman and Robin

Batman and Robin swinging on a rubber band
Batman told Robin, "I'm gonna buy you something to hide your ole cane."
Robin said, "Batman, I don't care
'Cause your mama is the one who stole my underwear."

Your Mama Don't Wear No Draws

Your mama don't wear no draws (yeah)
I see her when she take them off
She put them in the sink (yeah)
She put them on the line (yeah)
The sun refuse to shine
The sink began to stink
She put them on the wall (yeah)
The wall began to crawl

Kiss My Ass!

STATEMENT: Kiss my ass!

REPLY: Kissing your ass is like kissing your face
                 Kissing your face is a complete disgrace

The Food Chant

*[This chant is recited while pointing to the
appropriate parts of the body as the words dictate.
The beer and hot dogs refer to bodily waste.]*

Ice cold beer
Get it right here
Step around the corner
Get your hot dogs here

The Woodpecker

The woodpecker pecked on the schoolhouse door
He pecked and he pecked until he couldn't peck no more
He came back the next day but he couldn't peck
Why?—Because his pecker was sore

Put Your Foot on the Rock

Put your foot on the rock, s'ah—s'ah
Let the boys feel your cock, s'ah—s'ah
Don't be ashamed, s'ah—s'ah
'Cause your mother did the same, s'ah—s'ah

When You Get to Be a Man

When you get to be a man
Be a man in full
Let your balls hang down
Like a Jersey bull's

Mary Had a Steamboat

Mary had a steamboat
The steamboat had a bell
Mary went to Heaven
The steamboat went to . . .

Hello operator
Give me number nine
If you get no answer
Just stick it up your . . .

Behind the refrigerator
There's a piece of glass
And every time you step on it
It flies right up your . . .

Ask me no more questions
I'll tell you no more lies
A man got hit with a bottle of shit
Right between the eyes

A Geea, My Geea

A geea, my geea, a playing in a ditch
A gee, call my gee, a dirty son of a . . .

Bring down your children and let them play with sticks
When they grow older, they want to play with . . .

Dickie had a brother, they named him Tiny Tim
Put him in the piss pot, and learned him how to swim

He swim to the bottom and he swim to the top
Mimi got excited, caught him by his . . .

Cocktail, ginger ale, buy your sister a glass
If you don't like it, you shove it up my . . .

Ask me no questions, I'll tell you no lies
A man got hit with a bag of shit, right between the eyes

Boom, boom

Batman

Batman
I took her to the movies
Batman
The movies was closed
Batman
I took her to the park
Batman
The park was dark
Batman
I took her to my house

Batman
I laid her on the couch
Batman
I stuck it in greasy
Batman
It came out easy
Batman
Her mother was surprised
Batman
To see her belly rise

Down by the River

Down by the river where nobody goes
There lies Betty without any clothes

Along came Freddy swingin' his chain
Down with the zipper and out it came

Three months later, all was well
Six months later she began to swell

Nine months later out it came
Little Freddy Junior, swingin' his chain

Tra-la-la Boom-de-ay

Tra-la-la boom-de-ay
Have you had yours today

I had mine yesterday
From the boy across the way

He threw me on the couch
And stuck it up my crotch

Tra-la-la boom-de-ay
Tra-la-la boom-de-ay

My mother was surprise
To see my belly rise

My father was disgusted
To see my cherry busted

It took me nine months
To get rid of the lumps

Tra-la-la boom-de-ay
Tra-la-la boom-de-ay

Her Belly Began to Rise

No. 1
My story has just begun

No. 2
She told me what to do

No. 3
She laid me between her knees

No. 4
Then we were on the floor

No. 5
Her belly began to rise

No. 6
I inserted my big prick

No. 7
I thought I was in heaven

No. 8
The doctor was at the gate

No. 9
The twins were at her side

No. 10
Then we started all over again

Bang Bang Lulu

CHORUS: Bang bang Lulu
Bang bang Lulu
Who's gonna bang bang Lulu
When I'm dead and gone

Lulu had a boyfriend
Her boyfriend had a truck
Drove her in the alley
And taught her how to fuck

Bang bang Lulu
Bang bang Lulu
Who's gonna bang bang Lulu
When I'm dead and gone

Rich girls wear Kotex
Poor girls wear rags
Lulu's cunt is so damn big
She wears a burlap bag

Bang bang Lulu
Bang bang Lulu
Who's gonna bang bang Lulu
When I'm dead and gone

Lulu had a bicycle
The seat was made of glass
And every time she hit a bump
The seat cut up her ass

Bang bang Lulu
Bang bang Lulu
Who's gonna bang bang Lulu
When I'm dead and gone

Sing the Old Tunes

(a)

[Sung to the tune of "Carolina in the Morning"]

Nothing could be finer
Than to be in her vagina
In the morning

Nothing could be sweeter
Than to feel her squeeze my peter
In the morning

(b)

[Sung to the tune of "Honey, Baby, Mine"]

I got a girl in old Kentuck, honey
I got a girl in old Kentuck, babe
I got a girl in old Kentuck
She can't sing, but she sure can fuck
Honey, baby, mine

(c)

[Sung to the tune of "Good Old Summertime"]

Put on your old pink panties
That used to be your granny's
With the silver buttons on the side
And the hole in the middle
Where your grandpa used to fiddle
In the good old summertime

Baseball Bat

Sister, Sister what is that
Hangin' on Father like a baseball bat?
Sh! Sh!! Don't say that
Go ask your mother what is that

Mother, Mother, what is that
Hangin' on Father like a baseball bat?
Sh! Sh!! Don't say that
Go ask your brother what is that

Brother, Brother, what is that
Hangin' on Father like a baseball bat?
Sh! Sh!! Don't say that
Go ask your father what is that

Father, Father, what is that
Hangin' on you like a baseball bat?
Sh! Sh!! Don't say that
That's what made your mother fat

A Man Named Brockett

There once was a man named Brockett
Who put his dick in a socket
His wife was a bitch
And turned on the switch
And Brockett took off like a rocket

I've Been Told

I don't know, but I've been told
Eskimo pussy is very, very cold

I don't know, but I've been told
Granny ma hole is very, very old

I don't know, but I've been told
Chinese pussy is full of folds

I don't know, but I've been told
Catholic pussy is very, very holy

I do know and don't have to be told
Black pussy is very full of soul

I Was Walking Through the Jungle

I was walking through the jungle with my cock in my hand
I was a cool motherfucker 'cause I was a jungleman

I looked in the tree and what did I see
A dirty motherfucker trying to piss on me

I picked up a rock and skinned off his cock
And now I don't know if he's living or not

The Titty Shout

CHORUS: Tit-tit-tit-tit-tit
Tit-tit-tit-tit
Tit-tit-tit-tit

LEADER: Soul Duo Number One
Tell me why the titty
Is so much fun

DUO: The titty's soft, Oh! yeah!
The titty's round, Oh! yeah!
And when it's hard
You're off the ground

CHORUS:	Ungh! Ungh! Ungh! Ungh! Ungh! Ungh! Ungh! Ungh! Ah! Ungh! Ungh! Ungh! Ahhhhh!
LEADER:	Soul Duo Number Two Tell me what the titty Can do for you!
DUO:	The titty's big, Oh! yeah! The titty's bad, Oh! yeah! It makes you happy Never sad!
CHORUS:	Ungh! Ungh! Ungh! Ungh! Ungh! Ungh! Ungh! Ungh! Ah! Ungh! Ungh! Ungh! Ahhhhh!
LEADER:	Soul Duo Number Three Tell me what the titty Has done for you
DUO:	When I was young, Oh! yeah! It raised me up, Oh! yeah! And when I suck it It fills me up
CHORUS:	Ungh! Ungh! Ungh! Ungh! Ungh! Ungh! Ungh! Ungh! Ah! Ungh! Ungh! Ungh! Ahhhhh!
LEADER:	Soul Duo Number Four Tell me why the titty Makes you go for more
DUO:	The titty's black, Oh! yeah! The titty's bold, Oh! yeah! The titty's always Full of soul
CHORUS:	Ungh! Ungh! Ungh! Ungh! Ungh! Ungh! Ungh! Ungh! Ah! Ungh! Ungh! Ungh! Ahhhhh!
LEADER:	Soul Duo Number Five Tell me why the titty Makes you feel so alive

DUO: The titty's warm, Oh! yeah!
The titty's soft, Oh! yeah!
If you are hungry
You'll bite it off

CHORUS: Your titty! Your titty!
Your titty! Toooooo!

LEADER: Soul Duo Number Six
Tell us what the titty
Does for our dicks

DUO: It makes them hard, Oh! yeah!
It makes them long, Oh! yeah!
And when it does it
They sing a song

CHORUS: Your titty! Your titty!
Your titty! Toooooo!

LEADER: Soul Duo Number Seven
Tell me why the titty
Makes you feel you're in heaven

DUO: It makes you high, Oh! yeah!
It makes you fly, Oh! yeah!
'Til I know
I'm above the sky

CHORUS: Your titty! Your Titty!
Your titty! Toooooo!

LEADER: Soul Duo Number Eight
Tell me why the titty
Makes you feel so great

DUO: The more the ounces, Oh! yeah!
The more it bounces, Oh! yeah!
And when you squeeze
It wants to please

CHORUS: Your titty! Your titty!
Your titty! Toooooo!

LEADER: Soul Duo Number Nine
Tell me why the titty
Makes you feel so fine

DUO: It blows my mind, Oh! yeah!
It feels so fine, Oh! yeah!
You keep on licking
You feel divine

CHORUS: Your titty! Your titty!
Your titty! Toooooo!

LEADER: Soul Duo Number Ten
I really want to lick
That big black titty again

DUO: It's like a game, Oh! yeah!
Don't feel no shame, Oh! yeah!
I bite the nipple
It taste like "Ripple"

CHORUS: Your titty! Your titty!
Your titty! Ahhh!

Part II

RAPPING, SIGNIFYING, BOASTS AND THREATS

Man, I don't play.
I quit school because they had recess ...

Briefs

1. Man, I don't play. I quit school because they had recess.

2. I joke, smoke, snort coke, but I don't play. Took the knobs off my radio.

3. Nigger, I don't play that shit. I don't. I only buy things by the elevens and thirteens.

4. When I'm drinking my wine, I'll kill Jesus Christ and three other white men.

5. I'm a bad little diddy-bop don't take no sass
   Mess with me and I'll kick your ass.

6. You may be king of the jungle and lord of the sea
   But you gotta be a bad motherfucker to mess with me!

7. You're too womanish; I need to cut you down to a buttonhole lower.

8. If you don't shut your mouth I'll whip your head until it looks like okra. [*Variation:* I'll whip your head until you rope like okra.]

9. I'll beat you so bad you'll have to look up to look down.

10. I'll put my foot so far up your ass that it will take a twenty-mule team a week to pull it out.

11. You would rather stick a wet noodle up a wildcat's ass than to fuck with me.

12. You would rather go through hell in gasoline-soaked drawers than fuck with me.

13. Nigger, I'll beat you 'til my elbows catch on fire.

14. You would rather let a four hundred pound gorilla suck your dick in a telephone booth than fuck with me.

15. You would rather stand on your dick and whistle through your asshole than fuck with me.

16. Man, we will lock asses like two dogs if you mess with me.

17. Nigger, you don't know me, I'll knock you back up in your mother's womb.

18. Don't let your mouth write a check your ass can't cash.

19. Don't let your alligator mouth get your canary ass in trouble.

20. If I'm wrong, in my chest is where you belong.

21. Nigger, you keep messin' with me and I'll slap the cowboy pee out of you.

22. I'll hit you so hard you'll stink standing up.

23. Nigger, I'll lighten up your ass if you keep fucking with me.

24. Man, put your hands on me one more time, you'll draw back nubs.

25. Don't be fat mouthin' me, boy.

26. If you so bad, you better start throwing hands.

27. If you can't get along, get it on!

28. You'd better git while the gittin's good.

29. I can do more things with you than Carver did with the peanut.

30. Fuck with me and your ass is grass.

31. I'll cut you so low you'll have to reach up to touch bottom.

32. Don't be handin' me no chump change.

33. Every motherfucker got a theme song; sing yours.

34. If you like pushin' up daisies, keep messin' with me.

35. Keep messin' with me and you'll end up using your teeth for a saucer to set yo' teacup in.

36. Fuck with me and I'll twist off your leg and kick your own ass with it.

37. Keep fuckin' with me and I'll run up into your ass like a storm.

38. If you mess with me I will put both feet up your ass and tap-dance on your liver.

39. Mess with me and I'll stick my foot so far up your ass when you brush your teeth you'll shine my shoe.

40. Nigger, keep messin' with me and I'll slap you until yo' jaws rattle like tin pans.

41. You ain't crazy, nigger, now I know you ain't crazy. Hell, you'd rather walk in a lion's cage with a pork-chop jacket on than to mess with me.

42. Nigger, I ain't buyin' you nothin'! I ain't puttin' out nothin' but tombstones, and you have to be dead to get one of them.

43. Nigger, if you feel froggy, leap!
    [*Variation:* My father was so evil that when he said frog, I jumped!]

44. I'll run you down the street so fast you'll have to stick your fingers in your nose to keep the wind from cutting off your breath.

45. Nigger, I'll beat the black off you.

46. I'll beat you till your mother won't recognize you.

47. I'll punch you in the mouth so hard you'll be grinning out your ass.

48. Keep fucking with me and I'll light your ass like sterno.

49. Keep fucking with me and I'll introduce your head to the Municipal Lumber Yard.

50. I don't do no yodeling in the valley [eat pussy].

51. I'll fuck you up fast
    I'll fuck you up slow
    And if you keep on talking shit
    I'll fuck you up all over this damn floor.

52. Ya better stick yo' head in a jaybird's tail
    And put a stopper in yours
    'Cause when you mess with me
    You gonna have a shittin' good time.

Claim to Fame

"Van?"

"Yeah, that's my name, claim to fame.
Don't abuse it, misuse it, or otherwise tamper with it.
Now what the hell you want?"

There Is No Double

My name is Abel, there is no double
Don't let your mouth get your ass in trouble.

Plumber

Just call me a plumber
'Cause I lay mo' pipe
Just call me coffee
'Cause I grind so fine.

A Declaration of Friendship

You're my ace boon coon
You're my pride and joy
You're a ugly motherfucker
But you're still my boy.

Crying Blues

I was walking around the fairgrounds and this man stopped me and said, "Hold it! Here's ten dollars."

I said, "Ten dollars? What for?"

The man said, "The ugliest man on the ground get ten dollars."

I was proud to be ugly then, because I didn't have nothing then. I reached out for it like that and the man snatched it back and said, "Hold it! Here's a man back of you that's uglier than you."

And that's the kind of hard luck I had
If hard luck was music
I'd have the hottest band in town
If hard luck was money
I'd be the richest man in town
I got buzzard luck
Can't kill nothin' and won't nothin' die
And I'm slowly starving to death.

My Family

My mother never told me a story in my life. Every time she said something about she goin' to whip me, she did.

My people on my father's side, they all of them is in big business. My uncle and my aunt, they had a iron and steel business. My uncle went out and stole all night and my aunt stayed home and ironed. Yes, they was great people. I had another uncle. He was a great dancer. Last time I saw him, he was dancing on the end of a rope.

One thing about it, all of my people is honest. Of course, the judge didn't think so. One of my uncles stole a battleship and he got away with it. And went back to steal the ocean to sail it in and they caught him with the first bucket of water.

I never was angry but once in my life. But I never been mad. I had a dog that went mad and they killed him, so I just get angry and stops. I didn't want to get killed like the dog did.

Mean

Mean!! Is my man mean?!!
Can a duck make pancakes?
Does a bear fart in the woods?
Is fat meat greasy?
Do chitlins stink?

I Farts Freely

I farts freely wherever I be
'Cause it was the death of my father
But it won't be the death of me.

My Name, My Game

Tony is my name, and kicking a jive nigger in the ass is my game.
I laugh, joke and smoke, but I don't jive.
When I first came to New York there wasn't but a few bad niggers still alive.
When I got through doing my do the only one left is the one talking to you.

Joe Taylor

My name is Joe Taylor
My dick is a whaler
My nuts weigh 44 lbs.
If you know a fat lady
That wants a big baby
Just tell her Joe Taylor's in town.

I'm a Cool Cool Nigger

I'm a cool cool nigger
From a cool cool town
Take another cool nigger
To mow me down

You can roll your eyes
You can stomp your feet
But this is one motherfucker
You sure can't beat

You kin look me up
You kin look me down
But this is one motherfucker
You can't turn around.

My Legend Has Come to Pass

My name is Jody, and my legend has come to pass
Don't let your mouth make a check that your body can't cash

Don't mess around because you'll get your money took
Your mind shook
And your name written down in the undertaker's book

I might not always be right
But I'm never wrong

You got no rights
If you can't fight

I'm hitting hard, moving fast, breaking jaw and kicking ass
I'll stick my foot so far up your ass
I'll have to stop by the hospital to pick up my shoe.

Don't Mess With Me

My name is Blue and I'm going to get you
Fe fi fo fum here I come, who wants to shoot one
Bip bop bam here I am
Yeah, this is me and I'm ready as I want to be

I'm Ali Sock, the baddest motherfucker you'll ever see
Fury is my name
And sounding on sad motherfuckers like you is my game

You jive-ass faggot, I'm gonna put a cut in your strut
A glide in your stride
And remove that hole in your soul
I'm gonna put some pep in your step
And some pride in your stride

I may be five foot eight on the ground
But I'll be six foot seven and 667 lbs. in your collar.

I'm a Lover

I'm a love man
Yes, that's me, darling
Too slick to be tricked
Too cool to be fooled
Too old to be cold
A slice of life twice as nice

Five foot nine tall sugar
Weigh 140 lbs., curly hair
Ain't got a world to care
Caramel-colored shin, 18 years old
And I ain't never had enough of nothing
Young, black, bold, full of soul
And I'll rap to any girl that passes by

I've got a love that's as soft as tissue paper
As sweet as candy paper
As strong as aluminum foil

Pretty little thing, let me light your candle
'Cause, momma, I'm sho hard to handle
Got the power to give it to you
If you got the power to take it
What I don't have you don't need

Of the women I make frequently
Each holds in her heart secretly
That she is really making me a love man

One said the other night
That I make love like coffee
I asked how
And she said 'cause I grind so good

Another said last week
It was like Maxwell House
Good to the last drop

Boys and things are a dime by the dozen
But that ain't nothing but drug store love
I know I can love you better than them
So won't you bring your ass with me
Just take it off them and lay it on me
Where it ought to be.

If You Don't Like My Apples

If you don't like my apples
Don't pick from my tree
I didn't want your man
Your man wanted me

If you want your man
You better keep him by your side
'Cause if he wants to ride my train
I'm gonna let him ride

If you want your man
Keep him by your side
'Cause if he flags my train
I'm sure gonna let him ride.

When I Die

When I'm dead and in my grave
No more pussy will I crave
On my tombstone will be seen
A streamlined body of a fuckin' machine

When I die, don't bury me at all
Just pickle my balls in alcohol
Lay my prick upon my chest
Tell all those whores I've gone to rest

When I die don't bury me deep
Put a gallon of 'lasses at my feet
Cake and cornbread in my hand
So I kin sop my way to the Promised Land.

Ninety-Four Whores

Ninety-four whores standin' up against the wall
I swore to my God I could fuck 'em all

I fucked ninety-two, that's the best I could do
I went across the railroad track and ate some oyster stew
I came back 'n fucked the other two
I fucked and I fucked 'til I fucked down to hell
I fucked the devil's wife, and I fucked her well

Two little devils peeped over the wall
Sayin' take him out, daddy, 'fore he fucks us all

Twenty Women

I was walking through the jungle with my prick in my hand
I'm a cool motherfucker from Swaziland

I saw twenty women behind the wall
I bet you five dollars I can fuck them all

I fucked nineteen, and I had to stop
I had an operation and my balls got hot

When I die, bury me
Hang my balls on a cherry tree

If they roll, let them roll
I'll be fucking in the devil's hole.

Three Wine-Ole Bitches

Three wine-ole bitches walking down the street
Jim, hungry as hell and not a damn thing to eat

So, one bitch said, "Let's stop on the corner and have a glass of wine,"
And said, "I bet neither of you bitches got a bigger pussy than mine."

The first bitch said, "Whore, my pussy is big as the Chesapeake Bay,"
She said, "It holds two wagons loaded down with hay."

The second bitch said, "Whore, my cunt is big as the sea,"
She said, "Bitch, the whole Titanic could have sunk in me."

The last bitch said, "Whore, my cunt is big as the moon,"
She said, "Bitch, I fuck in January and come in June."

Fathers and Sons

1st Boy: My father is the best painter in the world.
2nd Boy: What did he paint?
1st Boy: He painted the White House.
2nd Boy: That's nothing. My father painted the Red Sea.

• • •

1st Boy:	My father smokes fifty packs of cigarettes a day and he blows smoke through his eyes, nose, and mouth.
2nd Boy:	That's nothing. My father smokes through his ass.
1st Boy:	His ass?
2nd Boy:	Yes, I ain't kidding. I always hear my mother telling my father she sees nicotine in his drawers.

• • •

1st Boy:	My father is the greatest hitter in the history of baseball.
2nd Boy:	I know my father is.
1st Boy:	Let me tell you something: once my father hit a ball out of the park and it landed in a house five miles away.
2nd Boy:	That's pretty good. But once my father hit a ball so hard it went up in the sky and out of sight.
1st Boy:	Out of sight? What happened?
2nd Boy:	The ball came down a week later with a note attached to it which read: *Don't disturb me while I am sleeping.* (Signed) *G. O. D.*

Dime

As I was standing on the corner of 48th and Vine
I happened to meet a friend of mine whose name was Pete

Pete asked me to loan him a dime
I said: Pete, I don't mean this for no argument and I don't mean it for no fight

But you have to be born blind and then naturally can't see
Have your legs cut off twelve inches above your motherfuckin knees

Shoot me a line of shit as far as I could see the railroad track
Then reach your hand up the camel's ass and snatch the hump out of his back

Find me the three Hebrew children that set the world on fire
Catch the zoom off that rock that killed Goliath

Jump off the Empire State Building on your motherfuckin head
Get up and do the twist to prove to me that you ain't dead

Then maybe I might introduce you to a friend of mine
That might loan you a nickel but never a dime!

DOZENS

How come your father don't live with you? . . .

GENERAL: "THE CONDITION YOUR DEAR FAMILY'S IN"

1. "Knock, knock."
   "Who's there?"
   "Yo." [*or:* "Joe"]
   "Yo who?"
   "Yo' ma!"

2. "Ain't yo mama . . .?"
   "Ain't my mama what?"
   "Ain't yo mama on the cornbread box?" [*picture of Aunt Jemima*]

3. "Hey man! How's your mama? I saw her last night. Her hair was kinky, her draws were baggy, and she was drunk as a skunk. She looked so bad she would have scared a baboon to death."
   "Say, man! That was your mama, who was looking so bad even you didn't recognize her."

4. "Hey, I saw your momma last night."
   "What do you mean, man? My momma was home last time I was there."
   "Coulda fooled me. I was down at the Paradise and I coulda swore I saw her up on the balcony with her drawers around her knees."
   "That's funny, 'cause that's how I saw your momma there last Saturday, only close-up. In fact she was so close I got cross-eyed."

5. "Hello brother! How's your momma?"
   "What you mean, how's my momma?"
   "Well . . . I woulda said how's the family, but I know your pappy ain't been home for a month."

"That's right, motherfucker, he been living over at your momma's place since my momma threw him out."

"That ain't your poppa, that's my momma's hound-dog who looks so much like your poppa that even you couldn't tell them apart."

"Shiiiiiit! I coulda sworn that was my poppa by the way your momma was letting him tell her what to do."

"That dog wasn't telling her what to do! My momma was just blowing a fart and you thought it was your poppa's barking mouth."

"You right. I shoulda known that my poppa was too good to bother hisself with a gas bomb like your momma."

"Shiiiiiit! My momma wouldn't even open the door to no trash like your poppa."

"That's news."

"What's news?"

"The news about your momma gettin' doors on her house."

6. "Hey man, ain't that your momma in that red, raggedy, stinky wig?"

"No, man, that's your momma wearin' army fatigues and combat boots."

"Dig, man, at least she can wear somethin' and ain't as fat as your mom."

"She may be fat but she sure is better than your skinny, bow-legged old lady."

"Your mom can't wear nothin' but orange iridescent circus tents."

"That's alright, at least she can wear something. Your mom is so skinny when she buys something it hangs like a gunny-sack."

"Man, your momma goes down to the beach wearing her tent and ships take her for a lighthouse."

"Ha, your moms goes to the beach and the waves take her away . . . at least my momma doesn't get knocked down by a grain of sand."

"Your momma, man, opens her mouth and everybody runs to hide. Oh, that breath!"

"Man, you are wrong, that was your mother's fault, she was walking down the street . . . boy, is she ugly!"

"No, man, your momma's so ugly she can make every window in the Empire State Building break, plus she can scare a gorilla."

"That gorilla is your daddy, and he didn't scare your momma too much, 'cause here you are.

7. Your mother is very athletic; she does knee-bends over fire hydrants.

8. How come your father don't live with you?

9. Your mother barks at the moon.

10. Hey man, didn't your mammy fight at the Battle of Bull Run?

11. My papa cussed out yo mama and told her to chew the seat of her dirty drawers.

12. Your mama took her own chair to the movies and sat with the rats.

13. Your mother is like an alka-seltzer; put her in a glass of water and she'll fizz to death.

14. Your mama talks so much her mouth runs like a sick nigger's butt.

15. Your mama chews tobacco.

16. Your mama dips snuff.

17. Your mama was standing on the corner and the garbage man picked her up, and it took her two hours to convince him that she wasn't garbage.

18. Your mother fought King Kong, and won.

19. Hey man, you ain't got no father. Actually I think you look like your mother's boyfriend. The one with the pink lips. Ain't he a wino?

20. Your mom is so little that I saw your pop chase her down the street with a can of Raid [*roach spray*].

21. Is that your mother over there? Quick, kill her before she multiplies!

22. I saw your mother last night. She was crawling up my wall. Lucky for her I couldn't find the roach spray.

23. A lady said to your father, "Your fly is open." Your father said, "You noticed my fly was open, did you see that big shiny black Cadillac?" The lady said, "No, but I saw a little Volkswagen with two flat tires."

24. Yo father's forever handin' out wolf-tickets [verbal threats], and yo mama's a gofa—she goes for all of his bullshit.

25. My momma an yo' momma was sittin' in a ditch
    My momma called your momma a dirty son-of-a-bitch.

26. You're up the ditch, you're down the ditch
    You turkey walkin' son-of-a-bitch.

27. Your father's name is Tricky Dick
    'Cause wherever he puts it, it never sticks.

28. I saw your papa coming across the field
    Slippin' and slidin' like an automobile.

29. I went down the street to get some butter
    And saw your father laying in the gutter
    I stuck a piece of glass up his ass
    And never seen a motherfucker run so fast.

30. "Go to hell!"
    "Hell is my home
    The devil is my brother
    The last time I saw him
    He was fucking your mother."

31. Your mother got hit by a flying turd
    She couldn't swim, she couldn't float
    So this here shit went down her throat.

32. Tootie, tootie
    Fruity, fruity
    Your mama's face
    Looks just like my booty.

33. Your mama wrapped her legs around the flag pole
    She lost her grip
    Her feet slipped
    Came sliding down and busted her asshole.

34. There goes your mother sittin' on a fence
    Tryin' to make a dollar outta ninety-nine cents.

35. Yo' mama's in de kitchen
    Yo' papa's in jail
    Yo' sister's round the corner
    Hollerin' "Hot stuff for sale!"

36. When your mama was young and sweet
    She called me Sweet Sweet Papa
    Now she's ole and lost her teeth
    She call me Weet Weet Wopper.

37. Jodie's got your gal and gone
    Ain't no use in feelin' blue
    Jodie's got your mama too.

38. Your mom is so funky she makes shit smell sweet
    She's so ugly I bet your father beats his meat
    She's so fat she wears XXX-large drawers
    To get her in the house they had to take off the doors.

    Her drawers are always stained with shit
    That's why when she called me to fuck her I had to split
    When she spread her legs and the funk started flyin'
    I took a deep breath and I just knew I was dyin'.

    Your mom's tits are so big and hang so low
    That she can pick 'em up and tie 'em in a bow
    Her ass is so big and round
    When she farts they can smell her in the next town.

    She's the major cause of air pollution
    A little soap and water is the simple solution
    If your mom would just wash once in a while
    People would stop calling you the son of a shit pile.

39. "The 7 o'clock bell just rung."
    "Yeah, and your mama rung it."

Poor

1. Your family's so poor you have to buy toilet paper on the lay-away plan.
2. I wonder where your mother went
   When the landlord came to collect the rent.
3. I saw your mother in the street singing
   "Don't be greedy, give to the needy."
4. Your family is so poor they don't have a down payment on a biscuit.
5. Your mama cannot afford a girdle.
6. Your father's on welfare meat.
7. Your mother goes to church, puts in a penny, and asks for change.
8. You're so poor you don't put cheese in your mouse trap.
9. Your mother's so poor she can't afford to go on welfare.
10. I hear you're so hard up that when your mama hangs out the laundry there ain't nothing on the line but clothes-pins.
11. Yo father's so broke he can't even pay attention.
12. You're so poor you can't pay attention.

House

1. Your mother's address is Sewer Seven, Pipe Eleven, Ash Can Drive.
2. "You live in the sewer."
   "So, you live in a cardboard box!"
3. You live on the sixth floor of a five-story building.
4. I remember you. Didn't your family used to live on the corner, second floor of the empty lot?
5. I rang your doorbell and the toilet bowl flushed.
6. Your house is so small that when I go in the front door I fall over the back fence.
7. I asked your mother were you home and she said, "Grab a vine and hang on."
8. I went to your house and had to use the bathroom. Your mother handed me a shovel and said, "Start digging."
9. When I was at your house I asked where the bathroom was and they said, "Third bucket on the right!"

10. When I went to your pad and put out my cigarette your mother screamed, "Who turned off the heat?"

11. Your house is so hot the roaches carry canteens.

12. Your house is so cold the roaches fart snowballs.

13. There are so many people in your house that they go to bed piggy-back.

Food

1. Hey man, your mother eats toilet paper.

2. When I invite you to my house I say, "Pull up a seat and have some meat." At your house they say, "Pick up a stone and have a bone."

3. I went to your house and asked for a drink. Your mother handed me a safari jacket and a shovel and said, "Good luck!"

4. At least you have variety in your menu. One day you have beans and rice, the next day you have rice and beans, the next you have beans then you have rice, then you have beans and rice again.

5. Your mother makes them touchdown beans and rough biscuits!

6. Your mother makes them hope and pray biscuits: hope you can make 'em, pray you can eat 'em.

7. You're so poor that when I went over to your house your mama chopped your papa's head off, put it on a plate, and hollered, "No hunks!" [nobody can have any]

8. Your family had ants for dinner last night, as usual.

9. For breakfast you eat bacon grease and scrambled egg shells.

10. For lunch you had a wish sandwich: two pieces of bread and wished you had some meat.

11. On Sunday you say, "Dear Lord, make me able to eat every damn thing on the table; if there's anymore in the pot, bring it on while it's hot."

12. The only blessing you say is:

    Good bread, good meat
    Good Lord, let's eat.

13. On Thanksgiving it's, "Our turkey 'tis of thee, sweet potatoes and cranberry," then everyone eats.

14. On Thanksgiving you ran in the house shouting, "Where's the turkey? I want a leg, I want a leg!" Your mother said, "Beans ain't got no legs."

15. You're so poor you eat beans for breakfast.

16. You had cornbread for your birthday cake.

17. Your family's so poor that you have cupcakes for Thanksgiving dinner.

18. I went to your house for dinner one night and asked your mother what was for dinner. She said, "Doze-offs." I said, "What's 'doze-offs'"? And she said, "The first nigga that dozes off, gets ate."

Rats and Roaches

1. "I went to your house and a rat came to the door and said, 'We don't want any.'"

    "I went to your house and a rat came up to me and asked for a cigarette. I offered him a Winston, but he said he only smoked Kools."

    "Aw, nigger, I went to your house and I was watching television when a rat walked up to me and said it was 10 o'clock and he wanted to watch *The Fugitive*."

    "So that ain't nothing. I went to your house and when I went to the bathroom I saw two roaches in the toilet bowl playing *Sea Hunt*."

    "So the rats and roaches pay rent in your house, motherfucker."

    "Aw, motherfucker, y'all got so many rats and roaches, your old man got to claim them as dependents."

2. In your house the roaches have to make room for the bedbugs, and the rats carry switchblades.

3. I heard that those rats have been with y'all so long, that when you sit down to eat they jump up on the table and say, "Pass the biscuits!"

4. You got so many cockroaches in your house that they jitterbug on your coffee table to entertain your company, and then run to beat you pulling up chairs at the dinner table.

5. Your family's so poor, I went to your house and saw a roach pull a switchblade on a rat for a piece of cheese.

6. I went to your house and stepped on a roach, and your mama cried, "Oh God! There goes dinner!"

7. You're so poor, you eat the crumbs from the roaches.

8. You ain't got no roaches in your house. The rats eat 'em all.

9. Your family is so poor the roaches leave at dinnertime.

10. You're so poor even the roaches starve.

11. You're so poor that when I went over to your house and sat down on a chair, a roach grumbled, "Move over, boy. I pay rent here!"

Clothing

1. Your mother wears her drawers all day and scrubs the floor with them at night.

2. Hey man, your mother don't wear no panties.

3. Your mama wears dirty drawers.

4. Man, your mammy wears government drawers.

5. Your mammy wears cement drawers.

6. Your mama wears bubblegum drawers with nicotine trimming.

7. Your mother wears iron drawers.

8. Your mama wears a one-legged steel drawers.

9. Man, your mammy's drawers so raggedy, she looks like a bowl of Chinese egg-drop soup.

10. Yo' mama wears ten-penny bloomers and wa-wa sneakers.

11. Man, your mammy wears sneakers.

12. Your mama wears high heel sneakers.

13. Your mother wore tennis shoes so long, she wore them down to the name on the ankle.

14. Hey man, your mother wears cleats! [football shoes]

15. Your mama wears Puerto Rican roach killers: shoes so pointy she can stomp roaches in a corner.

16. Your mother wears combat boots.

17. Your mama wears combat boots and a jock strap.

18. Your mother wears combat boots and khaki pants.

19. Your father got drunk and his pants got high [pants above the ankles].

20. That nigger must live below sea level. Look at them high-water pants!

21. I see you're wearing your high-waters today. Where you wading to, boy?

22. Where's the flood?

23. His floods were so high it made me sea-sick.

24. Your pants are so high you have to give them sugar and water to sweet-talk them down.

25. Your pants are so high your shoes should have a party and invite your pants down.

26. You must be wearing your church pants—sing "Holy [holey], Holy, Holy."

27. Where you sailing for? [large baggy pants]

28. Who made your pants, Ahab the tent maker? [for baggy pants]

29. Hey man, you made your pants out of old curtains. I can see right through them [for split or thin pants].

30. I see you're wearing a tablecloth around your neck; a chest protector [wide tie].

31. You're losing your soul, brother [shoes falling apart].

32. Your shoes are talking to you [falling apart].

33. The soles of your shoes are so thin you can step on a dime and tell if it's heads or tails.

34. Your mother wears Seymour hats: you can see more head than hat.

35. Nigger, you get your clothes from Robert Hall: Robert threw them out and you hauled them in.

36. You got that coat from Lord & Taylor's: tailor made it, and Lord knows you need it.

37. I see you got your Buster Brown shoes: brown on top and busted on the bottom.

38. You wear Dunlap shoes: they done all they could and lapped over.

39. I see you got your patten [patent] leather shoes: leather on the top and your feet patting the ground.

40. I saw your momma the other day and she looked like she had just gotten dressed in front of an airplane propeller.

41. Your mother had her only dress on last night.

42. Your mother got a bra from Woolworths for 99 cents.

43. Hey man, your socks are so holey they pray to you each night.

44. I can tell from your mama's socks
    That she robs from the poor box.

45. Yo' mama don't wear no draws
    'Cause I saw her when she took 'em off
    An' she washed 'em in alcohol
    Then she hung 'em in the hall
    An' they took her to City Hall
    For exposing them dirty draws.

46. Your mama wears dirty drawers
    I saw her when she took them off
    She put them in the sink
    The sink turned to ink
    She put them on the line
    The sun refused to shine
    She put them on the grass
    The ants refused to pass.

Ugly

1. Your mama's so ugly she hurts my feelings.

2. Your momma's so ugly she makes the Phantom of the Opera look like Cinderella.

3. Listen Jack, your moms is so ugly the wolfman wouldn't fuck with her.

4. She was so ugly, all she had to thank God for was that she was breathing.

5. Your sister is so ugly you have to walk her every day.

6. Your mama's so ugly she has to sneak up on a glass to get a drink of water.

7. Your momma is so ugly that she has to sneak up on a mirror.

8. Your mother is so ugly that she has to put a sheet over her head so sleep can sneak up on her at night. [*Variation:* You're so ugly your mother had to put a sheet over your head so sleep could sneak up on you.]

9. Man, you so ugly you can draw a blister on a rock.

10. He's so ugly he scares himself.

11. Your mother is so ugly that she scares the monkeys in the zoo.

12. Your momma is so ugly that your daddy goes to bed with a paper sack over his head so he won't have to look at her.

13. Your mother is so ugly your pops has to put a bag over her head when he does his thing.

14. Your mother's so ugly she uses Preparation-H for lipstick.

15. Your mother is so ugly, when she cries tears run down her back.

16. Boy, you're so ugly, you're going to ugly away.

17. Your mother looks like seven miles of bad road.

18. He looks like ten miles of rough shit.

19. That woman was so ugly she looked like twenty miles of unpaved road.

20. Your momma looks like her face caught on fire, and someone tried to put it out with an ice-pick (chain, brick, pipe, etc.).

21. Your momma's so ugly she looks like a baboon sucking on a lemon.

22. Don't snap on my moms, Jack, with yours looking like the son of King Kong.

23. Your momma looks like King Kong in a pair of red hot pants.

24. Your mother looks like a throw-back to the missing link.

25. You look like something the cats drug in.

26. Your mother looks like an accident about to happen.

27. Your momma looks like she was run over by a Mack truck.

28. Your mother's so ugly she looks like she's been beat with an ugly stick.

29. I've heard of people beaten by an ugly stick, but you were a victim of the whole forest.

30. Man, you so ugly you look like death eating a soda cracker.

31. Ugly!! She's so ugly she looks like death standing on a corner sucking a Life Saver.

32. Yo' sister's so ugly that when she smiles it looks like she's smelling her own ass.

33. It looks like your momma was in a hatchet fight, and everyone had a hatchet but her.

34. When you were born, instead of your father passing out cigars . . . he just passed out.

35. Man, I heard that when your momma was born she was so ugly that her parents went to the zoo and threw rocks at the stork.

36. When you were born your mother said, "Isn't he a treasure?" And your father said, "Yeah, let's bury it."

37. When you were born you were so ugly your mother threw you away and kept the afterbirth.

38. When you were born they put you on a step to see whether you were going to bark or cry.

39. You ain't ugly, you're yugly.

40. Let me tell you about ugly . . . your mama ain't got but one tooth, and it's a cavity; one eye, and it's crossed; one leg, and it's bow; and one hair, and it's nappy!

41. Q: Man, whose sister is that over there?

    A: You mean the one that just had the ugly attack?

    [*Variation:* Ooooh wheee, you look like you just had an ugly attack!]

42. I heard your momma tried to get a face lift, but when they saw what was underneath, they put it back on.

43. You could have been a movie star, but they stopped making monster flicks.

44. It's a woman's privilege to be ugly, but some take advantage of it.

45. "Did you get the number?"

    "What number?"

    "The number of the truck that ran over your face."

46. Y'all know the "Lee" sisters? Ug and Ly.

47. Your momma put the "u" in ugly.

48. If ugliness was holiness you'd be Jesus Christ.

49. If beauty is inside you need to put your liver where your face is.

50. If I had a dog with a face like yours, I'd shave his ass and make him walk backwards.

51. Black is beautiful, but you sure ain't.

Funky

1. Your mother smells like Gypsy Rose wine.

2. Your mother's breath smells like elephant farts.

3. Your mother's breath smells like she had diarrhea for a week.

4. Your mother's breath smells like wild ox farts.

5. Your mother's breath smells like wolf pussy.

6. Your mama's breath smells like a herd of wild sneakers.

7. You smell like the cool breeze from a buffalo fart.

8. Hey man, you smell like you want to be alone.

9. At least my mother don't walk down the street with stinkin', smellin', funky feet.

10. Your mom is so funky that as soon as she opens her legs, she funks-up the whole room.

11. Your breath smells so bad that I hate for you to open my icebox, 'cause every time you do all my food spoils.

12. Your father's feet stink so bad, he drinks Sneaky Pete to make them sweet.

13. Your mama is so funky that if we really wanted to get out of Viet-Nam, all we would have to do is put her on the front lines, out in the middle of the battlefield, and tell her to spread her legs.

14. Man, your nama's breath is so strong they use it to simulate elephant stink at the circus.

15. Man, I heard that you smell so bad that they had to put you on the dangerous pollution index list.

16. Hey baby, close your legs, your breath stinks.

17. Your uncle's name is Hal—hallatosis.

18. You smell so bad that the last time you took a bath the soap fainted.

19. You smell so bad you deserve a medal for standing yourself.

20. Your mama's pussy is so funky it makes a maggot gag.

21. If my breath smelled like yours I'd breathe out of my ass.

22. Tell your mama to keep her draws on around my dog. I don't want him to catch nothing.

23. When it was Christmas time your mother hung up stockings, and the health department made her take them down.

24. I heard that your soap was so bored from waiting for you to bathe, that it used to sit up and play solitaire.

25. Your house is so dirty the roaches wear combat boots.

26. Your house is so dirty the ants and roaches play wagon-train.

27. Your mama is so dirty that if she took a bath in the Harlem River she would leave a ring.

28. Give me liberty
Or give me death
Give me freedom
From your bad breath.

29. Scope only cost a dime
You need it all the time
Your breath smells like turpentine.

30. Your mother don't got no draws, funky bund
I see her when she took them off, funky bund
She put them in the sink
The sink refused to drink
She put them on the wall
The roaches refused to crawl
She put them in the bed
The bed bugs came out dead
She put them in the trunk
The moth balls came out drunk
She put them on the chair, funky bund
The chair said, "Give me some air!" funky bund.

31. Your mama smells so funky that they put her with the monkeys every time she goes to the zoo. Her funk is so bad that even had she washed, there would still be a residue.

32. Your mama smells so bad, I heard that your father had to wear a gas mask to their wedding. Her funk's so strong, and lasts so long, it saturates all of ya bedding.

33. I can tell by your mama's feet
That she don't smell so sweet
Soap is cheap, and water's free
So use them both—please—for me.

.

34. Your mama told the Chinaman her name is Annie
    And to put more soap in her panties
    The Chinaman told your mama, my name is Chinie
    And to put more soap on her hinie.

Age

1. Man, your mother's so old, when God said "Let there be light" she jumped up and cut it on.

2. Your mom is so old that she sleeps in a coffin just so she can be ready.

3. Your mama is so old that she farts cobwebs.

4. Your mother's so old, she farts dust and craps rust.

5. Your mama is older than water.

6. Some like it hot
   Some like it cold
   Some who like your mama
   Like it pretty damn old.

Size

1. Your moms is so skinny when she turns sideways she can hide between the edges of a razor blade.

2. Your moma's so skinny that when she turns sideways she looks like six o'clock.

3. Your mama is so skinny that she disappears if she turns sideways.

4. Man, she so skinny, she won't cast a shadow standing sideways.

5. Buster's sister is so skinny that on the block they called her "Death Valley Days."

6. Your mother's so skinny she can dodge raindrops.

7. Your mama is so skinny that she can't get wet in the rain.

8. Your mother so skinny she swallowed a pea and swore she was pregnant.

9. Your mother so skinny she can use a Cheerio for a hula hoop.

10. Your mother's so skinny she can run a mile aroun' a dime.

11. Your sister so fat and wrinkled, she has to screw her draws on.

12. I saw your moma the other day and she's so fat that people kept coming up to her and trying to shove letters into her mouth.

Height

1. Otis, I heard your mother so tall when she goes to bed she has to lay diagonally on the bed.

2. Your pop is so short he has to jump up on the sidewalk.

Hair

1. What's the matter, your hair hurtin'?

2. Your hair is nappy
   Who's your pappy?
   Ooh, you'se one ugly chile!

3. I saw your mama yesterday and she sure was look'n raggedy. Her hair looked like it just made a crash landing on her head.

4. Madam Walker [inventor of straightening comb] need to walk around your edges, child. And take it from the kitchen [back of the neck] straight up to the living room [front of head].

5. Hey, farmer, how's the crops? [Nappy, uncombed hair was said to look peasy.]

6. Your hair is so picky, I could use it for cooking peas with my rice.

7. Your hair is so nappy that when Birdseye sprayed their crops they sprayed your head thinking it was a pea field.

8. Not a kink, not a curl
   Konkaline rules your world.

9 Slicked back knots and B-B shots.

   [*Variation:* B-B shots, bring back knots.]

10. You got mailman hair; every knot's got its own route.

11. Your hair is so bad you need to carry a gun just to comb it.

12. Your 'fro ain't no bush it's an USH.

13. Her hair's so short I can smell her brains, see her thoughts; I mean her hair is so short, if she stood on her head, her hair wouldn't touch the floor.

Head

1. Talking about my momma? You ain't even got a momma. All you got is twelve bald-headed suspects.

2. Like a bear with no hair.

3. Your woman's so bald headed I can smell her brain.

4. Your mama's head is so bald that I can read her mind.

5. Goddamn, you sure got a big forehead; if you butt somebody you'll give them a tumor. Please don't butt me.

6. You got hills and lumps on your head.

7. He's got more lumps on his head than a camel.

8. Your mama has so many wrinkles in her head that she has to screw her hat on.

9. Head Names:

Headquarters	Head-head the modis	Head-head the mostest
Muscle head	Flukey-luke head	Trunk-key head
Plug head	Hammer head	Football head
Gibraltar head	Tank head	Cinderblock head
Bucket head	Skinhead	Saddle head
Forklift head	Galactus head	Meathead
Bonehead	Balloon head	Peanut head
Ape head	Baldie bean	Clean bean
Sunbeam	Potato head	

Teeth

1. Your mother's teeth so white, you can go dining at night.

2. Your mother's teeth is so brown, you could do the James Brown.

3. Look at the dude with all those missin' teeth—they ought to call him cumblin' gaps.

4. I heard of liar's gaps [space between front teeth] but you have a canyon.

5. Your mother's teeth are so buck that she can eat apples through a picket fence.

6. Your mother got whiskers on her teeth.

Titties

1. Your mama wears socks in her bra for titties.

2. Your mother has three tits, one on her chest and two up her ass.

3. Your mother's got two left titties.

4. Your mama's left tittie is gonna fall off.

5. Your mamny ain't got but one tittie, and it works by remote control.

6. Your moms is so flat they use her chest for a dart board / skate board combination.

7. Your momma's so flat-chested, she's a pirate's treasure . . . a sunken chest.

Dick

1. Your pop dick so big that the only thing he can fuck is an elephant . . . that's why he got your mother.

2. Listen, motherfucker, let me git this straight
   Your mother got a dick like a two-forty-eight
   Your father got a dick like a two-forty-nine
   So listen, motherfucker, don't you talk about mine.

Pussy

1. I heard your moms ain't got no snatch.

2. Your mama's pussy so big you could drive a train through it.

3. Hey man, when you see your mammy tell her to bring me back my wheel barrow. I left it in her cunt.

4. Nothing could be finer
   Than to see your mom's vagina
   In the morning.

5. Roses are red
   Violets are blue
   Your mother's pussy stinks
   And so do you.

6. Listen here, nigger, let's get it straight
   Your mama got a pussy like a B-48.

7. 2 – 4 – 6 – 8
   Your mama's got a pussy like a B-48
   Round as an apple, square as a pear
   Split down the middle and surrounded by hair.

8. Look here, man, dig, let me get you straight
   Your mother's got a pussy like a B-48
   She got somethin' call the "joo-jag-jam"
   It's hard to get, but it's good goddamn!

9. Ain't she cute
   Oh, ain't she cute
   She got bacon and eggs between her legs
   Now ain't she cute!

10. Ain't your mammy pretty
    She's got popcorn for her titties
    She's got scrambled eggs
    Between her legs
    Ain't your mammy pretty.

11. Ain't your mama pretty
    She got meatballs in her titties
    She got ham and eggs between her legs
    Ain't your mama pretty.

12. I hate to talk about your mother
    But she's in my class
    She has pom-pom titties
    And a rubber ass.

13. I hate to talk about your mother
    She was in my class
    She got popcorn titties
    And a brass asshole.

14. I like your mama
    She's a good old soul
    She's got a rubber-tire pussy
    And a brass asshole.

15. I hate to talk about your mother
    She's a good old soul
    She has a leather-lined pussy
    And a brass asshole.

16. I hate to talk about your mother
    She's a good old soul
    She has ten pounds of pussy
    In one grass hole.

17. I hate to talk about your mama
    She's a good ole soul
    She got humped-back titties
    And a rubber asshole.

18. I don't want to talk about your mama
    She is a good old soul
    She has a double-barrel pussy
    And a cannon asshole.

19. I hate to talk about your mother
    She's a good ole soul
    She's got popcorn titties and a rubber hole
    She's got knobs on her titties that kin open a door
    She's got hair on her pussy that kin mop the floor.

20. Your dear old mama
    Bless her soul
    She's got a ten-ton pussy
    And a rubber hole.

21. Don't talk about your mother
    She's a good old soul
    She's got a five-pound pussy
    And a rubber asshole.

Ass

1. Man, your mammy's ass is so big she has to wear suspenders to hold up her draws.

2. Your mama got a basketball for an ass.

3. Your mama's ass is so big that when she walks down the street it looks like two bears wrestling under a blanket.

Legs

1. Your mother has three legs, two she walks on and that wine bottle she has in her stockings.

2. Your momma's so bow-legged, if her legs were straight she'd be two inches taller.

3. Your mother's legs are so little, the dogs won't even bite.

4. Your legs look like posts.

5. Your legs look like baseball bats.

6. Your legs so fat, make an elephant jealous.

7. Your legs so skinny, they look like sticks.

8. Where are your wings? You already have bird legs.

9. Hey baby, you can sue your legs for non-support.

10. "Hey man, I heard that your poppa was really rid'n your momma the other night."

    "Why would my poppa be doin' something like that?"

    "Well, I hear that your poppa was saying something about your momma ruinin' his new chainsaw."

    "Now why would my momma be use'n my poppa new chainsaw?"

    "Well, from the looks of your momma, she was probably use'n it to shave her legs."

Feet

1. Check out those Seymours on that dude's feet—I see more feet than shoe.
2. His feet so big, when he walks north and south his feet go east and west.
3. He's got a good foundation [feet].
4. I can tell by your daddy's toes
   He's got buggers up his nose.

Hands

1. If I had your hands I'd throw away both my arms.

Work

1. Your mother is a construction worker.
2. Your moms used to ride shotgun for Pony Express.
3. Hey man, your mom ride shotgun on a garbage truck.
4. Your mother played second base for the Yankees.
5. I heard your mother played third base for the Husky Whores.
6. I heard your mother played fullback for Funky Harriet and Her Happy Whores.
7. Wow, I heard your moms so strong, she use to play pulling guard for the Green Bay Packers.
8. Hey man, your mother sells cufflinks!
9. Your mother sells Jet.
10. I heard your daddy works at Pat and Turner: pat his foot and turn the corner.

Role Reversal

1. Your momma bops and your daddy switches.
2. Your mother's a man.
3. You're not the man your mother was.
4. Your mother's a faggot.

5. Your father's a prostitute.

6. I saw your mother in a barbershop yesterday. She was getting a shave.

7. You look like your mother with that beard.

8. I understand you've been going through some changes, Jim. What size do you wear, 34B or 36C?

9. I heard your mama tried to get a job with a burlesque show, and they said, "We don't hire men here."

10. Your mama's dick so big it came in at eight-thirty, and the rest of her came in at a quarter to nine.

11. You got two fathers and one of them is pregnant.

Low Down

1. Your mother is so low she has to look up to tie her shoes.

2. Your mother's so low she has to look down to look up.

3. You're so low down you need an umbrella to protect yourself from ant piss.

4. Your mama is lower than whale shit—and that's on the bottom of the ocean.

5. I heard your mama pulled a hell of a trick
   She got down so low, she sucked an earthworm's dick.

Negative on Black

1. Wilfred, I heard your moms is so black your pops can't find her in bed when she turns off the light.

2. That ugly nigger looks like a black fright out of the night.

3. Do you niggers like midnight?
   You should, that's what you look like.

4. Let's play cards, Don; you'll be the ace of spades.

5. You're so black until I think I'll nickname you "eight-ball."

6. Your momma's so black she's blue [or purple].

7. Your mother's name is Smitty
   Big, black, and shitty.

8. Your momma's so black that if snow was black she'd be a walking blizzard.

9. Light skinned blacks are called "shit-colored."

10. You're so light until you look like an imitation Negro.

11. Man, your momma has such big lips that she can whisper in her own ear.

12. Man, your mother's lips are so big that when she smiles she gets lipstick on her ears.

13. There was a girl in our school who had such black skin, and she was real pretty too. But we said she was so black that if you touched her you would get a fever. So we called her *black fever*.

14. Other names for very dark people: Blue, Black Magic, Blue Magic, Pearl, Snowflake, Blackie, Midnight.

15. I went over the river to see Miss Lucy
    I gave her two cent to see her pussy
    Her pussy was so black
    I couldn't see the crack
    I said, "Damn, Miss Lucy,
    Give my two cents back!"

16. If you white, you alright
    If you yeller, you a good feller
    If you brown, stick around
    But Lord, if you black
    Stay the hell, way back.

STUPIDITY

1. Nigger, you ain't got the sense that God slapped up a goose's ass with a ten-foot pole.

2. You're so stupid that you got left back in kindergarten because you didn't know how to play.

3. You're so stupid you failed lunch.

4. Your sister's so stupid, when they were passing out brains she thought they said trains, bought a ticket, and left.

5. Your mother's so stupid she can't walk and chew gum at the same time.

6. You so light [dumb], if brains was food you'd starve to death.

7. If brains was heat you'd freeze to death.

8. If brains was sight you'd be Ray Charles.

9. If brains was light you'd be midnight.

10. If brains was dynamite your mother wouldn't have enough sense to blow her nose.

1. Yo' mother is a ho [*whore*]
   Everybody know.

2. Your mother's named Joe
   And she looks like a ho [whore].

3. Hey! Do you know his mama? You don't? I thought everybody knew
   his mama.

4. Humping your moms is like humping an elephant.

5. How's your wife and my kids?

6. Your mother and father were so happy when you were born that they
   ran out and got married.

7. They call your mother Juicy Lucy the Prostitucy.

8. I could have been your father—but I didn't have change for a nickel.

9. I could have been your father but I didn't have the correct change.
   The dude behind me did, so your mama took him over me.

10. I would have been your father, but a dog beat me over the fence.

11. Your moms was so good last night I even gave her a quarter when
    I was finished.

12. Hey, I heard Godzilla and your moms was getting off last night.

13. You're an all-American boy . . . you got a father in every state.

14. At least I have a father and not fifty suspects.

15. Your mother has had so many men she walks wide-legged permanently.

16. Man, me and your mommy was behind a tree shooting dice. She faded
    her ass for a half pint of moonshine.

17. More people have fucked your mother than cars have been through the
    Lincoln Tunnel.

18. Your mother was caught wheelin' and dealin' so the judge did some
    wailin' and jailin' to her ass.

19. Your moms enjoyed my cock so much she invited me back tonight.

20. I saw your mama last night. She was so drunk she tried to screw a
    gorilla.

21. Someone had to point out your mom
    While we was in town
    I didn't recognize her
    With her clothes on.

22. I saw your mama on the street today. She didn't recognize me—I had
    my clothes on.

23. Tell your mother I left her money on the table.

24. If you find a pair of slippers under your mother's bed, they're mine.

25. Tell your mother to move my slippers from under the bed.

26. Tell your mother I left my shoes under her bed.

27. Tell your mama to stop comin' around my house all the time. I'm tired of layin' her. As a matter of fact, you lookin' at your daddy right now.

28. Let's get off the subject of mothers, 'cause I just got off of yours.

29. Your mother would fuck a snake if someone would hold its head.

30. Your mother's great at playing road. She lies down and some nigger blacktops her.

31. "Hey man, your momma still working?"
"Yeah."
"On what corner?"

32. "Hey man, I saw your momma yesterday."
"What was she doin' when you saw her?"
"Well, she was runnin' down the stairs with a mattress on her back."
"Why in the hell would she be doing something like that?"
"Well, I asked her. I said, 'Lady, what are you doin' runnin' down those stairs with that mattress on your back?' And she said to me, 'Some dude said he wanted curb service.'"

33. Your mother's pussy is like a wall: everybody's written his name on her.

34. Your mother's like a coffee bean: everybody gets a grind.

35. Your mama is like the free library: open to the public.

36. Your mama is like Grand Central Station: everybody passes through her.

37. Your mama is like a balloon: always blown up.

38. Your mother's like an ice box: the meat goes in and out.

39. Your mother lays like margarine: she's so spreadable it's incredible.

40. Your mother's like a merry-go-round: everyone gets on and off.

41. Your mother's like a cup of coffee: hot, black, and ready to be creamed.

42. Your mother's like a railroad track: she gets laid all over the country.

43. Your mother is like a police station: dicks come in and out all the time.

44. Your mother is like a cake: everybody gets a piece.

45. Your mama is like a doorknob: everybody gets a turn.

46. Your mother is like a light bulb: everybody turns her on.

47. Your mama likes to do it with the whole damn gang
Anybody wants to can get a little poon-tang.

48. Your mama is a dog and she ain't got no class
Anybody wants to can stick it up her ass.

49. I don't play the dozens 'cause the dozens are bad
But I tell you how many children she had
Your mammy had one, she had two
But she had a dirty cocksucker when she had you.

50. I don't play the dozens
'Cause the dozens ain't the game
But the way I fuck your mother
It's a goddamn shame.

51. I don't know the dozens and I don't play the game
I fucked your mama on the passenger train.

52. I don't play the dozens
I play the six and a half
And the way I did it to your mama
Made your grandpa laugh.

53. I fucked your mother on an electric wire
The fire in her pussy made us both jump higher.

54. Fucked your mother on a bag of flour
She was shitting pancakes for a half an hour.

55. I fucked your mother in the deep blue sky
Scum dropped down in your grandfather's eye.

56. I fucked your mother on a railroad track
And she jumped up and said "Get back!"

57. I did it to your momma on the railroad track
And when her ass went up the trains went back.

58. I fucked your mother on the railroad track
Her pussy was so stinky the train turned back.

59. I fucked your mother on the railroad track
Her pussy was so hot even the train backed back.

60. I fucked your mother on the midnight hour
Baby came out screaming, "Black Power!"

61. I screwed your mother on a piece of cheese
A little rat came out saying, "Tip me, please."

62. I fucked your mother on top a hill
She came out the bottom like Buffalo Bill.

63. I fucked your mother on top of a house
She came out the bottom like Mighty Mouse.

64. I fucked your mother on a rusty fender
She stank so bad the Japs surrendered.

65. I fucked your mother on top of a post
She came out the bottom looking like a ghost.

66. I fucked your mother on top a train
    She came out the bottom like Jesse James.

67. I fucked your mother from corner to corner
    For a minute there I thought she was a goner.

68. I fucked your mother on top a bed
    Boy, did she have a nappy head.

69. I fucked your mother on top a table
    She came out the bottom like Clark Gable.

70. I fucked your mother in a jar of molasses
    You couldn't see nothing but two black asses.

71. I fucked your mother on the back of a truck
    Didn't nobody get it but me and Donald Duck.

72. I fucked your mother 'til she turned blue
    The baby came out doin the boogaloo.

73. I fucked your mother on a red hot heater
    Missed her hole and burned my peter.

74. I fucked your mammy between two shoes
    She had a little baby, looks just like you.

75. I fucked your mother from tree to tree
    The baby came out looking just like me.

76. I fucked your mother between the tree roots
    All she could do was wiggle and pooht.

77. I fucked your mommy in a pile of bricks
    She tried to come but I heard her shit.

78. I fucked your mother while drinking some wine
    I didn't get much pussy but she really could grind.

79. I fucked your mother till she went blind
    Her breath smells bad but she sure can grind.

80. I fucked your mama on a sheet of paper
    Put her ass in gear like a Studebaker.

81. I fucked your mama and your sister too
    I pointed my dick at your daddy, and that baldheaded nigger flew.

82. I fucked your mother from tree to tree
    The tree split, your mother shit
    And everybody got hit with a little bit.

83. I fucked your mother, your mother fucked me
    I fucked your mother up a sycamore tree
    The tree split, she shit
    And I couldn't get but a little bit.

84. I fucked your mother in a bowl of rice
    The baby came out shootin' dice.

85. Fucked yo' mama on a bag of rice
    Two babies came out shooting dice
    One throwed seven, other throwed eleven
    Know damn well they ain't goin' to heaven.

86. I fucked your mother in the middle of the road
    I said look out, baby, here comes a V8 Ford
    And made her pussy jump on the running board.

87. I fucked your mama like a dirty dog
    I fucked your mama like a funky hog
    I fucked your mama right through and through
    So mind your business or I'm gonna fuck you.

88. I fucked your mama till the sky turned green
    I fucked your mama till she let out a scream
    I fucked your mama till the sky turned blue
    I fucked your mama till she talked about you.

89. I fucked your mammy from Baltimore
    She had hairs on her pussy that swept the floor
    She had bumps on her ass that would open the back door
    Goddamn that bitch from Baltimore.

90. I fucked your momma last night
    That cock was sho' nuff outta sight
    I fucked her once, I fucked her again
    All for a cheap-ass bottle of gin.

91. Say, I hate to tell you this, man, but the other day
    I fucked your mama in a hell of a way
    I fucked that hole between a pile of bricks
    I made her pooht, I even made her shit
    Say I fucked her so good that the hole jumped up
    And taught me how to huckle-buck.

92. Man, your mama's pussy was a tight lid
    But I got to it before your daddy did.

93. Your daddy ain't no good and your momma's a whore
    I spotted you running through the block selling asshole from door
    to door.

94. Your father's a pimp, your mama's a whore
    I've had the bitch out on the corner a couple years or more.

95. I saw two cops sittin' on a bench
    Trying to screw your mother with a monkey wrench.

96. I saw your mother on top of the fence
    Sellin' pussy for fifty cents
    A bee came along and stung her ass
    So she raised the price to a dollar and a half.

97. Motorcycle, motorcycle
    Running through the grass
    After I fucked your mother
    She put her tongue up my ass.

98. On her honor she'll do her best
    To get a nigger to undress
    On her honor she'll do her duty
    To give up some of that big, black booty.

99. I saw your mother on top of the moon
    Fuckin' the hell out of Daniel Boone
    Daniel Boone didn't have no ass
    So she fucked the hell out of a piece of grass.

100. I saw your mother in a garbage can
    Fuckin' the hell outta Peanut Man
    Peanut Man didn't have no dick
    So she fucked the hell out of his walkin' stick.

101. As I walked through the jungle grass
    I looked down and saw your mama
    Sandpaper an elephant's dick
    Down to fit her ass.

102. Your mana's name is Valdosa
    I thought somehow I had lost her
    But when I looked in the grass
    I spied the print of her ass
    Where some hip son-of-a-bitch had crossed her.

103. I hate to talk about your mother
    Because she's in my class
    She got hair on her chest
    And my dick up her ass.

    She got a big black pussy
    That's soooo goood to me!!!
    So you better call me daddy
    But that's between her and me.

104. Down in the alley where nobody goes
    Lay your mother without any clothes
    Along came a man with a walking cane
    Pulled down his zipper and out it came.

Three months later was a great surprise
A month later her belly began to rise
Five months later out it came
A sharp motherfucker with a walking cane.

105. Down by the river where nobody goes
I saw your momma taking off her clothes
Along came Sonny swinging a chain
Pulled down his zipper and out it came.

Then three months later all was well
Five months later it began to swell
Then nine months later out it came
Little black Sonny swinging a chain.

TOASTS

He used to come in and lay his bar ... on the bar
And it used to be from here to thar ...

THE SIGNIFYING MONKEY

The Signifying Monkey (1)

... Then I had a stop in Africa. Why did I go there? I ran across this monkey,
and he was telling me this story about this lion that was always giving him
hell. I asked him, I said, "Monkey," I said, "how come you don't come out of
that tree?" And he said, "Well, I'll tell you." And he put it to me this way:

The Signifying Monkey said to the lion one day
"There's a baaad motherfucker a-heading your way

Now I knew from the start yo'all could never be friends
Because anytime you met somebody's ass would bend

Now I hate to say it, and put it this way
But he talked about your mama in a hell of a way

Now I want you to do something, and do it for me
When he start kicking your ass don't you call on me."

The lion shot by the monkey with such a breeze
His nose whistled and his ass sneezed

He collared up the elephant upside a tree
He said, "Look, you big grey motherfucker, it's gonna be you and me."

The elephant looked out the corner of his eye
He said, "Hunh! Go on, small fry, pick on somebody your size."

The lion made a terrific pass
The elephant sidestepped and kicked him dead up his ass

He broke both jaws and fucked up his face
And kicked his asshole dead out of place

The lion crawled back more dead than alive
That's when the monkey, he started his signifying jive

"Why, Mr. Lion, Mr. Lion, you don' t look so well
As a matter of fact you look like you caught all kinds a hell!

Look at you, with your ass all black and blue!
As tough as you are, that don't mean a damn thing to you

Look at you, you look like you had the seven-year itch
And you supposed to be king of the jungle, now ain't that a bitch!

Get up, get up from under my tree
I'll take out my dick and pee!

Shut up, shut up, don't you holler, don't you roar
I'll jump out this tree and kick your ass some more!"

Now the monkey was excited, he jumped up and down
His tail missed a limb and his ass hit the ground

Like a streak of lightning and a bolt of blue heat
The lion was on him with all four feet

The monkey looked up with a tear in his eye
He said, "Mr. Lion, I apologize."

The lion looked down with such a frown
Said, "Shut up, motherfucker, 'cause your ass is going through this ground."

The monkey said, "Now if you let me up like I know you should
I'll fight your ass all over this motherfuckin woods."

Now the lion didn't mind, he knew he had a sure fight
He was gonna kick that monkey's ass till the middle of the next night

Up the tree, up the limb, up the top of the tree flew the monkey
And he backhanded his old lady and said, "Bitch, that's for pushing me."
    [*Laughter*]

Lion said, "If you want to stay alive and be well for everyday
Up in that tree is where you better stay."

And that's where that monkey is to this very day.   [*Laughter*]

The Signifying Monkey (2)

Way over by the Congo way
Lived a signifying monkey who bullshitted all day

Up in a tree he stood on a limb
With his little grass house he kept close to him

It was during this hot sunny day
When Brother Lion came strutting along his way

"Hey, you son-of-a-bitch with all the hair
You must be the lousy motherfucker I heard about here and there."

Mr. Lion said, "Hey, you know, this is a goddamn shame
That drawed-up little bastard trusts to be calling me names."

The monkey said, "My friend told me how he kicked on your ass
How he scrubbed your damn face all in the grass."

The lion said, "It's a goddamn lie
The mother who told you this didn't have no alibi

You should have been there to see
How I made that motherfucker plead to me."

The monkey said, "You look mighty damn ragged to me
Anyhow, shut up, you hairy-faced bastard, I have to pee."

The lion said, "Hey, you little drawn-up clown
Stop talking that bullshit and hit the ground."

The monkey said, "I ain't no damn fool, you know
There's other places that I haven't visited, you know

He told me about your whole damn race
He even told me about your brother, your mother, and her fucked-up face."

The lion was so damn mad he was slobbing from the mouth
He said, "Show me this bad mother you are talking about."

The monkey said, "If you would just follow me
I'll have you there before you can count to three."

The monkey started to swing from limb to limb
While the lion walked through the path keeping his eye on him

The monkey said, "Hurry up, you know
There's other people who wants to see the show.

Yeah, I forgot to tell you what else he said
He said he fucked your mama and also your old Uncle Jed."

The lion was crying with tears in his eyes
He said, "I'm gonna kill this motherfucker for telling his lies."

The monkey said, "In case you never heard
This motherfucker eat three bales of hay and shit giant turds."

The lion said, "I don't give a damn
He's been trying to give my family the sham

So you don't have to say no more
When I set eyes on that motherfucker, we'll settle the score."

The lion was sure 'nuff mad
He popped his tail and slobbed like he never had

The monkey said, "It won't be long before you see
This big motherfucker who told this shit to me."

The lion didn't say a word
All he wanted was to meet this lying son-of-a-bitch who shits giant turds

The monkey said, "Hey, I see him in sight
Pick up a brick or a stick and go upside his head with all your might."

The lion said, "I want him to be face to face with me
When I start to slap his ass and teaching him about lying on me."

He jumped out of the brush popping his tail like a whip
He said, "Don't say nothing, big funky bastard, I'll bust your mother-
    fucking lip."

The elephant looked at him and didn't say a word
The lion said, "You're the motherfucker who says he shits giant turds

I'm going to teach you about fucking with me
'Cause all my friends here are witnesses to be."

The lion broke at the elephant and made a slip
The elephant was quick, he busted his fucking lip

He threw him down on the ground
Choked him, slapped him, and scrubbed his balls in the ground

The lion said, "Please, Mr. Elephant, don't do this to me
That signifying motherfucker, shit, there he is up there in that tree."

The elephant and the lion was putting on a show
The elephant said, "I ain't gonna take no chances, I'm gonna kick your
    ass some more."

The lion finally got away
But he'd never forget this ass kicking he'd had this day

The monkey jumped up and down laughing on the limb
When his motherfucking feet slipped from under him

The lion was on him like stink on shit
He gave his ass a whipping he'd never forgit

Yep! The lion put that signifying monkey in his grave
'Cause that was the only place he would behave

Up until today, this is all the witnesses can say
"That lion fucked up that signifying motherfucker on a hot sunny day."

The Signifying Monkey (3)

Deep down in the jungle where nobody goes
Lived the signifyingest monkey the world ever knowed

He told the lion one bright hot sunny day
"There's a big burly motherfucker a-down the way

Now you know, Mr. Lion, he couldn't possibly be your friend
'Cause he talked about the shape your dear family is in

He said your mother is a whore and your father is a punk
Your sister's got the pox and, motherfucker, you eat cock."

Now the lion listened on and he got so sore
He started popping his long bushy tail like a Colt .44

He tore off through the jungle like a terrific breeze
Knocking down Mr. Giraffe down on his knees

He came upon Mr. Elephant late that day
Lying on his ass and eating hay

"Hey, you big motherfucker, it's plain to see
That you're the big son-of-a-bitch that's been talking about me."

The elephant rolled over and looked out the corner of his eyes
Said, "Go on, you little wooly rascal, and pick on someone your own damn size."

The lion roared and made a pass
That's when that big motherfucker side-stepped and knocked him dead
    on his ass

They fought all night and they fought all day
I still don't know how that poor lion ever got away

He came through the jungle more dead than alive
That's when that monkey started his signifying jive

"Hey motherfucker! When you left here yesterday this jungle rung
Now you come crawling back, damn near hung

You look like a cat with the seven-year itch
And you're supposed to be the king of the jungle, ain't you a bitch!

Now don't come with that shit about you won
'Cause I had a ring-side seat when the shit begun

He kicked you in the side ninety-nine times and pulled your mane
Then he ran up your ass like a late freight train

LOOK OUT, motherfucker, don't you roar
I'll un-ass this limb and whip you some goddamn more!

Go on, motherfucker, get from under my tree
I've been drinking coconut juice and I might want to pee."

Now the monkey got frantic and started jumping up and down
That's when he lost his grip and his ass hit the ground

Like a streak of lightning and a barrel of heat
The lion was on this motherfucker with all four feet

The monkey looked up with tears in his eyes
And said, "Please, please, Mr. Lion, I want to apologize."

The lion said, "Oh no, motherfucker
I'm going to stop you from this signifying jive."

The monkey started crying and tried to cop a plea
"Please, Mr. Lion, you're hurting poor me."

All of this wasn't getting the monkey anywhere, so he said:

"Mr. Lion, if you let my nuts up out of this sand
I'll get up and fight you like a natural man."

The lion jumped up and squared off for a nice clean fight
That's when that monkey jumped damn near out of sight

"You big, stupid motherfucker, think I'll fight you fair?
I'll take one of these coconuts and part your motherfucking hair

Another thing, while you were getting your ass kicked
I was in your den fucking your wife and drinking your gin

I fucked her in the ass until she had to shit
So I grabbed your son, and made him suck my dick

While your father was busy licking his coat
I shoved my dick down your old mother's throat

Your father's ass hole was so juicy and tight
I fucked him the remainder of the night

Motherfucker, you might as well think of the future and forget the past
Because if you think I'm going to miss another limb, you're a lying ass."

The Signifying Monkey (4)

It was deep in the jungle, way back of the sticks
It was raining like a muthafuka and cold as a bitch

The monkey and the coon were sitting on the ground
Drinking corn liqour and bullshitting around

Now there hadn't been any shit in the jungle for quite a bit
So the monkey decided he'd start some shit

When out of the jungle came a mighty roar—
It was King Leo the Lion on all four paws

The coon poked the monkey in the side
He said, "That's one muthafuka we'll all let slide."

The monkey hunched the coon back and said, "What will you bet?
I'll have that lion's ass kicked yet."

The monkey jumped up. He yelled, "Leo, Leo, have you heard?
Have you heard the latest word?

Why, there's this fat muthafuka down the lane
That's been talking some shit that's a goddamned shame

He talked about your momma, he talked about your dad
Why, he said some shit that even made me mad

He talked about your sister, the one you love so dear
Why, he said the little whore would fuck for a small can of beer."

Leo jumped back with his jaws all fat
He said, "Where's the big muthafuka? Where's he at?"

Immediately, the monkey's tail pointed to the east

Like a ball of lightning and a ball of white heat
The lion set out on all four feet

He spotted Dimbo in a small clump of grass
He said, "Get up, muthafuka, I'ma kick your ass."

Dimbo looked out from the corner of his eye
He said, "You better go 'head, Leo, and fuck with somebody your own size."

The lion tried to hit him with a forward right pass
The elephant side-stepped him and kicked him in the ass

They fought for thirty days and they fought for thirty nights
And I still don't see how the lion got out of that fucking fight

Why, he crawled through the jungle on a cane and a crutch
Looking for that monkey that had to say so damned much

When high, high, in a coconut tree
The monkey yelled, "Hey, fuck-face, you looking for me?

Why you come past my house roaring and shit?
I ought t' kick your ass for that little bit

If I hadn't sprained my finger or broken my thumb
I'd walk with your ass from here to kingdom come."

Well, the monkey started laughing and jumping up and down
When his foot slipped and his ass hit the ground

The lion was on him with all four feet
He said, "I'ma grind this little muthafuka up to hamburger meat."

The monkey said, "Why, you just let me get my balls out the sand
I'll fight your ass like a natural man."

The lion jumped back all ready for a fight
And that's when that monkey jumped damn near clean out of sight

Since then there's been a lot of talk and a lot of lying
But I'll be goddamned if there's been any more signifying

Meanwhile, down at the bar having himself a ball
Cousin Baboon heard of Monkey's downfall

He looked at the crowd with a tear in his eye
He said, "That muthafuka Leo is just about my size."

He took a shot of whiskey, he took a shot of gin
He said, "I got a long way to go and little time to make it in."

The fight was about to start
Cousin Raccoon set it off with a fart

UUUuuurrt!

"In this corner, Cousin Baboon, a mean muthafuka
In this corner, Leo, king of us all!"

The bell rang, the whistle blew
Cousin Baboon was on Leo like a German on a Jew

Cousin Baboon turned his head to spit
Leo stuck close to him like stink on shit

The monkey jumped out of the tree and onto the grass
Just to see his cousin get kicked all in the ass

And like I said before, since then there's been a lot of talk and a lot of lying
But I'll be goddamned if there's been any more signifying.

The Signifying Monkey (5)

Said the signifying monkey to the lion one day
"There's a big bad motherfucker headed your way

I hate to talk about it 'cause I know it ain't right
But he said you two had one hell of a fight

He said he whipped your ass till you couldn't hardly walk
He said you tried to holler, and you couldn't hardly talk."

The damn lion roared and gave a sigh
He said, "That big motherfucker told a goddamned lie

If you don't believe me just watch and see—
Jump on my motherfucking back and ride with me."

The damn monkey saw that the lion was sad
And he thought up more shit to make him mad

"That ain't all that mother had to say
Man, he talked about your mammy in a hell of a way."

The madder the lion got the louder he would roar
He popped his tail like a .44

He got so mad he flew into a rage
Like a young cocksucker when he's puffing his gage

Like a streak of lightning, and a tornado breeze
He went sailing on through the jungle trees

All the animals were falling on their bending knees
Crying, "Please, Mr. Lion, goddammit, please!"

But he found the elephant leaning up against a tree
He said, "Wake up, motherfucker, it's going to be you and me."

The elephant just looked out of the corner of his eyes
He said, "Go on, chicken shit, and jump on something your size

Wise up, motherfucker, and let me be
Carry your hairy ass home and stop fucking with me

Because if you jump on me you just got to die."
The lion said, "That sounds like a motherfucking lie."

The lion ran up and made a jungle pass
The elephant stepped back and slapped him dead on his ass

Tears started meeting under the damn lion's chin
And the damn fool jumped up and tried that same shit again

This time when the lion started his pass
The elephant sidestepped and slapped a gut out of his black ass

He broke his back, he fucked up his face
He cracked all his ribs, and kicked his ass out of place

The lion said, "Ellie, ol' boy, this shit I can't take
Lighten up, motherfucker, I must have made a mistake . . .

If you just let me up like a good fighter should
Then I could fight your big ass as best I could."

The elephant let him up like a good fighter should
And that lion went sailing out through the jungle woods

As he ran through the trees he was bawling and crying
The damn monkey took to the trees and started signifying

He was clapping his hands and swinging his tail
He said, "Watch that scared motherfucker set sail!"

He said, "Wait, Mr. Lion, is that all you can do?
Run? You cowardly motherfucker, you!"

When the monkey found the lion, he was panting and blowing
He said, "Get up, motherfucker, you been used to roaring

Every morning I try to sleep a little bit
You come under my tree with that Grrrrrr! shit

Now get the fuck out from under my tree
Before I swing out over your ass and pee!

Now just open your damn mouth and try to roar
And I'll stomp your motherfucking ass some more!"

The monkey started shouting, jumping up and down
Then his damn foot slipped and his ass hit the ground

Like a streak of lightning and a ball of white heat
The lion lit on his ass with all four feet

He ripped that monkey from his ass to his ears
"Here is where I end your signifying career

When I get through with your goddamn face
They are going to kick your damn ass out of the monkey race."

The monkey looked up with tears in his eyes
He said, "Wait, you four-footed bastard, I apologize."

Right on his ass the lion lit
"Goddamn all this apologizing shit."

He grabbed the monkey by the throat and shut off his breath
And slowly the damn monkey crumpled in death

Mrs. Monkey walked up with her eyes all red
Mr. Ape said, "Don't worry, Mrs. Monkey, 'cause this motherfucker's dead."

They drug his ass out of the sun and laid him in the shade
The animals walked by and viewed his ass like GIs on parade

Later on that evening, just when it got dark
They laid that monkey's ass to rest, out in the jungle park.

The Signifying Monkey (6)

Said the monkey to the lion one bright and sunny day
"There's a big, burly motherfucker down the way

And the way he talks about your mother I know he ain't your friend
When you meet you're bound to bend

He talked about your momma and your grandma too
Said if you show up he'll talk about you

He talked about your sister and your cousins
And everybody knows you don't play the dozens

I'd have fought him myself," he said with tears in his eyes
"But the dirty motherfucker is twice my size."

Off ran the lion in a hell of a rage, creating a breeze which shook the trees
And knocked a giraffe to his knees

He saw the elephant resting under a tree
And said, "You big-eared motherfucker, it's you or me."

He dove at the elephant and made a pass
The elephant ducked and knocked him flat on his ass

He picked him up and stomped him all in his face
He kicked in his ribs and pulled his ass out of place

They fought all night and they fought all day
And I still don't see how the lion got away

He dragged back to the jungle more dead than alive
And that's when the monkey started his signifying jive

"King of the jungle! Now, ain't you a bitch!
All swelled up like you got a seven-year itch

When you came by here yesterday the jungle rung
Now you come back with your asshole hung

Shut up, you motherfucker, you better not roar
Or I'll come down there and kick your ass some more."

The monkey started laughing and he jumped up and down
His foot missed the limb and his ass hit the ground

Like a bolt of lightning and a streak of heat
The lion was on him with all four feet

The monkey looked up with tears in his eyes
And said, "Please, Mr. Lion, I apologize."

The lion said, "A signifying motherfucker always will
You gonna fuck around here and get somebody killed

You might as well stop all your hollering and crying
I'm gonna put an end to all your signifying."

The Signifying Monkey (7)

Deep down in the jungle behind five sticks
Was a monkey and a coon sitting in the breeze and drinking corn liquor

While down on the ground a lion came by and the monkey poked the coon
   in the side:
"There's one motherfucker I won't let slide."

He said, "Bro Lion, Bro Lion, you is the king of the jungle, that's true
But the elephant don't have too much respect for you

He sits in the land of the tall, tall grass
Hunched up high on his motherfucking ass

He talks of yo' mother, he talks of yo' father too
I don't think he has too much fucking respect for you."

Now the lion tipped down to the land of the tall, tall grass
Looking for that elephant who sat on his ass

He said, "Elephant, get up off yo' ass, 'cause when you do
It's gonna be me and you!"

The elephant peeped out of one eye and said, "Bro Lion, you may be the
    king of the jungle, that's true
But if you fuck with me yo' whole kingdom is through!"

The lion threw a false pass
But the elephant bobbed and weaved and kicked him square in the ass

They fought for forty days and they fought for forty nights
I don't see how the lion ever got outta the fight

The lion went back on a cane and a crutch
Looking for that monkey who had to say so much

He said, "Monkey, come down out of that tree
And when you do it's gonna be you and me."

The monkey peeped out of one eye and said, "Bro Lion, with yo' hair so
    knotty and yo' nose so snotty
If you don't know who you talking to, you better ask somebody."

As the monkey jumped from limb to limb, he missed and fell in the street
The lion was on him with all four feet

The monkey looked up and said, "Bro Lion, here I lay with my balls in the sand
If you let me get up, I'll fight you like a natural born man."

The lion stepped back, expecting a fight
But dush, dush, dush, that hairy motherfucker was outta sight!

The Signifying and Pool-Shooting Monkey (8)

Deep in the jungle, way back of the sticks
The baboon ran the pool hall, but the monkey was the slick

He wore big green suede shoes all trimmed in brown
A big Adams hat with the brim broke down

He was rather lean in stature, and as charming as a crow
Yes, this monkey could talk more than a Philco radio

I should mention that he was the only monkey that could shave without shame
He felt that trimming his moustache sharpened his game

My man wore big yellow sunglasses that hung about his face
The complementary stick pins and diamonds just seemed to fall in place

The cat had a gold watch attached by a long gold chain—
Actually there was more on his body than most monkeys in one life could
     obtain

The monkey would sometimes dance on one foot while making his body whirl
He would stop suddenly and let those white teeth gleam like pearl

Women were never a problem, or so it seems
For there were always more women around this monkey than Van Camps got
     pork and beans

With his turned down hat and his long zoot suit
He was the only monkey in the jungle that drove a convertible coupe

He has many a women, and was never anybody's fool
I suppose for these obvious reasons, others refer to him as Mr. Cool

Let me tell you, this monkey was for real
Whenever he approached the pool hall the whole damn town would just squeal

This cat was known by all as the Signifying Monkey, or so they say
For he could talk more shit than anyone, in a most implicating way

The monkey pulled up in front of the pool hall one day
And as sure as hell, animals started gathering from miles away

The monkey looked upon this gathering crowd with pride
As he strode past, his personal cue stick hanging at his side

The monkey walked up to the pool hall and through the swinging doors
His eye caught the baboon as he dollied across the floor

The monkey says, "Yes, Brother Baboon, soon we shall see
Who's the baddest motherfucker between you and me."

The baboon looked at the monkey without any sign of fright
As a matter of fact, he looked like he could play pool all damn night

The baboon tossed a coin—and for goodness sake
If you will, the Signifying Monkey won the break

He played the deuce in the far corner, the tray in the side
He banked the six off the nine and gave the eight ball a ride

Many of the animals turned their faces to the wall
They hated to see the monkey do his shit with the cue ball

The monkey said, "To all you motherfuckers standing on the wall
I realize I'm not so good looking, but I sure can play with them fuckin'
    pool balls."

He beat the baboon until it was a goddam shame
He threw his coat back, dipped his hat, and asked if any other mothers
    wanted the same

As the monkey looked around, a chilled hush fell over the crowd
It is my understanding, that every mother there was afraid to breathe out loud

The monkey, sensing this, strolled toward the door with pride
And of course he took his pool stick that had just given the baboon a slide

The monkey got to the door and made a quick spin
He showed all the teeth in his head, as he put on his best sophisticated grin

He said, "To show you dudes that this was in fun
I should like to tell you a few newly heard stories before I make my run

All the animals drew in close to lend an ear
They knew the Signifying Monkey could talk more shit than anyone could
    want to hear

The monkey recited:

> *The night was dark and the skies were blue*
> *Around the corner the shit wagon flew*
> *It hit a bump, a scream was heard*
> *A woman was killed by a flying turd*
>
> *Now here I sit in a world of vapor*
> *This shit-house ain't got no paper*
> *But why in hell should I sit and linger?*
> *Watch out, asshole, here comes my finger!*

As the monkey continued with what seemed a lyrical tune
His eyes shifted about and fell on the smiling baboon

"Hey, ugly motherfucker, wipe off that smile
Before I pick up my right foot and stick it in your weak ass awhile

I would feed you a shit sandwich, but it is often said
You're a funny motherfucker, and you hate eating bread

Now when I walk out don't try to nab me in the back
'Cause I'll turn around and let you have a left jab, dead up your crack

While I'm away perhaps you should practice your pool
And maybe next time you challenge me you won't look like such a goddam fool

And next time I see you don't tell me you've been sick
I won't buy that story, just remember you can't shit the slick

Now I must be off to the jungle to have a little fun
I just won't be satisfied till the elephant has that lion's ass on the run."

• • •

I can still recall the event, it was a day in May
The monkey ran across the lion as he went on his way

The jungle was very peaceful, there was nothing going down
It was so damn quiet one could hardly hear a sound

As the monkey approached the lion he put on his worst face, as though he'd
    been crying
When the lion caught his eye, the bullshittin' monkey started his signifying

"Hey, Mr. Lion, how can you take it lying down
While that lousy-stinking elephant is spreading lies about you and your
    family all over town

He called your mother a bulldozer, your sister a whore
He called your brother a little worm and your father a dinosaur

I wouldn't say nothin' about it, except I get so mad
To see that big fuckin elephant talking about your family and trying to make
    you look bad

Most folks think you'd do something about it, except you're afraid
The elephant will scatter your ass like paper in a New York parade

Pardon me, Brother Lion, I do understand your fear
And if I didn't sympathize with you I wouldn't be here

Just let all the jungle talk, and don't let it bother your head
'Cause if you fight the elephant it's your ass that will be kicked, and this
    we dread

Oh yes, he talked about your parents in a way that wasn't too neat
There's a few other little things I wouldn't even repeat

Please, Brother Lion, let the whole jungle keep on singing their tune
'Cause I'm afraid if you tangled with the elephant he's bound to lower
    the boom."

The lion stood up, his pupils as keen as a pin
It gave the Signifying Monkey such a good feeling to see the bullshit was
    sinking in

The lion said, "I'm the king of the jungle, and I won't let that pass
I'll find that elephant and kick his big rusty ass."

The monkey said, "I don't know, but I've been told
He usually hangs out at the water hole

And just to see that everything is fair and square
I'll get my shit together and get on over there!"

The monkey chuckled as he went to find a hiding place
He knew the elephant would beat the lion's ass to utter disgrace

It was about midday, or close to three
The lion crossed the elephant under the coconut tree

Brother Lion says, "You funky elephant, don't look at me out the corner of
    your eyes
The damn best you can do is apologize

Word's going around the jungle you're calling me names
By time I finish kicking your ass you'll want to retract them games."

As this argument got going and generated a little heat
The monkey sat looking innocent, perched on a ringside seat

The elephant said, "I don't know what the game is, and I wish you'd go away
I'd just like to lie here in the sun, it's such a beautiful day."

The lion says, "You don't get off that easy, hot shot
Time I mop your ass across this jungle floor you'll only be a big greasy spot."

The elephant says, "I see I won't get any peace, and this I regret
Till I slap you on your ass so you can knock off the threat."

The elephant hit the lion in the mouth, from his mouth jumped spit
He jabbed him in the ass, from his ass jumped shit

The lion thought, "Why did I let that monkey talk me into this jive?
Lord knows I'm lucky to get out of this shit alive."

He ran back through the jungle weeping, sighing, and there's no denying
That's really when the monkey started his signifying

"Ooohhhh! Bad motherfucker, you don't look too well
Looks to me like you been catching particular hell

When you left here a little while ago the whole jungle rung
Now you come back looking like you were damn near hung!

Walking around here calling yourself a jungle king—
Well, we all know now you ain't a goddam thing

Shut up, motherfucker, don't you roar
I'll snatch up one of these palm trees and whale on your ass some more

Yeah, you running around believing everything I say
I understand when you met the elephant you caught hell gettin' away

With me you definitely don't want a bout
'Cause I might just take my tail and knock all your fuckin teeth out

So if you thinking about tangling with me you better think twice
'Cause unlike the elephant, I won't be nice."

The monkey got frantic, jumped up and down
His four feet slipped and his ass hit the ground

Like a bolt of lightning and a streak of heat
The lion cut him from the top of his head to half of his seat

The lion stood on the monkey's back, and on his ass he pounded
He then moved around the monkey so fast, he felt as though he was surrounded

The monkey looked up with tears in his eyes
He said, "Please, bad mother, I apologize

And understand, Brother Lion, you didn't know hell
The public saw me when I slipped and fell

And if you'll let me get my left nut out of the sand
I'll fight your ass like a natural man."

The lion backed up to let the monkey get squared away to fight
At that point the Signifying Monkey jumped almost out of sight

I jumped up into the coconut tree and tied his tail in a knot
He swore by God and three other responsible people he never would drop.

STAGGER LEE

Stag-a-Lee (1)

From across the water, from the deep blue sea
Came a ragged motherfucker named Stag-a-Lee

He wore baggy pants and beat up shoes
He talked more shit than the *Daily News.*

Stagolee (2)

Over the mountain, across the street
There's a bad muthafucka named Stagolee

He got beat up pants 'n raggety shoes
'N talk more jive than the *Daily News.*

Stagger Lee (3)

Across the ocean, across the sea
There's a tall motherfucker named Stagger Lee

He's tall as an oak and dark as a crow
And he talks more shit than the radio.

Stagolee (4)

May 18, 1944, I had a pick-up Ford, rode through shit, rode through mud
Rode through this place called a Bucket of Blood

I said, "Bartender, Bartender, give me somethin' to eat."
He gave me a muddy glass of water and a fucked-up piece of meat

I said, "Bartender, Bartender, you don't realize who I am."
He said, "Frankly, punk, I don't give a damn."

Before he realized what he had said
He had a .38 slug in his motherfuckin' head

One lady popped up and said, "That's my brother, he can't be dead!"
I said, "Check that slug in his motherfuckin' head."

Another lady jumped up and said, "Stop that man! Call the law!"
I was forced to knock her in the jaw

Looked at my watch, it was a quarter to eight
Figured it was a-gettin' late

This slimy ole lady said
"Come in the room, I'll set you straight."

There was fuckin' on the table, fuckin' in the chairs
And this couple was even fuckin' on the floor

Then Mr. Harris walked in the door
He said, "Who killed this man, who can the murderer be?"

That scaredy-assed Mister Peabody said, "Not me
It was that bad motherfucker, Stagolee."

Stackalee (5)

Back in '72 when the times was hard
I carried a sawed-off shotgun and a crooked deck of cards

Wore blue suede shoes and carried a diamond cane
Had a six-inch peck with a be-bop chain

Had a one-button robe and a lap-down hat
And everytime you saw me I looked just like that

Well, the times was gettin' hard and the weather was gettin' cold
My wife said, "Move on, motherfucker, your love's grown cold."

So I decided to take a walk down 42nd Street
'Cause that's where I heard all them mean motherfuckers meet

Well, I waded through six inches of shit and ten inches of mud
And came upon a place called The Bucket of Blood

I told the bartender, "Give me sumpin' to eat."
He gave me a muddy glass of water and a tough piece of meat

I said, "Look, son-of-a-bitch, you know who I am?"
He said, "Frankly, I don't give a damn."

I said, "Well, motherfucker, you better wake up and see
I'm that mean son-of-a-bitch they call Stackalee."

He said, "Yeah, I've heard of you from down the way
But I meet you motherfuckers most every day."

Well, that's all he said
'Cause he lay behind the bar with six holes in his head

Bitch walked in, said, "Bartender, if you please."
I said, "He lays behind the bar with six holes in his head."

She said, "I don't believe he's dead!"
I said, "You can count the holes in his ragged-ass for yourself."

She said, "Better be gone when Billy Lyons comes back."

Spotted a bitch over at the next table
Rushed right over and grabbed me a seat

I said, said, "Hey baby, I don't wanna seem square
But who's this stud they call Billy?"

Well, she opened her billfold and pulled out a picture

Said, "Well, he's tall, dark and neat
The meanest motherfucker on 42nd Street."

I could see she was stuck on this stud
So I said, "Move over baby, I'm laying you on the floor."

Bitch over at the next table smiled at me
I rushed right over and grabbed me a seat

She said, "Hey, look like you ain't had no ass in quite a while."
I said, "Yeah, my wife threw me out, and I've been looking 'round for some
     other whore."

She looked at her watch, it said half-past eight
Said, "Come upstairs and I'll set you straight."

When we got upstairs I threw her on the floor
I was anxious to get some ass off that frantic whore

When we got back down to where we had been before
Well, they was fucking on the tables, they was fucking on the floor

In walked Billy Lyons . . .

He said, "Who might the murderer of my good man be?"
I said, "It's me, son-of-a-bitch, I'm Stackalee."

A punk jumped up, said, "Go for the law."
Somebody hit that punk dead in the jaw

Another punk went for the lights
But it was too late, I had Billy dead in my sight

When the lights come on, Billy lay at rest
With a clip of my bullets dead in his chest

Well, we fucked all the whores, we drank the place dry
I lay in the corner with blood in my eye

Next morning when I woke I saw the judge and twelve good men

The judge said, "What might the charge on my good man be?"
Cop jumped up and said, "Rape, murder and drunk in the first degree."

Bitch jumped up and started to shout
Judge said, "Sit down, motherfucker, you don't know what it's all about."

Judge said, "Well, I'm gonna have to let you go, Stack
'Cause I don't want to wake up with triple A's in my back."

Stackolee (6)

My name is Stack, Stackolee
Baddest motherfucker this world will ever see

I was born in a whorehouse, raised in a cave
Fightin' and fuckin' is all that I crave

I got a green pin-striped suit, and a broken-down hat
A forty-five pistol and didn't pay for that

I jumped off the Empire State Building and landed on my head
Got up and did the boogaloo to prove I wasn't dead

I swam the Mississippi and failed to sink—
That water was too shitty to even try and drink

Now I waded through water and I crawled through mud
Till I came upon a place called The Bucket of Blood

So I went inside to cop something to eat
The bartender gave me a muddy glass of water and a stale piece of meat

So I shouted, I screamed, "Do you know who I am?!"
He said, "Frankly, son, I don't give a goddamn."

I said, "My name is Stack," this I did say
He said, "Well, I heard of you, son; you from across the way

But let me tell you this, my good man
I been kicking ass like yours all over the land."

Now after he had finished what he had said
There laid two holes on that motherfucker's head

A whore screamed, "Is he dead? Is he dead?"
I said, "Whore, dig the holes in that motherfucker's head."

Then Stack began to rave and shout
He said, "I am at this bar and I want forty bad motherfuckers to throw me out

Now everybody up against the wall and don't make a sound
Else I kick a lump off all your asses that weigh a thousand pound."

Then a whore screamed, "You shot the bartender dead!
You put the holes in the bartender's head!

You did it without a fear of a sin
But you better not be here when Billy Lyons walk in."

I said, "Bitch, time will come and time will pass
And I'll be done bust a cap in Billy Lyons' ass."

So she reeled on her heels and flew for the door
That's when Stack was approached by this beautiful whore

Across her face was ... huh ... well, one of those smiles
She said, "Stack, you have any pussy in a good little while?"

So they went upstairs and they rustled and tussled
He shot fourteen inches through that whore before she moved a muscle

Then people downstairs started fighting and tearing up the place
Stack made it back down to investigate

Things got so quiet you could even hear a pin
Doors flew open; Billy Lyons walked in

He had on a six-button Benny, a four-button lounge
A stingy brim hat with the brim turned down

A brand new pair of kicks just came from the store
And in his hand was a long .44

That's when a whore screamed, "Billy, please! Billy, please!"
Billy up and bust a cap in both of that bitch's knees

Then a stud hollered, "Call the Law! Call the Law!"
Billy up and bust the cat dead in his jaw

"Who shot the bartender dead?
Who put the holes in my man head?"

Stack said, "It was I, Stackolee, without a fear of sin."
And that's the time that the lights gave in

Then the lights came on, Billy lied at rest
Two .45 slugs engraved in his chest

So the next day Stack knew what he had to do
He went to tell Billy's Ma, her name was Miss Lou

He said, "Miss Lou, Miss Lou, what a terrible thing I've done!
I've shot down Billy, your no-good son."

Miss Lou said, "Well, Stack, that can't be true
For you and Billy was friends for about a year or two."

He said, "But I know. If you don't believe what I confess
Go down to the bar and count the holes in his chest."

So Miss Lou threw on her raggedy-ass dress
And made it to count the holes on Billy Lyons' chest

So as time went on Stack figured he'd settle down
He went out and picked him the finest whore in town

Her father was the mayor; he protested, said he'd rather be dead
So Stack shot the motherfucker and had the ceremonies read

So one day he came in tired, and peeped in the room and dug the whore
    with her legs up in the air
Now if she wasn't fucking she just wasn't there

So he went downstairs, got a book and he read
Got disgusted and dashed back up and filled that whore full of lead

Next morning went out to cop himself a news
There was a lawman on the corner just looking for clues

He said, "Stack, did you shoot that whore dead?
Are you the rotten chump that filled your wife full of lead?"

Stack said, "It was I, Stackolee, without a fear or doubt
You got a warrant for my arrest? Go on, read it out."

So he snatched Stack in his chest
He said, "Yep! I got a warrant for your arrest."

So the next day in the court house, in the bull-pen
They had Stackolee handcuffed and guarded by ten armed men

In front of the judge his moms let out with a scream
He said, "Sit down, Ma, this is only a dream."

Then his lawyer got up and started to talk
He said, "Sit down, motherfucker, my time can't be bought."

Then Stack began to rave and shout
The judge said, "Ninety-nine years should straighten you out."

He said, "Shit, Judge, that ain't no time
I got a brother in Sing Sing doing one-ninety-nine."

Then out in the corridor was a crashing sound
The doors flew open, in walked Cocoa Brown, another one of Stack's boys
    from the west side of town

And much to everybody's surprise
He threw Stack two shiny .45s

They blast their way to the courtroom door
Tipped their hats to all the whores

Waiting outside was his little man Benny Green
And they hopped in his long black limousine

They rode uptown, downtown, crosstown, all about
Till they came upon this place called The Ole Hideout

Now this here place was known for nothing but sin
Because five minutes later the Law bust in

But Stack shot many motherfuckers dead
Firing from the hip over Benny Green's head

But all of a sudden everything went black—
Some rotten motherfucker shot Stack in the back

And upon his grave grew vine and honeysuckle
Engraved on his tombstone said:

> *Here lies the bones of a bad motherfucker*
> *He had a tombstone disposition and a graveyard mind*
> *Stackolee was the baddest motherfucker who didn't mind dying*

Yeah!

Bad, Bad Stack-o-Lee (7)

From the golden gates of California to the rocky shores of Maine
There was some bad motherfuckers and I knew them all by name

Take Billy the Kid, he had a groove of his own
He was a fast motherfucker and bad to the bone

And across the border from Mexico
Came throat-cutting, ass-kicking Geronimo

He shot his dad, and killed his best friend
He said, "I'll close the books on the nation and bring the world to an end."

Then up from hell came gun-slinging Sam
He was a black motherfucker and didn't give a damn

He had a little boy who was born to be the baddest motherfucker on land
    or sea
And the little boy's name was Stack-o-Lee

When Stack-o-Lee was just one day old
His dad kicked his ass till his blood ran cold

The very next day after Stack was born
He shot the tittie out of his mouth and made him drink pure corn

When Stack-o-Lee was at the age of five
He saw the white folks burn his daddy alive

This was in Mississippi where your black ass was mud
And them crackers was looking for niggers' blood

He walked to the grave and he didn't shed a tear
He said, "If you take over in hell, Pop, Stack will damn sure rule back here."

He got back home at 4:44
His blood was boiling when he knocked on the door

Although his mother's heart was breaking, she met him with a smile
She said, "We're left alone, my son," then she cried just like a little child

He walked on past his mother, and looked up over the door
That's when he buckled on his daddy's two famous .44s

He said, "I love you, Mother, but I got to go away
But before I leave this town, there some goddamn debt I got to pay."

He rode through Marshall, Texas, when the sun was going down
He said, "Reach, you motherfuckers, because I know my way around."

The undertakers called a conference and they began to smile:
"This little nigger will bring us plenty business, although he's just a child."

Billy the Kid said, "Stack-o-Lee, I think you're out of class."
Stack shot Billy the Kid, and kicked Geronimo's ass

Then he rode on out across the western plain
He's the only black man that ever robbed Jesse James

The white folks said, "Let's hang Stack's Mother, while Stack's not around."
But what they didn't know, this black nigger had eased back into town

They called his dear old Mother bitches, and a no-good Southern whore
And Stack fell outside blazing, with a brand new .44

This time he started shooting, fiery tears was in his eyes
And them motherfuckin peckerwoods was dropping dead like flies

But one old red face peckerwood ran from tree to tree
He took a lead and fired, and he dropped poor Stack-o-Lee

He said, "I got that nigger boy, and I got him on the run."
But what he didn't know, there was one more bullet in Stack's gun

He ran and stood up over Stack, and then to his surprise
He stopped that last damn bullet, right between his goddamn eyes

His mother ran out to him, while Stack was on the ground
He said, "You had better call the doctor, Mom, for your son is slowly going
    down."

She called the old peckerwood doctor, and they put him in the bed
They put two blankets on him and put two pillows under his head

He said, "Look, little nigger boy, is there anything you'd like to say?
Your temperature is rising like hell, you won't live to see the break of day."

Stack said, "All you peckerwoods are going to hell for sure
And I'll be there waiting on your ass, with a brand new .44."

Then Stack's chick came running in, she said, "Stack, I am your girl
Don't you want some just before you leave this world?"

She crawled on top of Stack and got the fucking of her life
She said, "Don't die now, daddy, for I want to be your wife."

She left his bedside crying.

She said, "Stack said tell you peckerwoods he'll take on any bets
Stack don't owe a motherfucker here, Stack paid off all his debts."

Stagger Lee and the James Brothers (8)

Way back in the 1800s, you know
Lived two brothers who didn't give a damn about the poor

Robbing and conniving, they thought they were right
And the ones who thought different had to put up a motherfucking fight

Frank and Jesse was their names
They were the last of the family called James

It was on this particular night you see
They set out on this big destiny

Frank rode a horse by the name of Shine
Who could piss, shit and run at the same time

Jesse rode a big pinto called Mack
Who got mad as hell if Jess broke wind on his back

Away in the night they rode like fools
Couldn't nobody tell 'em that they wasn't cool

As they rode and rode they watched the moon
Man, that damn train would be there soon

"Jesse," said Frank, "Let's wait on that hill
So we can hear that Iron Bitch when she makes that squeal."

Jesse said, "Brother, check out your .44
We can't have no bullshit when we kick in the door."

Just at the nick of time
That big funky train gave a sweet whine

"O.K., Brother, cover your face
We can't have no recognition after we have fucked up the place."

They rode like hell to catch up with the train
But that was all in the work of the James

"Jesse," said Frank, "pull your .44
When I count three we'll break in the door."

Wham!! Them fucking James boys jumped in the door
Passengers screamed, shouted and all in a uproar

Jesse said, "Shut up this goddamn noise, you hags
I'll blow your fucking heads off and put them in the bag!"

Jesse said, "Frank, you guard the rear
While I go up front and pick on the fucking engineer."

Way over in the corner as far as Frank could see
Sat a black shiny nigger. Who can this be?

Up jumped the nigger out of fright
Shouting, "Come on, motherfucker, you got a fight!

I'm going to teach y'all about fucking with me
Cause my name is Stagger Lee."

Frank said, "Nigger, ain't you ashame
You mean you never heard of the Brothers called James?"

Stag said, "It don't matter about a name
When I finish whipping your ass you'll be in the Hall of Fame."

Frank said, "Nigger, don't fuck up, you know
I got a friend who don't give a damn about you called .44."

All of a sudden Frank made a slip
And Old Stag cocked him in the lip

Yeah, Old Stag was on Frank like stink on shit
This ass whipping he'd never forgit

He shouted, "Please, black man, don't hit me in the face."
Stag said, "Shut up, motherfucker, before I pull out my case."

The passengers were jumping up and down with glee
Cheering for this black hero called Stagger Lee

Just about that time old Jesse came back
But Old Stag was quick, he ran Casey Mae up his crack

Until this day the James boys can say:
"If you see this black nigger coming your way

Please, please let him be
'Cause this bad nigger is Stagger Lee."   [*Laughter*]

THE TITANIC

...And Shine Swam On (1)

... And Shine swam on.

Then Shine came across a shark
And the shark said, "Shine, Shine
You're doing fine
But if you miss one stroke
Your ass is mine."

And Shine swam on.

He came across an old lady
She was gasping for breath
And pretty near death
She said, "Shine, Shine, please save me
I'll give you more pussy than you ever did see."

"Pussy on land
Pussy in the sea
But pussy on land is the one for me."

And Shine swam on ...

The Titanic (2)

The 4th of May was a hell of a day
When the great Titanic sailed away

Old Black boy work'n round deck
Had it made up in his mind not to be part of that historical wreck

Bow broke open, water started to flow
Shine thought it was time to let the captain know

Shine jumped up from the deck below, said, "Captain, Captain, I want you
    to know
The water done rose up to the first floor."

Captain said, "Shine, Shine, have no fear
I have ninety-nine pumps to pump the water clear

Now carry your black ass back down below
Before I beat your ass with this two-by-four."

Shine went back and he started to think
He said, "This motherfucker is about to sink."

Shine went up from the deck below
Said, "Captain, Captain, the water done rose to the second floor."

Captain said, "Shine, Shine, have no doubt
I got ninety-nine pumps to pump the water out

Now carry your black ass down below
Before I beat your head with this two-by-four."

Shine said, "Captain, Captain, can't you see
This ain't no time to bullshit me

I have no fear and I have no doubt
But I think it's time to get my black ass out."

Shine jumped overboard and he started to stroke
Making waves like a motor boat

He swam on his back and he swam on his side
He saw a whale and hitched a ride

Just about that time the captain came running cross the deck, crying,
    "Shine, Shine, save poor me
I'll make you the greatest black man you could ever be."

Shine said, "You hate my color and you despise my face
Jump your ass in this water and give these sharks a race."

About that time the captain's daughter come running across deck
With her draws around her ankle and her bra around her neck

Cried, "Shine, Shine, save poor me
I'll give you more pussy than you'll ever see."

Shine said, "Pussy on land, pussy on sea
Pussy on land is good enough for me

Now I know you're pregnant, about to have my kid
But you better hit the water like old Shine did."

Then all of a sudden a passenger came on deck crying, "Shine, Shine, save
poor me
If you can't save me please save my child. Come up here on the deck and rest
for a while."

Shine looked at the boy with a tear in his eye
"I'm sorry, little fellow, but every motherfucker is born to die."

Shine ran up on this shark, Shine said, "Nearer my God to Thee."
Shark said, "Bring your black ass to me."

Shine said, "There are fishes in the lake, the ocean, in the sea
You have to be a swimming motherfucker to out-swim me."

Shark said, "Shine, Shine, you're doing fine
Miss one stroke your black ass is mine."

Shine said, "Oh if I had my razor and a little notion
I'd spread shark shit all over this ocean."

By the time the news hit the land the Titanic had sunk
Shine was in Harlem at the Rooster dead drunk.

The Titanic (3)

Well, you know . . . I can remember a time back . . . Oh around the fourth of May
That was a hell of a day, when the great Titanic hit the bottom of the bay

Shine popped up from the deck below, he said, "Captain, this motherfucker
is gonna overflow."
The captain said, "Have no fear, Shine, we got forty-nine pumps to pump the
water low."

Shine went back down, popped up again, said, "Captain, the water's coming
in on the whiskey."
Captain said, "Shine, I told you before, we got forty-nine pumps to pump the
water low."

Shine said, "Shit, I can't swim and I can't float
But when I hit that water I'll be gone like a motorboat."

Shine was up and a-splash
A wave came and like to broke his ass

The captain came from the twenty-one deck, he said, "Shine, Shine, save
    poor me
I give you more gold than you ever did see."

Shine said, "Gold on the water, gold on the sea
Gold on land is more better for me."

Shine kept going.

The captain's daughter popped out from the twenty-second deck
With her titties in her hand and her drawers around her neck

She said, [*falsetto*] "Shine, Shine, save poor me
I give you more pussy than you ever did see."

Shine said, "Pussy, pussy! I could do it in slow motion
But that ain't shit at the bottom of the ocean."   [*Laughter*]

Shine passed a swordfish doing a hundred and five
That swordfish said, "Shine puttin' down some jive."

He passed a whale as big as a boat
He said, "Pop! [*finger snap*] You show one teeth I cut your goddamn
    throat!"

He passed this shark, the shark said, "Ha! ha! ha! ha! I'm king of the ocean
    and I'm king of the sea
And out here your black ass belong to me."

Shine said, "You might be king of the ocean and you might be king of the sea
But you gonna have to be a swimming motherfucker to make a sandwich out
    of me."

Shine did what no man did before
He got up and *ran* to the next show   [*Laughter*]

When the news got to the harbor that the ship had sunk
Shit, Shine was on easy street getting sloppy drunk.   [*Laughter*]

That was the Titanic, that was one day! . . .   [*Laughter*]

The Tee-Ti-Tanic (4)

Gimme a few minutes and I'm gonna tell ya
About the Tee-Ti-Tanic and what all was in it

When the captain called Shine from the deck below
He said, "Water done broke between the boiler room floor."

He said, "Shine O Shine, feel no doubt
I got forty-eight pumps to keep the water out."

Shine said, "You may have forty-eight pumps, it's true
But that shit you talkin', Captain, just won't do."

That's when the captain called the maid from the upper deck
And the bitch came with her drawers all up around her neck

You could tell she was big by the shape of her belly
'Cause her ass was shakin' like a bowl full of jelly

This is when Shine jumped overboard and began to swim
There was a thousand millionaires lookin' after him

This is when a broad yelled, "Shine, please come and save poor me
'Cause I got as good a pussy as pussy will ever be."

Shine said, "Yes, the hole in your cunt may be good, it's true
But them holes on dry land got good pussy too."

This is when Shine really began to swim

The sharks and porpoises was swimmin' mighty fast
But Shine said, "You motherfuckers won't get my black ass."

When the news got to town the Tee-Ti-Tanic had sunk
Shine was at my house damn near drunk.

The Tenth of May (5)

I don't know, but I think I will
Make my home in Jacksonville

I don't know, but so they say
The tenth of May was a hell of a day

The captain and his mates were mumbling a few words
As the great Titanic knocked hell out of that first iceberg

Up popped Shine from the decks below
And said, "Captain, the water is at my boiler room door."

The Titanic

He said, "Get, Shine, and do your act!
I've got forty-two pumps to keep the water back."

But before Shine could mumble another word
The great Titanic knocked hell out of that second iceberg

Over went Shine and he began to swim
Three thousand millionaires looking dead at him

The captain jumped up from the deck and called,"Shine, Oh Shine, please save poor me
I'll make you richer than any Shine will ever want to be."

Shine said, "Your money is good as far as I can see
But this ain't no shit for me

There's whales in the ocean and there's fish in the sea
Bring your red ass over and swim like me."

Up popped the millionaire's daughter upon the deck
With her titties in her hand and her kotex round her neck

She said, "Shine, Oh Shine, please save my life
On the tenth of May I'll be your lawful wedded wife."

He said, "I don't know, so I'm told
The gals on the other shore has the same peehole

The whales in the ocean are making it rough and tough
And if I get to the shore, it'll be damn good enough."

Shine swam for three days and three nights, when up popped the whale from the bottom of the sea
And said, "You black motherfucker, you're trying to outswim me."

Shine said, "You swim good and you swim fast
But you'll have to be a swimming motherfucker to catch my black ass."

When news got to Washington the great Titanic had sunk
Shine was on the corner of 125th Street damn near drunk.

At half-past four, Shine came in on the B and O, and rolled up to the whores, and "Don't you pout
'Cause I'm a peter-pushing papa, and a water trout

I measure thirty-six inches across the chest
And I don't borrow nothing but sickness and death

I've got a tombstone disposition and a graveyard mind
I'm one motherfucker that don't mind dying."

When Shine was dead from drinking his gin
The devil said, "You're a long time coming, but you're welcome in."

He sent the devil for a glass of water
When the devil came back he was fucking the devil's daughter

The devil stooped over to pick up the glass
He rammed his dick in the devil's ass

Two little imps standing against the wall said
"Get that black motherfucker out of here before he fuck us all."

The King, the Queen and the Whore (6)

There was a ship, and on the ship there was a king, a whore and a black cook
named Shine. The boat was sinking and the only one that could swim was
Shine. He was swimming and he passed the king and the king said:

> "Shine, Shine, save me, Shine
> And I'll give you all the money in the world."

Shine said:

> "Money good but money don't last
> Shine gotta save his own black ass."

So Shine swam on and passed the queen and the queen said:

> "Shine, Shine, save me, Shine
> And I'll give you all the jewels in the world."

Shine said:

> "Jewels good but jewels don't last
> Shine gotta save his own black ass."

So Shine swam on and passed the whore and the whore said:

> "Shine, Shine, save me, Shine
> And I'll give you all the pussy in the world."

Shine said:

> "Pussy good but pussy don't last
> Shine gotta save his own black ass."

So he was a hundred yards from shore when Shine heard:

> "Shine, Shine, swimming fine
> Miss one stroke your ass is mine."

So Shine replied:

> "You might be the king
> of this deep blue sea
> But you gotta be some motherfucker
> to out-stroke me."

Shine, the Devil and His Brother Sammy (7)

Shine was on a ship eating black eye peas and rice
Everything was fine, everything was nice

Till the water rose above his knees
Therefore Shine started to sneeze . . .

Hold it. We going to go into it a different way—

Shine was on the Titanic and the Titanic was sinking.
At that same time Shine's ass was stinking

Shine ran to the Captain. He said, "Captain! Captain!
The first deck is flooded!"

The Captain was fucking. He said, "I don't give a fuck.
We got a second deck."

Shine said, "Captain! Captain! The second deck is flooded."
He said, "I don't give a fuck. We got a third deck."

Shine said, "I don't give a fuck about you!"

He dove off the ship and into the ocean
Met a shark with only one good notion

Shark said, "Shine, Shine, you stroking fine
Miss one stroke and your ass is mine."

Well, Shine was a real cool cat
He wasn't the kinda person you'd call dirty or a rat

But he replied, "If I had a knife and a very good notion
I'd cut shark shit all over this ocean."

Shark was very bright
Waved goodbye, said goodnight

Shine stroked on . . .

Shine ran into the whale and said, "You may be king of the ocean, king of
    the sea
But you got to be a fast swimming motherfucker to outstroke me."

And Shine stroked on . . .

After a while he ran into the captain, he said, "Shine, Shine, please save me
I'll make you Captain of all the Seven Seas."

Shine said, "Being Captain's good, while it lasts
But if you can't swim, that's your ass."

And Shine stroked on . . .

He ran into the Captain's wife, she said, "Shine, Shine, please save me
I'll give you all the pussy that your eyes can see."

Shine said, "Pussy is good, while it lasts
But if you can't swim, that's your ass."

And Shine stroked on . . .

Well, to cut it short, Shine got to land and he died 'cause he had a fly up his
asshole. And he went to hell where the devil had just married a new woman.
Devil said, "I'm going to give one of you motherfuckers a chance to get back
to earth, if yo'all can name something I can't do."

One guy said, "Make me a castle of marble." The devil made him a castle
of marble.

Another guy said, "Make me a ring with all precious jewels." The devil
made him a ring with all precious jewels.

Finally he got down to Shine. He said, "You's a new motherfucker down
here, ain't you?"

Shine said, "Hell, yeah!"

He said, "Well, I might as well give you a chance too."

Shine said, "Well, git me a can."

Devil got him a can and said, "Is that all?"

Shine said, "Hell no, motherfucker! Put about fifty holes in that can and
move out the way." Devil put fifty holes in the can. Shine made a terrific fart,
and after the gasses cleared Shine said, "Now, which hole did that fart come
out of?"

The devil must have looked at that hole for two hours. Finally he said,
"That hole."

Shine said, "You's a goddamned liar 'cause it came out my asshole!"

Devil said, "We goin'a give you a week's worth of luxuries, then we going
let you go back to earth."

Now that was on Monday
On Tuesday the devil lined up eighty-eight women

Shine fucked eighty-four
Got a glass of Tiger Rose, and fucked four more

On Wednesday the devil was getting a glass of water
Came back and Shine was fucking his daughter

On Thursday, the devil bent over for a handful of coal
Turned back up, and Shine stuck his rusty dick up his asshole

On Friday the devil was sharpening his knife
Came back and Shine was dicking his wife

By Friday the devil called a meeting, he said, "All you motherfuckers,
  big and small
We got to kill this motherfucker before he fuck us all!"

Well, Shine was hip to that
Now he decided it was time to go back to earth.

Now, a lot of people heard of Shine, but not too many people know Shine
had a brother by the name of Sammy. Well anyway, Shine was coming home
and Sammy saw him walking down the road. He ran and said, "Mammy
Mammy! Shine's home! Shine's home!" They were so happy to see one another
he said, "Listen, Shine. I'm going to go down here and git some of this white
man's money, 'cause it's payday. And then me and you's going to have a good
time."

Sammy was walking down the road singing:

> *"Just Mary and me
> under the tree . . ."*

And his boss heard him. He said, "Nigger, sing that goddamn song right!"
He said:

> *"Just Mary and me
> under the tree . . ."*

He said, "Hey listen, you black motherfucker, if you don't sing that song
right, I'ma hang you."

He said, "Hold it! Hold it! Boss, hold it! I know what you want. You want
that classical shit:

> *"Just Mary . . ."*

Well anyway, they was going to hang the motherfucker. So finally Shine
was coming down the road, and he saw Sammy sitting on a horse about to be
hung up. He said, "What's . . . what's happening?"

Sammy said, "I don't know, Shine. I was just singing

> *"Just Mary and me
> under the tree . . ."*

Shine said, "What! Didn't you know Mary was a white lady?" Sammy hollered,
"Hold it! Hold it!

> *"Just Mary and yo'all
> and not-a-me at all . . ."*

The Three Women (8)

Shine was on a ship one day with all these chicks and it was three chicks he was digging on. It was a Chinese chick, a white chick and a black chick. He was going around rapping to them every night trying to get over, but he couldn't get over; for three days Shine was rapping but he couldn't get over.

Then the fourth day a storm came up and lightning hit the ship and everything started to get fucked up and the ship started turning over. So, everybody jumped overboard. Shine was on a raft, sort of swaying along. These three chicks were hanging on different pieces from the boat in the water. So, Shine jumped off the raft and started swimming for shore, shore was a long way off. First thing he saw was this Chinese chick who he had been rapping to real hard. She went:

> "Shine, Shine, please save me
> I'll give you all the tea that you can see."

Shine said:

> "Tea on land, tea on sea
> Tea on land is best for me."

And Shine kept right on swimming.

Then Shine swam on for about a mile. And he ran into this white chick he had been rappin' to. She said:

> "Shine, Shine, please save me
> I'll give you all the money that you can see."

Shine said:

> "Money on land, money on sea
> Money on land is best for me."

So Shine kept swimming on and they all drowned. Shine kept swimming on for about two miles. Then it was the black chick he had been rapping to. She said:

> "Shine, Shine, please save me
> I'll give you all the pussy you can see."

Shine said:

> "Pussy on land, pussy on sea
> Pussy anywhere is good to me."

So, Shine stopped swimming and climbed on the raft, fucked the chick, and then he jumped back into the water and she drowned. Then he started swimming for shore.

So, he was three miles off shore and he kept swimming and swimming. Then this big fucking black whale came swimming up behind him.

The whale said, "Shine ..."
Shine said, "What you want?"
The whale said, "Shine!"
Shine said, "Leave me alone!"
Whale said:

> "Shine, Shine, you doing fine
> You miss one stroke, your ass is mine."

Shine started pulling up faster and stroking hard. Two miles from shore,
Shine started swimming powerful.
The whale said, "Shine ..."
Shine said, "Leave me alone!"
Whale said:

> "Shine, Shine, you're doing fine
> You miss one stroke, your ass is mine."

Shine started going faster; he was one mile from shore. Shine got tired,
real tired, and he didn't think he was going to make the last mile. The whale
started grinning and he came up closer and closer, whale was about three feet
from Shine, and there was five feet from shore and he didn't think he was
going to make it. So, he said:

> "When I die bury me deep
> Bury my dick beneath my feet."

Then he started swimming on and a wave washed him on shore.

Years later ...

Son of Shine (9)

Years later, Shine gets married and has a son, Shine Jr. Down South the coun-
try fair comes once a year and they love all kinds of contests. They have con-
tests for cows, for poultry, for livestock. So, Shine Jr. wanted to join a contest
but he didn't know what to join. Because he didn't do anything; he was a South-
ern city slicker. So Shine Jr. said, "Mom, I'm going to the fair to get in this
contest."

"Okay son, if you can find a contest get into it. I know you can win it."

So, he went on to the fair. He looked around for a contest but there was
nothing he could qualify for. So, he came up to this one contest. It was a dick
contest, and it was all these big dudes standing around, trying out for dicks.
This woman would go around measuring them. So Shine was in the audience
looking at what was going on. So, the first dick was about eight feet long. Shine
said, "Awh that ain't nothing." Everybody started yelling and women started
falling out, screaming and everything.

Woman went to the next dick. She measured that one and it was eight and a half feet. Everybody started screaming, "Yea, yea, yea." Shine said, "Awh that ain't nothing."

Then, she went to the third dick and measured and that was about nine feet. Shine said, "Awh that ain't nothing."

Somebody said, "Man, since you don't think it's nothing, why don't you get up there and be in on it. So Shine went up there and they measure Shine's dick. Shine's dick turns out to be ten feet long. Everybody started screaming and falling out.

Word got back to Shine's mother that Shine was showing his dick around. She was very tight. Shine came home that night. She said, "Shine, I heard you were in this dick contest."

Shine said, "No, ma, I wasn't in no dick contest."

"Shine I heard you were in this dick contest."

"Yeah, mama, but don't worry, mama, don't worry. I didn't show 'em the whole thing."

DOLEMITE

Let me tell you about the little bad motherfucker called Dolemite

Now Dolemite was from San Anton
A ramblin', scamlin', gamblin' little young motherfucker from the day he
        was born

Why, the day he was dropped from his mammy's ass
He slapped his pappy's face and said, "Cocksucker, from now on I'm running
        this place."

At the age of one he was drinking whiskey and gin
At the age of two he was eatin' the bottles it came in

Now, Dolemite had a uncle called Sudden Death
Killed a dozen bad men from the smell of his breath

When his unk heard how Dolemite was treatin' his own ma and pa
He said, "Let me go and check this little rascal 'fore he go too far."

Now, one cold, dark December night
His unk broke in on Dolemite

Now, Dolemite weren't no more than three or four
When his uncle came breaking through the door

His unk said, "Dolemite . . ."
He said, "I want you to straighten up and treat your brother right

'Cause if you keep on with your dirty mistreatin'
I'm goin' to whip your ass till your heart stop beatin'."

Dolemite sittin' in the middle of the floor playing
He said, "I see your lips quiverin', Unk, but I don't hear a cocksuckin' word
      you're sayin'."

This made his uncle mad.

He let off with a right that made lightning flash
But Dolemite tore his leg off, he was that damn fast

Now all the men of San Anton gathered around that night
To see if they could do something about that little bad rascal called Dolemite

It took a hundred of the boldest, the ugliest men in town
Finally rode Dolemite's ass down

They put him in jail
They held him without bail

If you think his mammy was happy
You should have seen his pappy

Now it's been eight long years since Dolemite's been fed
The average motherfucker would have long, long been dead

Now the warden called Dolemite
Said, "Dolemite, I'm goin' to tell you what we goin' to do

We goin' to give you a dollar and a half and a damn good meal
If you promise to leave us alone and get your bad ass out of San Anton."

Dolemite took the dollar and a half and the damn good meal
Said, "I'm goin' to tell you old jive, moldy, ancient, decrepit motherfuckers
      how I feel

Yo'all can suck my dick, balls and ass down to the motherfuckin' bone
'Cause I ain't never comin' back to San Anton."

Now Dolemite wasn't more than thirteen when they let him out the gate
He said, "I think I'll go across the sea and try my fate."

He got a job in Africa
Kickin' lions in the ass to keep in shape

He got run out of South America for fuckin' steers
He fucked a she-elephant until she broke down in tears

Now Dolemite worked for five years and a day, got his pay
He said, "Well, I believe I'll go back to that jive-assed USA

The news of the heavyweight fight was being broadcast that night
And a special bulletin said, "Look out for storms, atomic bombs and
    Dolemite."

Now the first thing Dolemite encountered
Was two big rocky mountains

He said, "Mountains, what yo'all goin' to do?"
They said, "We goin' to part, Mr. Dolemite, and let your bad ass through."

Now Dolemite went on down to Kansas City
Kickin' asses until both shoes were shitty

Hoboed into Chi [Chicago]
Who did he run into but that bad-assed two-gun Pete

He said, "Move over and let me pass
'Fore they have to pull these triple A's out your ass."

Went on down to 42nd Street
Not for no shit but some place he could sleep and eat

Run into that Chi Mable, of all the whores she was the boss
She suck you, fuck you and jack you off

She said, "Come on down to my pad, Dolemite,"
Said, "We goin' fuck and fight till broad daylight."

Dolemite said, "Bitch, I had a job in Africa
Kickin' lions in the ass to stay in shape."

Said, "I got run out of South America for fuckin' steers,"
Said, "I fucked a she-elephant until she broke down in tears."

Mable said, "I don't care where you goin' or where you been
I'm layin' to wrap this good, hot, juicy pussy all around your bad-assed chin."

Dolemite said, "Bitch, it's best you not fuck with me,"
Said, "I'd better run you down some of my pedigree."

Said, "I swimmed across muddy rivers and ain't got wet
Mountains has fall on me and I ain't dead yet

I fucked an elephant and dared it to mutter
I can look up a bull's ass and tell you the price of butter

I fucked another elephant down to a coon
Even fucked that same damn cow that jumped over the moon."

Said, "I rode across the ocean on the head of my dick
And ate nine tons of cat shit and ain't never got sick

And you talk about wrappin' your good, hot pussy all around my bad-assed
    chin
Bitch, you ought to be blowin' up my ass tryin' to be my friend."

But Mable farted
That's when the fucking started

She made her pussy do the mojo, the popcorn, the turkey and the grind
Left Dolemite's ass nine strokes behind

She threw pussy up Dolemite's back, come out of his ear, down his side, run
    out of his pocket
Damn near put his asshole out of socket

But Dolemite suddenly made a mojo turn
Had the crabs around that bitch's asshole hollerin' "Burn, baby, burn!"

The next morning they found Mable dead
With her drawers wrapped around he nappy head

And the crabs was madder than a motherfucker
To see Dolemite beat them out of their goddamn supper

But Dolemite kept right on kickin' asses and fuckin' up in the fall
Until finally his roll was called

They had his funeral, Dolemite was dead
But his dick was still hard

The Preacher said, "Ashes to ashes and dust to dust,"
Said, "I'm glad this little bad motherfucker called Dolemite is no longer here
    with us."

DEATH ROW

Heard they fried Big Tony last night, dude who said he wasn't afraid to die
But we all heard that big faggot cry

Before they even pulled the switch
He broke down and cried like a scaredy old bitch

The old-time mobster said he was tough, huhnh
He sure had me fooled with his bullshit bluff

Well, today is the first, and at ten I go
Today is my day to be the star of the show

Then comes Jo-Jo, then Fat Red
But the main event's over after I'm dead

When I'm gone there'll be very little action
Because I, Dirty Eddie, will be the main attraction

And you can quote me, fellows, there'll be no yells, no pleas
No holding on bars or crying on my knees

When it comes to time to walk that wing
I'm gon hold my head high like a proud ancient king

Well, I had my supper, which suppose to be my last
Jo-Jo threw his up, Fat Red had to fast

I downed peas and potatoes and a big T-bone steak
A half gallon of ice cream and a large piece of cake

I had strawberry shortcake and roast pheasant under glass
I didn't let a motherfuckin crumb slip past

And when I asked for seconds the warden stood a-lookin'
I said, "Give it to me raw, chump, and let the chair do the cookin'."

Then I laid back on my bunk and lit me up a smoke
And listened to the hack run down some dirty jokes

Then my mind jolted, wandered, I thought of my woman on the street—
Jack, I heard she's run down and looking kind of beat

I heard she's going with my main man Moose . . .
I'm glad I cut that dirty bitch loose

We'd vowed to be together through all types of weather—
Come to think of it, me and her suppose to walk this last mile together

I heard that Moose turned her into a stomped-down whore
Well it wouldn't be so bad, but I killed for the broad

Now I'm glad I shot that storekeeper dead
I said, "Give up your life, or your motherfuckin bread."

And he started screaming and just wouldn't cease
So I shot him five times with my steel-blue piece

Now I'm extra glad I killed that cop
Because he shot at me first because I wouldn't stop . . .

Ah well, these are memories long before my trial
Now I must get ready to walk this long last mile

Wait ... what's that I hear? ...
Footsteps approaching? ...

Who's that cat in that funny-time hat, that black suit and white collar band?
What's that he's carrying, a short-ice book in his hand?

"... Oh, it's you, Father Brown!
I don't know why you keep comin' around

I told you I don't wanna hear about Good Friday, Resurrection or Easter
Take that book and shove it up your keester

Go 'way, Father, you put anger in my heart
The gate is about to open, the show is about to start ..."

So I hopped off my bunk, scratched my head and rubbed my chin
And on my face was still that nasty-assed grin

I stepped next cell to say so long to Teddy
"Get off my arm, punk, I told you I was ready."

As we proceeded down that long stone hall, still I boasted, still I bragged,
    but still I was cool
The warden told the Father, "The man is a goddamn fool."

And as we approached that big steel door and I happened to look within
I didn't mind the silence 'cause the lights was so dim

And then I dug my lawyer ... maybe reprieve, maybe good news!
Maybe the electric chair blew a fuse! ...

... What, no reprieve? ... No good news? ... Electric chair in good workin'
    order?
"Call back that guard, I want a glass of water!

Guard, Guard, I'm dying of thirst!
Let Jo-Jo or Fat Red go first! ...

Father Brown, Father Brown, please say you will
You tell 'em I'm a good man and didn't mean to kill!"

No, Father Brown strolls slowly over to my chair
He took out his book and he began to read a prayer

He said, "God forgive him, for he know not what he did ..."
I said, "Stop canting that shit, tell 'em don't burn the kid! ...

God! God! Unstrap my wrist! ...
I need a ... I wanna ... I gotta take a piss! ..."

Meanwhile, back on Death Row—

"Hey, Rabbit! Hey, Rabbit! Did you hear that scream?"
"Yeah, but that couldn't have been Eddie, 'cause Eddie was too mean."

"But, Rabbit, I swear I recognized his voice!"
"Naw, that sounded more like my sister Joyce."

Then the hack came back to ran down the game
He said, "Your man Eddie turned out to be a jive-ass lame

He called on his ma, he called on his pa
Then he gave up all connections and he called on the Lord

He sat there and hollered like a jive-ass bitch
And what makes it so bad, the motherfucker died before they even pulled
    the switch."

... Well, that's a little "Death Row," ran by the one and only ...

DORIELLA DUFONTAINE

*Now I'm gonna cut you into a little "Doriella DuFontaine" ... which happens
to be ... eh, true ... what you can say ... episode or chapter of my life. Hmn.
I don't open these pages to many people, but I seem to be in a pretty intimate
crowd, so there's certain things I reveal to my so-called intimates. So, you're
it. Well, let's get down with this thing.*

Now I was standing near the corner, by McKinley Square
I made some arrangements to cop some reefer there

Now I was some kind of fly, and fairly well high
Standing there pinning the whores
When I dug my man, Big-Money Van
Pull up in a 98 Olds

As Van got out, looked about
Dug me and began to speak
From the other side with a long sexy stride
Walked a broad who looked real freak

She wore a white chemise dress that was one of the best
Her hair was long, glossy and black
Skin light copper tan, prettiest eyes in the land—
This bitch was a queen for a fact

Now she wouldn't have to hunt for someone to eat her cunt
Because, like I would oblige her anytime
Believe me, Jim, she was shapely and trim—
Man, this bitch was fine

Now as I spoke to Van and shook his hand
I cracked, "Is this your honey?"
With a bit of a sigh he made this reply:
"She's yours if you want you some money

"Now she's real down, known all around
Her name's Doriella DuFontaine
She's real slick, knows every trick
One of the best in the game

"Now, I seen her work, she's no jerk
She's cool and uses her head
Because once when I was up close, way out on the coast
Sal, she made me a whole lot of bread."

Now, Van wore a Panama straw, a Corona-Corona stuck in his jaw
And a suit that looked real silky
Loafers made in one piece, and imported from Greece
That would have made Leighton's feel guilty

Now I too was pressed in some of the best
But I couldn't compare with Van
Though my taste was good as his, the main reason is
Van was a big-money man

"Say, fellows," said Dee, "I'm starved as can be
Let's go for a bite to eat."
So we all agreed on a real boss feed
At Zoakos' right down the street

Now Zoakos' was a delight, and this was our flight
We was clean as the Board of Health
Three players true, sporting ribbons of blue
We painted a picture of wealth

Then a waiter named Abel showed us to a table
And brought us some ice-cold wine
Dry champagne from the cellars of Spain
Vintage 1849

Then we ate humming-bird hearts, some other choice parts
Turkey a la king
Hawaiian sweet peas, Viennese salad leaves
Sprinkled with butterfly wings

Then some ice cream went in a bowl of creme de menthe
Along with strawberry cake upside down
I smoked a cigarette while Van paid the debt
And we went out to paint the town

And all the while we been dining Van was unwinding
Running down my pedigree
And I happened to note as we left Van's boat
Huhnh, this whore was pinning me

"Say, fellow," said Doriella
"About meeting you I'm kind of glad
How about meeting again, say, Saturday night about ten?
Here's the address to my pad."

Now, Saturday night I got fly
And went to see Miss DuFontaine
Stopped off at Joe, a dealer in snow
And copped two caps of cocaine

Now, when I got to the pad it was some kind of bad
And was filled with a real boss scent
On the floor was a three-inch carpet imported from the market
Somewhere in the Orient

Now the stereo was wailing, but, fellows, I was failing
I just couldn't rap to this deb
I wasn't too bold until she broke out some soul
Some dynamite Panama Red

Now with coke on her thumb she massaged my gums
And gave me some wine to sip
You should have heard her purr when I grabbed hold of her
And massaged her gums with my lips

Now she didn't beat around the bush
Here's what this freak whore said:
"Sal, daddy, I dig you, you're the most
And like coke you go to my head

"If you'll be my man I'll comb the land
And be your own true bitch
Though you might have to lend me to some other men
With their money I'll make you rich."

Well, you know where I'm at, I really bought that
And took this freak whore off to bed
And me and this queen made love supreme
And I flipped when she gave me some head

Now I was schooled by this girl in the arts of the world
And games that I never dreamed
I learned very well, and can't begin to tell
How this fabulous whore could scheme

Then one day she said, as we laid in bed
"Sal, we been sleeping all day!"
So we got our heads bagged up fly and left the pad
And went out in the streets to play

And it was at the Copa Club where I made a big rub
In a game called the Japanese Fan
I took off a fool real nice clean and cool
Who was solid gold ten grand

And the stud was a square, he wanted me to lay odds
Because he owned a haberdashery
That's when Dee showed and said, "Don't let him go!"
And when I did she got warm with me

But at home she was at ease where she dug the ten G's
As I laid it on the bed
"Sal, darling," she chimed, "I'm glad we combined
Van said you was a cold thoroughbred."

But the truth of the thing, this was my first big sting
Though I'd scored now and then
It was through this slick chick that knew all the tricks
That the big money kept rolling in

One day she said, "Sal, stay in bed
Because money I'll make plenty of
You don't have to buy me rings, fur coats or fancy things
Just give me the strength of your love."

Now my eyes got big, I just couldn't dig
This freak whore romantically uptight!
But my nose was open too, so what could I do
Except treat Miss Doriella right?

So we lived fly, stayed high
Until things were never a bore
We were both real hearty—Jack, life was a party
As for money we could always get more

Then one night about one, while having some fun
In a club called The Hours of Joy—
Yeah, I met Dixie Fair, drug store millionaire
And international playboy

Said Dixie Fair, "Who's the woman over there
The one in the red mini-dress?
Introduce her to me and I'll give you a fee."
I did, and Doriella did the rest

Now, that morning in bed, "Sal, darling," she said
"I can get all Dixie's dough
But you have to lay for me real patiently
Down in sunny Mexico

I don't want you around when I take off this clown
And snare him in my den
But when I'm through I'll come to you
And we'll never have to hustle again."

So I got my two bank books, my vine off the hooks
And we made love all that day
And at eight that night I was on my flight
On luxurious TWA

Now my stay wasn't bad, I had a boss pad
And I cut into some fabulous whores
I pulled Carmen LaVista who had a big keester
First cousin to the Mexicali Rose

Now the climate was hot and there was plenty of pot
And the tequila was stone dynamite
But I just laid in the cut on Carmen's big butt
And kept on my knees all night

Then one day a postman came my way
With one of those cablegrams
It read:

>   SAL DARLING STOOD IN THE BOX AND WAITED
>   AND HIT US A COLD GRAND SLAM
>
>   LEAVING ON FLIGHT 59 PAN-AMERICAN LINE
>   JET COMET NUMBER 3
>   ARRIVING TIJUANA AT 4 CAN'T SAY NO MORE
>   LOVE YOUR WOMAN DEE

So I had Carmen bathe me in some milk, put on my grey Italian silk
And went out to cop me some wine

Bought a *New York News* that rocked me in my shoes
When I dug the bold headlines

It said:

DIXIE FAIR, DRUG STORE MILLIONAIRE
COMMITS SUICIDE
LEAVES ALL HIS GAINS TO MISS DUFONTAINE
WHO WAS SLATED TO BE HIS BRIDE

So I made it on to the airport
And as I arrived the loudspeakers blared
And I got inside the Waiting Room
And just in time to hear:

ALL PERSONS AWAITING FLIGHT 59
JET COMET NUMBER 3
PLANE, PASSENGERS AND ALL ABOARD
JUST CRASHED IN THE HILLS OF CHILE

When the rescuers arrived they found one alive—a young woman, age about
    twenty-five
Hair long, glossy and black
Skin light copper tan, prettiest eyes in the land
And she knew there was no turning back

She told the rescuers just before she died: "Tell my man Sal . . . how hard
    I tried . . .
Dixie Fair had made me rich! . . .
And I was bringing him all the money . . .
Like a real down bitch."

Then she called my name . . .
Screamed and cried . . .
Coughed up blood . . .
Trembled, and died . . .

But I'm back on the corner
I'm broke and I'm sick
Shit, things haven't been the same
Since I lost my chick

But I'll pull through like all good hustlers do
And I'll continue to play the game
But God knows there'll never be another whore for me
Like Doriella DuFontaine.

This Is Your FBI (1)

Well, here's a little something about one of the big-time spenders in the narco game. I'm sorry it is not complete, but as far as it goes you'll get just what I mean. Alright. It goes by the name of "Honky-Tonk Bud."

Now Honky-Tonk Bud, the hip-cat stud
Stood digging a game of pool
Those pockets was bagging and he wasn't bragging
'Cause he knew he looked real cool

He was choked up tight in a white-on-white
Wore cocoa front that was down
A candy-striped tie hung down to his fly
And he sported a gold-dust crown

It was the fifteenth frame of a nine-ball game
As Bud stood digging the play
With a casual shrug he looked up and dug
A strange cat coming his way

He was a funny-time cat, wore a messed-up hat
That looked to be nine years old
He wore S. Klein vines and needed a shine
And shivered as though he was cold

Now Bud pinned as the cat moved in, and measured him up for size
To all other cats he was an ordinary flunky
But to the well-trained eyes from many past highs
The hip cat dug he was a junkie

Now Bud pinned as the cat moved in
And asked if he knew Joe
Joe wasn't around 'cause his bags was down
And he had went to his man to score

He said, "You look sick, as if you need a fix
Maybe I can do some solids for you
I'm Honky-Tonk Bud, the hip-cat stud
From over on 8th Avenue

Now if you wanna cop let's talk shop
And I'm sure I can help you to score

But you need a bill because my man is wholesale
And he's the best connection I know."

Now the cat looked down with a half-assed frown
As though he was trying to make up his mind
"I'm leary," he said, "but I got the bread
I just want the best I can find

Still I don't want to spend all of my ends
Till I know that the stuff's alright
'Cause there's three other cats put money in the hat
And they don't want it out of their sight

Still if you've got the bag and if the stuff's no drag
We'll get you to cop some more
'Cause we need a full load to take on the road—
We're traveling boosters, you know."

Now, Bud hesitated because he had underrated
And thought he could pull a big sting
But now he knew a shuck wouldn't do
And he had to produce the real thing

He said, "Wait in the shop while I go cop,"
And he wasn't gone for long
For he too was sick and needed a fix
And they went to his pad to get on

Now, he broke out some hypes, broke out some spikes
And rolled up some dollar bill G's
Cooked a small taste on a kitchen match blaze
And they both rolled up their sleeves

Now the cat tried real hard, but he was so scarred
He just couldn't find no room
But when he finally struck red ole Honky-Tonk said
"Easy, 'cause the stuff's real gone."

Now they both jacked until they tasted smack
And blood began to cake up hard
Chins began to lag, and conversation sagged
And Honky-Tonk went into his nod

Now Bud sighed as the cat untied
"Dig it, baby, I'm high."
That's when the cat made a pass and flashed the gold badge
And said, "This is your FBI."

The Hip-Cat Stud (2)

Honky-Tonk Bud, the hip-cat stud
Stood there digging a game of pool
His bags were bagging, but he wasn't bragging
'Cause he knew he looked real cool

He was choked up tight with his white-on-white
And his cocoa front brown was down
Had a candy-striped tie that hung to his fly
And wearing a gold-dust crown

It was a fifteen frame of a nine-ball game
As Honky stood digging the play
With an outer shrug, he suddenly dug
This strange cat comin' his way

He was a medium-type cat with a funny-time hat
That looked about nine years old
Had a messed up vine and needed a shine
And shivered as if he were cold

Now to all the other cats but Honky-Tonk Bud
This cat looked like a regular time flunky
But, with many highs and well-trained eyes
Honky-Tonk knew he was a junky

Honky-Tonk pinned as the cat moved in
To measure him up for size
With a shivering hand he wiped his brow
And tears ran down his eyes

Honky-Tonk said, "You might still be in hope, for I think I've still got
     some dope
But, first I must get over my high."
The guy bobbed and weaved, touched his toes
Copped him to the nose and said, "I'm from the FBI."

The high was gone. The trial was on
As the judge said, "What do you have to say?"
Honky-Tonk said, "Your boy did his bit, now let's get through with this shit
So my lawyer can take me away."

As the trial progressed it became a hell of a mess
But Honky-Tonk's lawyer stayed cool
He said, "Your boys didn't catch him with no shit, so don't give me no lip
'Cause I've made you all look like goddamned fools."

THE FREE SNORTER

Alright. This here is about a typical guy that's ... eh ... there's one in every neighborhood, so I've heard it said. And being in the Life somewhat myself, well, I've kind of like experienced one of these lames in every neighborhood, you know, from gettin' around. So maybe some of you know a guy like this. But, if you're in the Life chances are you do. Now his thing goes like this: "The Free Snorter."

Now he's always in the block, so he'll dig you if you cop
And no matter how you try you can't get past
And you never leave his sight, and he'll greet you with the light
And say something like, "What's happenin', jazz?"

Now, needless to say, he'll know by the attitude you show
You don't want him nowheres around
But he'll take you by the hand and tell you you look grand
And pretend not to hear if you sound

So you stop and chat with the group that's hanging on the stoop
And hope this lame will pass you by
But he'll do odd things like re-tie his shoe strings
And stay, no matter how you signify

Now you can't hold out much longer because the urge to get high is
    stronger
But the free snorter is still on your trail
So you go upstairs with a frown 'cause you wants to knock 'em down
But you dig that it would be to no avail

So you shoot him this old line that just pops to mind
"I'm sorry, but the pad belongs to Joan
And her paps is on the scene and, Jim, he's some kind of mean
He don't allow no strangers in his home."

But he knows this isn't true, almost as well as you
Because somewhere he heard this line before
So he looks you in the eye, because he caught you in a lie
And it's him, not you, knocks on the door

Now the door's open wide and you both step inside
He's the first to take off his hat and coat
Then he sits in the easy chair and he won't get up from there
And he just stares at the coke and gloat

Then he starts to sound the girls about how they wear their curls
And all the session through he criticize
And all the session through you hear what others should do
And everytime you say something he's wise

Then he start to chat about where he bought his coat and hat
And he claims his shoes come from Spain
Now while he's bragging about his vines you shoot him this ole line
"Now tell me where you cop your cocaine."

Now this time he wasn't wise, you caught him by surprise
And everybody's peeping the conversation
You know you got him down, on his face there's a frown
And no one gives him any consolation

So he says, "Eh . . . Oh, I cop from Stan . . .
You know, the big-time dope man
Why, this morning I copped two caps, but it didn't last long
A few snorts and it was gone. . . . ."

Now he expects you to believe that! . . .

Then he start to talk about his girl, claim she's out of this world
And all the while he's holding the pack
And between each word a snort can be heard
And he makes no arrangement to give it back

Now the coke is goin' around, but, Jack, it's goin' down
Because the snorts he takes are rather huge
Five minutes later the broads split, you know he made them sick
And that leaves just the free snorter and you

Now he's sittin' in the house as timid as a mouse
And you're wondering how long he's gonna stay
'Cause there's a bad flick at the show and you really want to go
But you might have to pay this fool's way

So you cut on a radio, not loud but rather low
And he ups and sound you, "Jack, get Sid" ["Symphony Sid" radio show]
And then he falls back on the couch and goes into his crouch
And you calmly tell him, "I just did."

Now he's scratching everywhere while Sid is on the air
So you sound him, "Look, Jack, be cool!"
And the thing that makes you sick, everytime Max Roaches kick
He starts scratching like he's on the record too

The Free Snorter

So you sound him, "Go get a head. I know you got some bread
And don't come up with a charlie [dollar] or two
Because you've been in on many of my sessions it's about time you learned
    your lesson
Now let me get a high and walk for you

'Cause you got a nasty habit, when you see stuff you grab it
Whether you know what's shakin' or not
Well, I'm certainly wise, and I hope you realize
You'd be better off going back to smoking pot

Yeah, you was a down stud when you was in the club
But the club broke up in '57
That's why I'm setting you wise and I hope you realize
That I don't get my pennies from heaven."

Now he doesn't go for that, he ups and grabs his coat and hat
And looks at you as if you came up wrong
And you sound him, "Don't come back until you produce some caps
Because of you all my coke is gone."

So he walks out of the pad looking kind of sad
He's high but he didn't put up no bread
He was one of the fellows, it's true, but let me school you
Tomorrow he'll be back for another free head.

PETE REVERE

Pete Revere (1)

I remember one time in Mexico, we were sittin' in the bar
This man named Pete Revere . . .

He used to come in and lay his bar . . . on the bar
And it used to be from here to thar . . . [*Laughter*]

But it was a sad sad day for poor ole Pete
As Sadie the whore came walking her beat

Ole Pete's prick looked like Venetian blinds
As he watched the slow curves on Sadie's behind

As she passed ole Pete pat on her big ass, he grabbed her by the tit
Sadie backhanded him and said, "Pete, you ain't shit!"

At this point Pete's dick fell
'Cause he knew Sadie was gon give him hell

Sadie challenged Pete for a duel
Over the mountain and down by the pool

People came from miles around
To see that girl Sadie put her fuckin' down

Scumback Nelly from Tennessee
Was there to referee

Pork-n-Bean Annie blew a loud loud fart
And that was the time for the fucking to start

First, she threw him a Spanish curve
Pete held on to it but it took much nerve

Then she dropped and threw him a sinker
That showed Pete was a quick thinker

Then Sadie rared back and gave Pete the Texas grind
Pete came up both bleedin' and blind

With his ass still pumping and his dick still hard
They drug his black ass to the nearest graveyard

Pete's last words on his dying day
Was, "Good pussy brought me, now it has taken me away."   [*Laughter*]

Yessir!

Big Pete (2)

Pete was a man big and strong
Had a dick on his body eighteen inches long

Sadie the whore came into town one day
She started to walk old Pete's way

Pete reached over and touched her tit
She said, "Hands off, motherfucker, because you ain't shit."

Challenged old Pete to a fucking duel
Suppose to be held by courthouse rules

Old drunk Jock Mississippi
Was to act as judge and referee

When old Jock let out a fart
That was the signal for the fucking to start

Sadie led off with an English grind
Left old Pete ten strokes behind

Pete Revere

Pete came back with a Spanish twist
Said, "Hold on bitch, 'cause you ain't shit."

She killed poor Pete, the dirty bitch
But she shall die of the seven-year itch

When they carried old Pete to the graveyard
His ass was still wiggling and his dick was still hard

Last words old Pete was heard to say
"Lord, pussy brought me here, and it sure took me away."

BIG DICK WILLIE

I'm from the Middle West
I came by New York just to take a rest

I saw an ad in the paper the other day, said there's a big affair in Chicago
That's where all the big men like to go

So I grabbed the 20th Century Limited, and went to that big affair
Where a pretty little maid was waiting there

She said, "Excuse me, mister, for being so fresh
But would you like to go to my address?"

I said, "Excuse me, miss, for being so slow
But my money is kind of low."

She said, "Where I live there's a hundred doors
And a hundred whores

A thousand dollar bet upon the wall
That no one man could fuck them all."

Now you can tell by my vest
That I come on in any contest

So I hoist my wings and grabbed this dame
And down we strolled through the shady lane

We came upon a whorehouse and knocked upon the door
The landlady answered like a .44

She said, "Who is knocking and won't come in?"
I said, "Big Dick Willie, and I came to win."

I entered the house and there's a hundred whores lined against the wall
They knew I came to fuck them all

I dropped my pants below my knees
That's when the landlady came to see

But when I took out dick by the foot
That's when the whores took their look

I fucked ninety-eight straight without a stop
That's when my dick got red hot

I jived the landlady out of an oyster stew
And promised her faithfully I'd fuck the other two

I ate this oyster stew
Quite naturally I had to fuck the other two

I reached up on the wall to grab this bet
She said, "Hold it, Jack, you ain't won yet!"

So I grabbed the landlady by the waist and upon the bed I threw her
And between her maiden thighs I began to screw her

I threw her this way, I threw that way
And asked if it suit her?

She said, "You can ram it, and you can jam it, just as long as you can
    bear it
'Cause I've got a Goodyear Rubber pussy, and I'm damn sure you can't
    tear it."

I said, "I'm going to make it, and I'm going shake it, just as long as you can
    take it
'Cause I've got a hickory stick dick, and I'm damn sure you can't break it!"

BLACK JACK TUCKER

Two niggers lived in Texas, an old man and his son
And he taught that boy a thousand tricks on how to use a gun

Cowboys rode in from everywhere
To watch him shoot bumblebees down out of the air

He was just nineteen and the west was young
When he rode up to a tree where his dad was being hung

As he cut his dad down, his dad called his name
He said, "Black Jack, I've got to take a ride on that hell-bound train

But I want to tell you this before I go
I've taught you every motherfucking thing that you need to know

And always remember this, my son
From now on you've got to live by the speed of your gun."

When he laid his dad to rest his eyes was sad
But he had learned every trick of the trade from his dad

He saddled his pinto up in front of his home
And said, "It's good bye, Texas, for Black Jack must roam."

His dad's two .45s decorated his side
That motherfucker could shoot and that nigger could ride

As he rode along, tears was falling like rain
And he thought about his dad on that hell-bound train

That night he slept under the stars on the plains
And he dreamed about his dad on that hell-bound train

The very next morning at the crack of dawn
That nigger saddled his pinto and that nigger was gone

He rode up to a little one-horse town and stopped
He saw two white men bury a nigger behind a rock

They said, "Look here, nigger, you'd better turn around
This black motherfucker tried to ride through town."

His guns blazed twice, and he on his way
He shot shit out of Cheyenne Brady, and killed Doc Holliday

As he rode the next day he was singing for a change
Him and that goddamn pinto, admiring the range

He rode into Dodge City, on a hot summer day
They asked, "Who is this damn nigger from down Texas way?"

As he rode the sun was going down
He pulled up to the hitch rock and slid to the ground

His teeth were like pearls that was edged in gold
He was six feet tall, and now twenty years old

A broad smile covered his handsome face
Till them peckerwoods tried to make him feel out of place

No goddamn quicker than the news got around
Cowboys started gathering from all over town

They were laughing and talking about having some fun
Like shooting at this nigger's feet, and watching the motherfucker run

Each man waited and took his turn to shoot
Bullets plowing up dirt around that motherfucker's boot

He folded his arms and slowly walked away
He said, "Okay, motherfuckers, that's all for today."

They began to whisper as this nigger strolled past
With his two .45s swinging low on his ass

His silver spurs were clinking a tune
Keeping up with the music from the Nugget Saloon

He bat open the doors and strolled up to the bar
Johnnie Ringo said, "Nigger, you're going too goddamn far.

Nigger, this is a goddamn white man's town
Hit leather and start riding before the sun goes down."

He said, "Ringo, you must be edging for a fight
I've been riding all day and I am spending the night

When I rode in I came from the south
I killed a motherfucker today about his goddamn mouth."

Johnnie Ringo hit leather and that's where he fell
He cashed in his chips, 'cause it was pay in hell

That nigger whirled around with his back to the bar
And said, "Draw, you motherfuckers, whoever you are.

These pearl-handle colts that's hanging by my side
Says that hell-bound train is waiting, who is the next motherfucker to ride?"

The doors swung open once again, the cowpokes spun around
He said, "Nigger, my name is Wyatt Earp, I'm marshall of this damn town

Things were quiet and peaceful here, just before you came."
Earp made with his famous draw, so he died and caught that hell-bound
    train

That nigger stood up over Earp with his thumbs down in his belt
You can imagine to yourself, how them motherfuckers felt

Bret Maverick rose up from his chair, he was gambler known by name
He said, "Nigger, two to one is damn good odds, that says this time you'll
ride that train."

Old nig began to laugh like hell, thoughts spinning through his brain
So he issued out another pass to Maverick's ass, and he died and caught that
hell-bound train

Matt Dillon busted through the door, with Chester by his side
He said, "It's two of us this time, black boy, and I bet you'll take a goddamn
ride."

Matt Dillon's gun cleared leather, and when he tried to aim
That nigger sent a pass to Dillon's ass, and Dillon caught that hell-bound
train

Chester didn't fuck around too long, as soon as Dillon fell
That nigger's blast grazed Chester's ass, and Chester's leg got well

The bar-keeper grabbed a six gun that was lying on the shelf
But that bastard got so goddamn scared, he shot his motherfucking self

A big-legged blonde came walking in, old nig began to smile
She said, "Nigger, get a drink on me, and let's go upstairs and fuck awhile."

She said, "Listen, nigger, tell me, what the hell could be your name?"
But when he shot his load up her she died and caught that hell-bound train

He walked back downstairs to the bar, there was dead men all around
But he stayed that night to keep his word, and calmly rode on out of town

He was the baddest nigger that ever lived, there were no bad men left
Black Jack was so goddamn bad, he had to shoot his fucking self

They laid his ass out on boot hill, where only bones remain
But he issued a lot of passes to many asses, that died and caught that hell-
bound train

I don't know what your thoughts will be about old Black Jack Tucker
But I'm sure you'll join me when I say, he was a shooting motherfucker.

INVECTIVE

Bitch, you're a lying motherfucker and a sack of shit
And under your dress is cunt, both nuts and dick ...

Put-Downs

1. She's got that nigger's nose so wide open if it rained he'd drown.

2. You think you hot stuff, but you ain't nothin' but cold diarrhea. In order for you to light anybody's fire you need a book of matches and some kerosene.

3. You can toot your whistle
   You can blow your horn
   But the man I love
   Can make a dead woman moan.

4. You can scramble in the kitchen
   You can scramble in the hall
   If you can't wash the dishes
   Take your hands off my balls.

5. Yo' eyes may shine, yo' teeth may grit
   But none of this good thing is you gon' git.

Pimpin' Sam

While sittin' and thinkin' in deep meditation, shuckin', jivin', lollygaggin',
    eatin' chitlin' stew
I'm reminded of a girl I once knew

She wasn't no bathin' beauty and she didn't have long black hair
But she was a stone good mud kicker and her mug was fair, baby

I pimped this little chick
And moved out west and settled down out there

When I first met her, baby, I thought she was a little girl just out of school
You listen close I'll tell you how bad I was fooled

While playing small towns back east my bankroll got low
She said, "Look here, pretty papa, you can't jive me," she said, "I've forgotten
   more than you'll ever know."

Said, "I'm Wicked Nell
The Coast Guard's heart from burnin' hell

When you first met me you tried to fill me full-a bull
But you can't look up a mare mule's ass and tell how big a load she'll pull."

She said, "Baby, I'm goin' to tell you what, I beat chumps for their money
   and their clothes too
I would've beat them for the tobacco but all fools don't chew."

She said, "I've been from New York to the Frisco Bay
I've fucked all pimps like you with the game you tryin' to play."

She said, "But you a good lookin' kid and look alright in your clothes
But, baby, you'd better corner yourself a mule 'cause you ain't shit tryin' to
   pimp whores."

This made Pimpin' Sam mad

He said, "Shut up! Shut up, bitch! Don't you say another motherfucken word
If you do I'll put my foot in your ass about something I heard

Now you're running around here with your nose all snotty
If you don't know what the game is all about you better ask somebody

Now your tits is hanging down like a shithouse bucket
And your pussy's so funky even a dog wouldn't suck it."

Pimpin' Sam looked at her and said, "Bitch, there's a tick! Catch it, catch it
   quick!
And you better catch it if you've got to suck its motherfucken dick."

She said, "Look here, daddy, I ain't got on no clothes."
He said, "Catch it out the window, bitch, you ain't goin' out the door."

Then he looks at her and says, "So you that little girl they call Wicked Nell
The Coast Guard's heart from burnin' hell?

Bitch, I'll jump up in your pussy like a storm
'Cause I'm that notorious hustler called Pimpin' Sam."

Said, "I've been from the Golden Gate of California to the shores of Maine
I know all the whores, the bulldikers and cocksuckers by their natural names

I've been from New York City to Eagle's Pass
Playing society whores and kicking your kind of bitches in their no-good ass

Now you were alright down home with the few nickels you knocked
But, bitch, out here you're squarer than a block

If you're goin' to play the game and have success
You'd better ask me about it, goddamn Buldike Bess

To tell you the truth, bitch, you should be back on the farm to your uncle
      Ned
'Cause the only way you can make a pimp like me a dime is to go out of your
      motherfucken head

And furthermore, I'll tell you what whores do for me every day you could
      never do
That's fuck me, suck me and give me that money too

I've got eight or ten whores standing in a line, and ain't a day go pass
I don't kick five of them in the ass

I'll pull a bitch like you out of the bed at half past four
And make you jump in Lake Michigan if it's 90 below

And you'd better not shiver when you come to shore
'Cause if you do I'll make you jump off there and swim some cocksuckin'
      more

Now the pistol's on the dresser and the razor's in the drawer
And if you think about nary one of them, I'll break your motherfucken jaw

And bitch, don't you roll your eyes and give me no sass
'Cause I'll make these brand new Stetsons sing a song in your ass

Now if you ever think of goin' home to Chitlin' Switch
I want you to tell everybody you met Pimpin' Sam, a bad, bad sonofabitch."

On the Corner

Say, I was standing on the corner about two one day
And I sure I seen a bitch I once knew from down the way

I said, "Good afternoon, lady. Is your name Lorraine?"
She said, "No, funny-face motherfucker, and you I've never seen."

I said, "Bitch, you're a lying motherfucker and I should kick your ass
Bitch, I remember when you left Florida on a train with a pass

Whore, I remember when you quit Brown and went for Bill
Whore, I even remember when you moved to Forest Hills

Whore, Brown is the motherfucker who split your lip
Beat your ass, put you out and put stitches in your hip

Bitch, you're a lying motherfucker and a sack of shit
And under your dress is cunt, both nuts and dick

Bitch, you got the nerve to say you've never seen me before
Bitch, I know who turned you out and made you a whore

Bitch, if I didn't have to be somewhere at exactly three
I would kick your ass until you pee, and make you testify that you do know me

But being that time is running out fast
Fuck you, bitch, and kiss my ass."

PREACHER TALES AND PARODIES

David slew Goliath, he didn't beat the shit out of him ...
And we do not refer to the Father, Son and Holy Ghost as
Big Daddy, Junior and the Spook ...

Preacher Man

(a)

Some people say that the preacher don't steal
I caught two in my corn field
One had a sack, one had a hoe
Stealing my corn row by row.

(b)

Who that say that preachers don't steal?
I caught two in my melon field
Eating up the melon and throwing away the rind
Shouting, "Hallelujah, children, this is fine!"

A Prayer

Lord, this is your humble servant coming before you once again, knees bowed and body bent to ask for thou's blessing and grace. Coming to you like an empty pitcher waiting to be filled. I come to you this morning thanking you for waking me out of sound slumber by touching me with your finger of love.

I want to thank you for hovering over me and protecting me last night, like a hen hovering over her roost on a cold and frosty night. I want to thank you that the four corners of my bed wasn't the four corners of my grave, and my mattress wasn't my cooling board and my covers weren't my winding sheet.

Father, I want you to look down in my heart this evening and if you find anything that shouldn't be, take it out and throw it as far as the east is from the west, so that it will not be held against me on Judgment Day.

I know I only have a few more risings and a few more settings of the sun, but when my day comes, take me in thy powerful arms and place me on the old Ship of Zion so that I might cross that old river Jordan and take my rest.

AMEN.

Telephone to Glory

Going around with a hung down head and a mighty aching in my heart. Little man Jesus came riding by, made me laugh, made me cry, told me that my time was now.

Planted a sword in my right hand and told me to go on the field and fight. Fight until every foe was made to heel or fall down among the slain.

Ten thousand devils may tangle my feet, but none can hold me fast. He's my lily of the valley, he's my bright morning star. He's my rock in a weary land, my shelter in a time of storm. He's my bread in a starving land, my water in a desert sand.

If I was going to call from here to Chicago I'd have to place my long distance call through the operator. If I was going to call from here to California I'd have to call the operator. But I got a telephone in my bosom and can call my Jesus anytime. Don't have to dial no operator, just fall down on my knees, pick up my receiver and say give me my Jesus.

The New Priest

The new priest at his first mass was so nervous he could hardly speak. He asked the old priest what he should do. The old priest said he should put a little gin or vodka in his water glass before the mass and this should relax him.

The next Sunday the new priest filled his water glass with gin and he talked up a storm. After the mass he asked the old priest how he did. The old priest said, "You were relaxed enough, but there's a few things we must straighten out:

- There are ten commandments, not twelve.
- There are twelve apostles, not ten.
- David slew Goliath, he didn't beat the shit out of him.
- We don't refer to Jesus Christ as the late J.C.
- Next Sunday there's a taffy-pulling contest at St. Peter's, not a peter-pulling contest at St. Taffy's.
- And we do not refer to the Father, Son and Holy Ghost as Big Daddy, Junior and the Spook."

The Visiting White Preacher

Somewhere around the city of Leesburg, Georgia, there was a custom of ultra-liberal white preachers visiting black backwoods churches. On this Sunday morning, a white preacher by the name of Reverend Camden Cameron visited Mt. Olive Baptist Church. His sermon this Sunday morning was: "We're all God's children, and we're all going to the same heaven."

So Reverend Cameron began: "Now, listen, you colored folks, you're going to heaven, too. But remember, when you get there, you're not going to sit up front with us white folks.

"And you're not going to have milk and honey like us white folks. You're going to have molasses and cornbread. But you're going to be in heaven, just like us white folks.

"So you just keep praying and being good. 'Cause God loves us all." With that he closed his sermon.

Deacon Alonzo Jones offered this prayer following the sermon: "Oh Lord, we don't want to sit up front with the white folks, when we get to heaven. We don't want to drink milk and honey with the white folks. Just let us get to heaven, and we'll do as we damn please!   AMEN."

The Baptism

(a)

Once there was this guy who lived in the South. He was the type of person who didn't go to church or didn't do anything others did. But one day he decided to change and join a church. At the River of Baptism the Preacher dipped him in the water, and as he came up he asked him to profess his faith.

PREACHER: Do you believe?
INITIATE: Yes, I believe.

The Preacher dipped him a second time, holding him down in the water a little longer.

"Do you believe?"
"Yes, I believe."

The Preacher dipped him a third time, holding him still longer in the water. He came up gasping for breath.

"Do you believe?"
"I believe . . . I believe . . . I believe you're trying to drown my ass!"

(b)

Two brothers went to the river for baptism. The Preacher would hold the candidate leaning back into his arms, and dip him in the water. As he was doing this the guy got loose and he couldn't find him. So he said, "Well, that is one Brother going to heaven by water!" Then he turned to the second brother. "All right, come on, Brother." The brother said, "Unh, unh, I'm goin' by land!"

Ghosts

One year, at a big church convention the delegates were so numerous that they couldn't hardly take care of all of them. There was three preachers left didn't have nowhere to stay: there was a Baptist, a Methodist and a Holiness preacher. Since this was a Baptist convention, they stayed at the house of a Baptist woman, who neglected to tell the ministers that the house was haunted.

They came home that night to eat, all three of them plus the woman with whom they stayed. Eventually the haunts began to come in. The Baptist preacher began singing. The more he sang the more the haunts came in. The Holiness minister began to pray. The more he prayed the more the haunts came in. He turns to the Methodist minister and tells him that it's his turn to do something. The Methodist minister screwed up his eyes as if in prayer and decided to say, "Let's take up a collection from everyone," and those ghosts began to leave.

Smart Preacher

Sometimes it happened that the preacher don't do no other work except preaching; often the way that worked was that he be tricking the boss. The preacher was the smartest man in colored town and he always seemed to be able to steal the boss's animals without getting caught.

One day the boss asked, "How is it that you always slip by me no matter what it is that I do?"

And he answered, "I bet I could slip by you tonight here while you watching."

"No," said the master, "you may be slick, but you can't do that. But if you can," he laughed, "you won't have to do all that ol' hard work."

"All right," the preacher said, "I'll steal your clothes tonight."

That night about nine o'clock the boss laid out a suit of clothes and told his wife about the deal. While they were laughing about the stupid preacher, the boss heard the mules and horses in the stable running like someone was after them.

"Here, wife," said he, "you take this gun and keep an eye on my suit. I'm going to see who out there."

Preacher, who had started the ruckus to attract the boss's attention, now eased on up to the house. All that public speaking had made him a good mimic and in a voice that sounded just like the boss, he cried, "Woman, give me my clothes, that nigger might steal them while I'm gone."

The wife, thinking that it was her husband asking for the suit of clothes, handed it out the window to the preacher.

Last Will and Testament

Now it often happened that ministers during their tenure, divinely inspired, of course, acquired by the standards of the day, considerable wealth. Often this wealth was in the form of material goods, rather than in human love and appreciation. One such minister, a Reverend Johnson, had a large membership and a good tract of bottom land. Since he had begun to preach rather late in life, it wasn't long before his health started to fail. He had a young woman for a second wife, and she wanted him to be sicker than he actually was. So she called all the children around his bedside and asked the Reverend to make his will.

One of the children ran to get the Judge and the wife began to record the will with paper and tablet. First of all he said: "I wants my wife and children to have all the good bottom land, all of it up to Meeks Hill."

His wife cried, "Lord, children, listen, your daddy sho is dying with his good senses."

The Reverend said, "I wants my wife to have all my milk cows and chickens, 'cause she'll sho need those to live lak she's been used to living."

His wife reached down and hugged her children and shouted, "Children, it's wonderful, your daddy sho is dying with his good sense." All the children agreed that it was wonderful.

"I gots two carriages," he said, "and I want my wife to have both of them."

"Lord," the wife said, "it is wonderful that my husband is dying with all his senses."

"Now, my wife," that minister said, looking out of one eye, "the las' thing I'm a puttin' in mah will is that I nevah wants you to marry no more."

When he said that, his young wife wailed, "Lordy, Lordy, children, you sho better run and get that doctor 'cause yo' daddy is talkin' out of his head again."

Fresh Air

There was this preacher who loved to drink. He just couldn't do without his whiskey. He would even take a bottle to church to nip on during his sermon. He would hide it under the steps of the church, and he would say to the congregation:

> Sing me one more song, say me one more prayer
> While old Rev go out and get him some fresh air.

And he would duck out and get a drink.

He was going out and getting his fresh air so regular, one day one of the deacons got hip to what was going on and went and stole the whiskey from under the steps. The preacher as usual said to the congregation:

> Sing me one more song, say me one more prayer
> While old Rev go out and get him some fresh air.

He ducked outside and grabbed for his bottle and found that it was gone. So he rushed back into the church and yelled:

> Stop them songs and stop them prayers
> 'Cause some sonofabitch done stole all Rev's fresh air.

The Preacher and the Ducks

There was an old man who had a daughter, and he and the daughter had invited the preacher to the house. He told his daughter that he was going down to fetch the preacher and that the two ducks that he had baked that morning were not to be eaten. The daughter promised not to eat them, but as soon as her father left, she got to tasting and tasting and ate them ducks.

When her father came home the girl knew she was going to get whipped so she met the preacher in the sitting room. Her father was out back in the kitchen sharpening the knives and things for the dinner. Anyway, she was alarmed and already crying, thinking on the whipping she was going to get. So when she came into the room the pastor asked her what was wrong. She said, "The only thing wrong with papa is that when he invites the preacher to the house he goes and sharpen the knives to cut off their ears."

The Reverend, hearing the knives out back, cried, "Girl, get my hat quick!" And that pastor was beatin' it on up that road.

The girl called her daddy and said, "Daddy, the preacher done took the ducks and gone."

The man of the house ran to the door and asked the preacher where he was going and why he was running off so fast. And the preacher answered, "Damned if you'll ever git either one of these."

G. Y. B. A. P. C.

The youngest and spoiled son of a farmer had to make a decision. A decision as to what to do. That year, however, his father had a real good crop and it seemed his decision had been made for him already. He moaned and groaned around for several days, took his Bible and sat under the cool shade trees (with a cool one in hand), then with closed Bible and closed eyes, he seemed to be thinking.

When time came to gather the crop he told his father he couldn't do it; he felt the Lord was calling him to preach. Indeed, one day he pointed to the side of the barn where the letters G.Y.B.A.P.C. had mysteriously appeared. He called his father, mother and brothers to witness the miracle. After several anxious minutes the boy spoke up and said, "Well, I guess I'm called. Those letters mean:

"GO YOUNG BROTHER AND PREACH CHRIST."

His father watched him slyly and said, "I read them letters to say:

"GET YOUR BLACK ASS PICKING COTTON."

I Want to Testify

This preacher was preaching and this lady hadn't ever been to church. She was a drunk, so everyone was glad to see her in church. So the preacher really got into it: "Thou shalt not sin, I said thou shalt not sin. Tell your trouble!"

The lady began to get happy. This made the preacher feel good, and he really preached. The lady began talking, saying, "I want to tell it, oh, I want to tell it!"

Then the preacher said, "Tell, good sister, please tell God," and the lady began to flop around on the floor, shouting, "I want to tell it!"

The preacher said, "Tell God, sister, please tell God!" But she was so happy she couldn't talk. The preacher kept repeating, "Sister, please tell God!"

Then she jumped up from the floor and hollered: "I'm so goddamn drunk I don't know what to do!"

Make a Joyful Noise!

Way down yonder where the cotton fields grow
Lived a black greasy preacher by the name of Reverend Boe

The Lord called Boe when he was very small
He said, "Nigger, I want you to preach the gospel and all."

Down through the years as he grew
Reverend Boe never knew

That one day he'd be proud to say
"Come one, come this here damn way."

Yes, he thought he was the best
Talked shit to all the women when he massaged their breast

Yea, Reverend was known through the South
He didn't give a damn where he went, he never shut his mouth

So one day while passing down the way
Reverend met an old friend by the name of Jessie Mae

She said, "Good evening, Reverend Boe
If you ain't busy we can get it on, you know."

Reverend said, "Hey! Hey! Hey! I feel the same
I've always been good at this kind of game."

So they laid down on the ground
And began to hump, grind and make all kinds of sounds

Old Sister Jessie was humping with all her might
She said, "When I'm finished humping you, goddamn it, you'll sleep all
        night."

Just about that time Reverend began to hum a little tune
'Cause he knew that good feeling would be there soon

He said, "The Lord, He is our shepherd
He maketh us want to lie down in green grass and get stains on our ass

He maketh this woman to relax my soul
Her hole and my staff have comforted me

I anointed her breast with oil
And her honey runneth over

We shall feel at ease
'Cause our minds have been pleased

Surely this goodness will be with me all the rest of my life
Ummmmmmmm!! . . . . Aaaaahhhhhhh!!!"

Sister Jessie said, "Reverend, how do you feel?"
Reverend Boe said, "Be patient, Sister, you'll know when I make a squeal."

Just then the Sister grinded with all her might
She squeezed, kissed and held him tight

Reverend said, "Jessie, in case you never knew
The Lord called me to teach you how to screw

But I don't guess that he was aware
How you had learned to throw this body here and there

Maybe the Lord wouldn't mind to see
How you're throwing this body on old poor me."

Jessie said, "Reverend, I don't have time for reciting and games
Will you please get off your cookies? Damn! You must be lame."

Reverend started to hump up and down
He was holding on to the grass that grew in the ground

Reverend said, "I think I'm getting close, you know
My balls are beginning to get a little sore."

Rev started to grumble and mumble
"Make a joyful noise and hold your hand."

He said, "To serve you all with gladness
To come before y'all in the presence of nudity."

Then Rev said, "Sister, sister, hold on, sister
Hold on, hold on, sister, hold on."

At that time old Rev began to breathe
"Hu, hu, hu, hu, hu, hu, hu, hu, hu, hu."

The sister said, "It's about time, you know
Goddamn it, I don't think you never made a score."

The Reverend said, "Please, Sister, don't be mad at me
I can't 'member the last time I laid with thee

But I will promise you one thing
If you come around again I'll learn how to sing

'Cause the way you put this body on me
I'll go out and tell the whole world what a great big black preacher came
    to be."

Mock Sermon

*[The preacher greets his congregation and
bawls them out at the same time]*

PREACHER

Good evening, ladies and gentle mules, dogs and cats. You bowleg mosquitoes
and you cross-eye bats. I did not come here to address you, I came here to
undress you. I did not come here to talk about your welfare, I came here to talk
about your filthy underwear. Where were you last night when I done preached?
I know where you all were, out in the moonlight courting the gals and forgot
all about you're going down to the gap of hell. There is too much sin in this
little hell town. All you folks need is the eye of an eagle and the eagle of an owl.
Put some turpentine upon your lips so you can say the right word. Put some
voodoo power in your shoes so you can dance to the right music. Drink the
right kind of liquor so you can sing the right songs and blow yourself up with
the dynamite of hell-fire. Hallelujah! That's all.

A VOICE FROM THE CONGREGATION

When we folks kick the bucket we better take our liquor with us because they
ain't handing out nothing but cold hard corn liquor down there.

PREACHER

Now we will be led in prayer by Brother Buzzard Foot.

PRAYER

Our devil who are in the kitchen, hallow will be in the dining room, but lead
us on into the bathroom. Deliver us all from the stomach-ache of all those
black-eye peas, collard greens and corn bread. And at last, Oh Devil, when I die
do not bury me so deep. Put a hoe cake of corn bread at my head and a jar of
syrup at my feet so I can sop my way on down to hell. All women.

CONGREGATION SINGS

> Amazing grace!
> How sweet it taste
> The polecat peed
> In the possum face.

PREACHER READS THE SCRIPTURE

I call your attention to the Book of Do You Ramble?, 6th chapter, 8th to 12th
verse. The devil is our leader and we shall follow him into the fiery furnace of
hell and on through the quake of everlasting beauty. May the devil add a bless-

ing to the reading of his word and may it sink deep into our hearts and souls and find a lodging place and spring forth in due time and do us good this day and henceforth days to come. All women.

Down in the valley where nobody goes
There stands the sisters without any clothes
Along came the brothers swinging their chains
Pulled down their zippers and out they came
Three months later nobody knows
Six months later they began to grow
Nine months later out they rolled
Rolled, brothers, rolled
Rolled, sisters, rolled.

PREACHER'S TEXT

My brothers and sisters, I had hope to speak on the subject of "What Are We Waiting For?" But since I heard the choir sing, I judge from that I am the only one waiting. So I changed my mind about the text and decided to use for my text, "And They Played Upon a Harp of a Thousand String," taken from the Book of Action, 10th chapter, 3rd verse. I like to use the last clause of that 3rd verse, "Thousand-String Harp."

A VOICE FROM THE CONGREGATION

All women! Preach on, preach! I know that you could do it!

ANOTHER VOICE FROM THE CONGREGATION

Preach, preacher! That's what I'm here for, to hear that preaching preacher! I was told that you sure knows just how to swing that chain!

ANOTHER VOICE

You are so right, sister, because I have one of the link from his chain on my lap.

A MAN LEADS THE CONGREGATION IN A SONG

Well, my hair still curly
And I got the rhythm too
I can still swing my chain
Like I used to do.

ANOTHER MALE VOICE

My chain is on fire and I am hot all over. So hot I feel like I can wing and fly.

All women!
Yes!
That's alright!
Hallelujah!
Fly on, brother, if you want to!

[*Ushers trying to keep order*]

PREACHER

Leave them alone, Ushers. I am enjoying that kind of carrying on.

[*A sister in the all-women corner gets happy and her husband
goes over to hold her, and she tells her husband:*]

WOMAN

Go back, Caesar, go back! Don't come near me! I got the movement in my hole
and I want Deacon Honeycutt to know!

[*After this a moment of silence, and the preacher
continues with his text*]

PREACHER

My text: "And They Played Upon a Harp of a Thousand String." Now, there are
a great number of strings in the world. First there are strings likened to thread
which women mend their clothes with. Then there are the strings of the harp
and guitar which we like to play upon. Then there are the strings which we
lace our shoes with; they are called shoe string. But I am talking about a sym-
bolic string on a harp that reaches from here to hell well. Ah! my brothers and
sisters, Ah! that well is filled with bottles, and in those bottles are liquor and
each bottle has a string tied around it so whenever I am thirsted all I got to do
is pull on the string. Ah! my brothers and sisters, do you know what I am talk-
ing about? Now, have you ever tried pulling on that string? Ah! if you pull on
the string I am talking about you will never need to thirst again. Ah! this string
is an everlasting string and it is tied to a bottle in the everlasting well of liquor.
Ah! that liquor can't be beat! Ah! just try drinking some of it every once in a
while! This string is not just for the white or black but it's for all who want to
pull on the string. When Satan comes back for his congregation he's not look-
ing for color, he's looking for those who pulled on the string daily. Ah! the only
way I know who they are is because every time a man get ready to pull on the
string he roll up his sleeves. Wherein the ladies get on their knee and look down
into the well. Ahhh!!!

I wish I was near that well now; I would not just look down into it but I would take wing and fly down into the well and climb back upon the strongest string. All women! Preach on, preacher! I knew you could do it! Fix it up now, that's alright!

ANOTHER VOICE

Yes, fix it up for us! You are preaching now! Go on, talk about it! That's alright! Go ahead, I'm enjoying that sermon!

PREACHER PROCEEDS WITH HIS SERMON

Now my brothers and sisters, they tell me that that string that I am telling you about today is the string that is not only for us just to climb upon, but the mouse and cat play on that string also. Ah! I know another man who when just a shepherd boy he played on that same string. Ah! do you know the story? His name was Navel. Navel played on the string from morning till night. One day Navel got tired playing on the string so he laid it down and went on home to claim his rightful place in the well and receive his share of bottles that had been drawn up by his strings daily. Ah! I am glad that I am laying up treasure every day beside my bottles. Because one day when this old hole of mine get tired down here I can go on and get my reward from each bottle that I have a string laid beside. Ah! I know that my name will be on every string. Ah!!

ANOTHER VOICE FROM THE CONGREGATION

All women, preacher! You are a preaching fool! But I know you could do it, you sure know how to fix it up! I know that I am going to have some bottles on those shelves!

PREACHER CONTINUES

In my concluding statement, I know that will be a great day for me and all of us who pulled on the string daily. When all of the strings from every nation join together to make their final report of all who pulled on the string, Ah! but I am so glad that I know my name will be on the roll. I know a place has been reserved in that well for me. Ah! I am not worried about my journey, I am not worried about my seat. I am not worried about my bottles. I paid the price a long time ago. And at the close of my day I am going to say: "Tell everyone that I am on my way. My battle is fought, my victory is won. My string is broken, and now it's time for me to say well done." Ah! Church, will you be there? Somewhere around the table? Meet me there to listen to The One Who Is In Charge call the roll.

VOICE

That's alright, preacher! I knew you could do it! You didn't have to do it for me to prove that you could do it, but I am glad you did do it to prove to the congregation that I was right about that link from your chain sitting on my lap, and your sermon just proved to the congregation that this is a link from your chain!

ANOTHER VOICE

Let the word fly, preacher, let the word fly!

CHOIR SINGS

Hold to the string on your bottle
If that string break
Get another one before it's too late
The bottle is on the string and the string is in your hand
All you got to do is try to make it to the well of our promised land.

PREACHER

Ladies and gentle mules, I know you all enjoyed the sermon because I heard the ladies in the congregation say: "Let the word fly!" The money word is ready to fly now.

A VOICE FROM THE CONGREGATION

Never mind, preacher, let the word walk now. I am going home. I got what I came here for.

ANOTHER VOICE

I am going to pay my quarter because money talks these late days.

PREACHER

You are so right, Sister. Money talks.

DEACONS COME FORWARD FOR COLLECTION

Well, folks, I know if you all got what I got you enjoyed that hole-stirring sermon.

ANOTHER VOICE

I am glad you enjoyed it, Ralph, and I am glad you finally told me you enjoyed it. Because that was my hole you was staring in.

[Deacons continue taking up money. Congregation is silent]

All rise and come to the table with your offering. I am going to start the offering off with a quarter.

What can a quarter buy nowadays? That's the reason you have been turned down in so many ways by some of these old maids. Here, I am paying twenty dollars.

She's just showing off. She can't afford it.

Are you kidding? That lady have spunk, and she sell it for top price, not for just four or five coppy cent but for big G. I know.

[After the collection, Deacon says:]

I like to thank you all for one hundred seventy-five dollars and forty-two cents.

PREACHER BLESSES THE OFFERING
The offering is not for the swift
The offering is not for the strong
It's all for me
I have done no wrong
All women!

ACKNOWLEDGMENT OF VISITORS
VISITOR:	It's good to be here; I enjoyed everything.
ANOTHER VISITOR:	I feel good! Hallelujah!
PREACHER:	Thank you all! Come again soon!

CLOSING SONG
Blessed be the string that ties our hearts
To our bottles in the well
From the bottle we will drink and never sink
We will fellowship with those who have gone on before us.

BENEDICTION
May the string remain in your hand.
It will pull you direct to the well to land.
ALL WOMEN!!!

Jonah and the Whale

Now the great Lord was sitting
in his rosy rocking chair one halleluiah morning
And when the Lord has special favors
                                    he call on special children

And the Lord called to Gabe
And Gabe put down his horn and he swung with the book

And the Lord flipped the pages
A . . . B . . . C . . . D . . . E . . . F . . . G . . . H . . . I . . . J . . .
And it was Jonah getting his kicks on the beach

And Jonah said,
"Ain't it crazy out here on this here beach!"
Said, "A man's got a lot of room
                        to groove
                        & a sunshine
                        & everything is serenity
                                    & fine

Hhhmmmmmmmmm!

Make you want to
                jiggle and wiggle!
Make me want to
                strrrrrrrrrrrretch
my wings and
                rrrrrrrrwwwwwwwwwwaayyyyyyy!!!! . . .

Good morning, Lord!"

And the Lord said, "Good morning, Jonah.
Jonah, I got a favor . . ."

Jonah said, "Ain't that groovy! . . ."

Lord said, "Jonah . . .
I want you to
cross the Red Sea
        & put the message
        on the Israelites
They're squaring up
        over there."

Jonah said,
"You don't mean that big pool, do you, Lord?

RRRRRRRRrrrrrrrrrrHHHHHHrhrhrhrhrhrhrhrhPOOOOOMMMM!!!!!

Look at them waves!

WWWHHRRRRrrrhrhrhrhrhrhrhrPOOM!!!"

He said,
  "Don't you mean
      some little ole
      Jonah-sized pool?"

And the Lord said,
"Jonah, put your nose in the wind
    and the message will come to you."

And Jonah did:

He put it in the East Wind
      fffffffffrhwhwhwhwhippppppp!
           it was not there!
He put it in the West Wind
      ffffpphhhhwhwhwhwhrrhipp!
          it was not there!!
He put it in the North Wind
      ffffrrhrhrhrhrhrqtgqtgdjrqdop!
         it was not there!!!
But when he put it in the halleluiah South Wind
      ffffffrrrrrrrghwbnnccvrrripp!
          it was there!!!!

And Jonah rode for twenty-one day & fifteen minutes
And he stopped and saw
    a group of cathedral-like trees
Lifted in supplication of the Master

And down at the bottom of these green sequoias
Jonah saw growing a strange green vine

And Jonah said, just like Brigham Young
"Pop! [*finger snap*] This is it!"

And he sat down beside it
       & he observed of it
And he selected of it
       & he rolled of it
& he swung of it

And Jonah said,
"Phffphff!
Where's that fool pool Lord want me to dig?"

Look out, here come Jonah
                    hhmmmmmmphBOOOM!
Making a beeline
          through the best of the waves!

And fatigue hit Jonah
And he laid in the arms of Morpheus [sleep]
He was goofing on his eyebrows

And as sleep came to Jonah
When he woke, what did he see?
                    He saw a WHALE!
What did he say when he saw this whale?
                    "Get me from this sea
                              IMMEDIATELY!!"

And the whale said
"Whhey! Whaaa! Whhey! . . . [*Laughing*]
Everytime I stick my nose out this pool
               I sure dig me some crazy jazz."

Jonah said, "What do you mean, Mr. Whale?"
Whale said, "Look at that, it talks too! . . . Ha! Ha!! Ha!!!" . . .

He said, "Of course I talk, Mr. Whale
Ain't you hip to marine news?
I'll groove my way, you groove yours
               I'll swoop the seas and dig you later."

Whale said, "Now, wait a minute
I got the good mind to gobble you up."

And Jonah said
          "O don't you do that, Mr. Whale
'Cause if you do
          I'm gonna knock you
          In your most delicate gear!"

And the whale said
"That done it!"
BOOM!
He swallowed Jonah

And here's Jonah slipping & sliding
                    from one side to the other
Of this great sea mammal
Can't go out the front & afraid to go out the back   [*Laughter*]

And he fell on his knees on this great blubbery rug
And the prettiest sound came from Jonah

Jonah said [*moaning*]
"Loooooooord! . . . Loooooooord!
Can you dig me in this here fish?"

And the Lord said
"I got you covered, Jonah."

Jonah said
"Lord's sure got a crazy sense of humor
He ain't got me covered, he got me
                              surROUNDED!"

And the Lord said
"Jonah, reach into your water-tight pocket
And get some of them cigarettes
That you rolled from the
strange green vine
And courage will return to you."

And Jonah did.

There's Jonah watching the pistons
                              pounding
Watching the walls
                   spanding and expanding

And the whale said, "Ehhhh . . . Jonah! . . ."

And Jonah said, "Pspshff! What is it, Fish?
        Hmmnhn! What is it, Fish?
You heard what I said, Fish!
        F-I-S-H, Fish!
You got a new captain
on this mast now
        Fish!
I ain't on the outside no more
I'm on the inside now
                FISH!!"

The whale said
"Jonah, what in the world's you smoking in there?
I'm headed for the Canary Islands
You got me two minutes off the Panama Canal
This jazz has got to go!"
He said, "Jonah, whyn't you just sit down
                              and cool yourself
You gettin' a ride for nothin'!"

Jonah said
"I'll walk all over this room all I want."
He said, "What's this over here?"

He said, "Jonah, don't you go fuckin'
          with equipment
          like that there,
          boy!"

He said, "What's this over here?"

He said, "Jonah! Jonah!
                    That's my Full Speed Ahead lever!
My Full Speed Ahead! . . .
                    Jonah! . . . Jonah! . . .
Look out for the rock on the right! . . .
The rock on the right! . . ."

He said, "We're in shallow water . . ."
Jonah said, "Cool."
He said, "It ain't cool at all! . . ."

Jonah pushed the Sneeze-O-Meter
WHHAAMM!!!
Shot him out on the cool sands of serenity . . .

And, like Confucius say
          I sai tui e sum sau
Translated mean:
          If you get to it
          and you cannot do it
          Then you jolly well off
                    aren't you? . . .

                              [*LAUGHTER*]

Part VII

JOKES

If the pilgrims had shot a wildcat
instead of a turkey
we might have been eating pussy on Thanksgiving Day . . .

> WELCOME TO
>
> MULESHOE, MISSISSIPPI
>
> SPEED LIMIT 35
>
> NIGGERS 90

Suicide!

A friend of mine wrote and told me of a Southern town where he was stationed while in the military. He said the town wasn't exactly bad for negroes but . . . the sheriff found a black man shot twenty-three times in the back and he told reporters it was the worst case of suicide he'd seen in twenty years of service.

Southern Hospitality

There once was this Northern white man who was driving through the South. He happened to have an accident in which he hit two blacks who were walking down the road. The first man was knocked clear of the car into a nearby cornfield, and the second wound up in the windshield of the car.

When the Highway Patrol arrived, the Northerner driver was quite upset. However, the Southern patrolman attempted to put him at ease.

"Okay, now, we gonna take care of you. Now, you see this nigger in the windshield?"

"Yes," the Northerner replied.

"Well, we're going to charge him with destroying private property. And you see that nigger over there in that cornfield?"

"Yes."

"We're gonna charge him with leaving the scene of an accident!"

Oink!

Two men decided to go and steal this white man's hog. They sneaked in the hog pen and got the man's biggest hog. The white man spotted them and called the police. They were afraid, so they decided to dress the hog up like a man and sit it in between them in the car. So, as they were driving down the road the police stopped them and said, "Hey, you niggers, what's ya name?"

The driver said, "Jim," and the police asked the other guy his name and he said, "Tom."

Then the police said, "Hey, you nigger in the middle, what's your name?" So then, one of the men pinched the hog and it said, "Oink."

The police said, "What?" and the guy pinched the hog again and it said, "Oink! oink!"

The police said, "Goddamn niggers, get the hell out of here."

So the police went back to his partner and said, "Two of those niggers are alright, but that damn one named Oink is an ugly sonofabitch."

Help!

It seems one Southern town was receiving more than its share of bad publicity concerning its racial policies. Therefore it decided to find a local darkie and put him on television to prove to the world that its darkies were treated well.

The television cameras panned the face of a congenial-looking negro (right off the Uncle Ben's box) and coaxed him to tell the world that ole massuh was a good boss. When it came time for the black man to make his speech, he turned to the moderator of the program and asked, "Suh, can dey hear me in Germany?" To which the answer was "Yes."

"Can dey hear me in France?" Again, the reply was affirmative.

"And can dey hear me in Russia?"

Getting a little impatient, the moderator replied, "Yeah, shit, nigger, they can hear you all over the world.

The old man said, "That's all I wanted to know . . . HELP!!!"

The Nigger Announcer

On the radio program called *The Shadow*, there was always a deep-voiced prologue to the weekly episode that went like this: "Who knows what evil lurks in the hearts of men? Only the Shadow does." Now the man who gave this deep-voiced presentation quit his job and the producers were looking for a good substitute. They found it in a black man who had come in one day for a try-out. First they looked at him skeptically, because they didn't expect a nigger. Then he recited for them in a beautiful purple-plum, velvety voice: "How Now, Brown Cow?" They hired him on the spot.

Finally came his first day on the job. He got in front of the microphone, cleared his throat and got the sign to begin. He took a deep breath, steadied himself and boomed in his magnificent bass voice: "Who knows what evil lurks in the hearts of men? Only the Shadow *do!*"

The Nigger Ape

The Philadelphia Zoo found that their star attraction, the gorilla, had suddenly died in its sleep. "Well, what we gonna do?" asked one manager of another. They decided to put an ad in the paper for a job at the zoo with good pay, room and board. All kinds of white men came in for the job but were turned down. Finally, a big, muscular black man came in. The managers took one look at him, nodded to each other and gave the colored man the job.

"Wait a minute," said the colored man, "what do I gotta do?"

One of the white managers pulled out a gorilla suit and said, "All you gotta do is put on this gorilla suit and get out there in the cage and put on a show. You know—jump up and down and growl, and swing around a little and just act like a gorilla."

The colored man thought it over and took the job. "But look out," warned the white man, "there's a lion cage right next to yours with a vicious lion in it, so don't go too near him."

The colored man put on the suit, got out in the cage and started to monkey around. He was jumping up on the bars, growling at the people, swinging all round the cage, eating bananas and in general just acting like a big monkey. Sure enough, the colored man got to enjoying himself and forgot all about the lion in the cage next to his. He swung so hard that he swung right on over into the lion' s cage and landed flat on his back. The lion jumped up and was on him snarling and growling. The colored man forgot he was supposed to be a gorilla and started yelling, "Oh please, somebody help me!"

The lion looked down on him with hard blue eyes and said, "Shut up, you dumb nigger, you want both of us to lose our jobs?"

Who Is the King of the Jungle?

(a)

There was this big old lion who used to just strut around the jungle all day long thinking that he was the baddest dude that ever was. He would spend all day just strutting through the jungle saying, "I'm the baddest cat there ever was in this jungle and if anyone ever forgets it, I'm gonna throw them the beat'n of their life."

Well, one day the old lion was strut'n around the jungle asking every other animal just who was the king of the jungle. First he came up to a little monkey and asked, "Hey, Monkey, who is the king of the jungle?"

"You sure is the king around these parts, Lion," answered the monkey. He knew if he was to say anything else that old lion would turn him into something that looked like a pile of dirty laundry.

Next the lion came up to a zebra. "Hey, Stripes, who do you think is the king of the jungle?"

"You are for sure, Lion," said that old zebra.

Then the lion walked over to a giraffe who was eating leaves out of a tree. "Hey, Stretch," yelled the old lion to the giraffe, "who is the king of this here jungle?"

"Well, I do know for sure that you are the king of this jungle," snapped the giraffe.

Then the old lion decided to ask a big, loud elephant just who he thought was the king of the jungle. He walked up to the big old elephant and hollered, "Hey, you big ol' tub o' guts, just who is the king of this jungle?"

That big old elephant didn't say a word. He just reached down with his trunk and grabbed the old lion around the neck. Then he picked up the lion and threw him against a tree. He started to jump up and down on the lion and did the boogaloo, the cha-cha and the twist right across his forehead. Then he ripped out one of the lion's front legs and he ripped out one of his back legs. He started to beat him over the head with both of them. Then he stuck the front leg where the back leg used to be and the back leg where the front leg used to be. Then he dropped an elephant-sized load right on the lion's head. That old lion just laid there looking as raggedy as a pile of dirty laundry. He looked up at the elephant and said, "You didn't have to get so mad just because you didn't know the answer."

(b)

One day the lion woke up feelin' mean, 'cause he hadn't got no pussy from that sweet little thing last night. He got pretty and strolled through the forest lookin' for some ass to kick. First thing he ran into was a bear so he grabbed the bear and demanded, "Who is king of the jungle?"

The bear whined back, "You are, O mighty Lion."

The lion slapped him aside and nodded smugly. He walked some more and ran into a tiger. He yoked the tiger and growled, "Who is the motherfuckin' boss of this jungle?"

The tiger cowered and said, "You are, O mighty Lion."

The lion threw him aside saying, "Damn right!" Being a nigger lion, he still wasn't satisfied, and he walked until he ran into a snake. He stepped on the snake's chest and roared, "Who is king of the jungle?"

The snake had a shit fit crying, "You are, O mighty Lion."

The lion still wasn't satisfied and so he walked until he ran into an elephant and demanded: "Who is boss of the jungle?"

The elephant collared the lion and broke both his legs, then he knocked his asshole out of joint, busted his nose, cracked his jaw, splintered his ribs, broke his back and then tossed him into the dust. The lion struggled weakly to lift his head up, looked at the elephant and said: "Damn, man, just 'cause you don't know the answer is no reason to get so rough."

Reno's Comin'!

One day the baboon was up in his tree cooking up some sausage and eggs when he saw an elephant come tearing through the jungle. "What's wrong with you?" asked the baboon.

"Shit, man, Reno's comin', you better run," answered the elephant.

"Who's Reno?" inquired the baboon.

The elephant looked at the baboon in disbelief and said, "He's only the meanest, baddest, ugliest motherfucker in this jungle."

"Well, fuck him, I'm the hungriest motherfucker in the forest, and I'm eatin', I don't give a fuck who's comin'.'"

The elephant ran on.

Then the baboon saw a lion come running through the jungle. "What you runnin' from?" asked the baboon.

"You ain't heard, man? Reno's comin'!'"

"Aw, fuck Reno, I'm hungry," was the baboon's defiant reply.

"Alright, don't say I didn't warn you," said the lion.

Next, a gorilla came lumbering through the forest. The baboon looked up in disbelief. "Goddamn, you runnin' from Reno too?" he asked.

"Hell, yeah!" cried the gorilla, "and if you was smart you'd be makin' it too."

"Shit, man, I'm hungry, I don't give a fuck who's comin'.'"

"Okay," said the gorilla, "see you later."

All of a sudden the baboon heard a thunderous roar echo through the jungle. He looked up to see a huge hairy beast ripping out trees to make a path, and heading straight for him. The hairy beast reached down and grabbed up the baboon's hot eggs and sausage, drank the hot grease with one gulp and wiped his ass with the sizzling frying pan while the baboon cowered, shivering. The beast looked down at him with mean eyes and said, "Shit, man, you better make it—Reno's comin'!"

The baboon broke his ass gettin' out that jungle.

You Ain't Shit

"You think you sompin' because you goin' to dat big-time college. Nigger, you ain't shit. Dey ain't teachin' you shit, nigger. Nigger, I remember you when you was running the street with the rest of dem little hoodlums. You ain't shit nigger, you ain't nothin . . . Let me have a dollar!"

Books and Authors

Sailor Beware . . . Don Ben Over
The Yellow Stream . . . I. P. Daily
By a Waterfall . . . U. P. Standing
The Wild Cats' Revenge . . . Claude Balls
The Bride's First Night . . . Peter B. Kyne
Blood on the Picnic Ground . . . Buster Cherry
The Sex-Mad Russian . . . Ivan Toretittsoff
The Rooster's Mistake . . . Rhoda Duck
Rip in the Mattress . . . Mister Completely
The Disappointed Old Maid . . . Dickie Small
Love Thine Own Self . . . O. E. Pullit and Howie Pullit
The Perfect Husband . . . John Everhard

The Faggot and the Truck Driver

A faggot walks across the street against the light and almost gets hit by a truck. The truck driver starts cursing at the faggot; the faggot calmly turns to the driver and says, "I would call you a bastard, because you are too ugly to be called a love child."

Lucky Strike

Early one Kool morning Miss Pall Mall strolled down Chesterfield Lane. There she met Mr. Phillip Morris who took her to the Marlboro Hotel. They got into an Old Gold bed. She put his king-size L&M into her flip-top box. If she doesn't look like a Camel in nine months, it will be a Lucky Strike. Kent said it couldn't be done, because he had a filter tip. Winston said it's what's up front that counts.

You Want the Indians to Hate Us?

It seems a few old-timers were gathered around the pot-belly stove down at Maude's place chewing the fat, and one old gentleman who had obviously seen more days than the rest of them commented, "Why don't they never talk about us? Hell, we fought the Indians!" To which one of the younger members replied, "Shut-up, motherfucker, ain't we got enough trouble? Damn, you want the Indians to hate us too?"

Bowels

There once was an Indian named Bowels who lived in a little teepee on the side of a hill. This hill was overlooking a very beautiful valley. One day the government came up the hill and decided to take this land away from Bowels because they wanted to build houses on it. So they went and said, "Bowels, you'll have to move."

But Bowels said, "Bowels no move."

So he decided to go to town and find a lawyer or someone who could help him. But mistakenly, because Bowels couldn't read, he went to the town physician. So he said, in very broken English, "Bowels no move. Bowels no move."

The doctor said, "Bowels no move? What do you mean bowels no move? Here, take this laxative and come back in a week."

So Bowels went home and he took the one pill the doctor had given him. The following week he went back to the doctor because the government was still bothering him.

"Bowels no move. Bowels no move."

"Bowels no move? Again? What's wrong with you? Here, take two! Come back in a week."

Bowels went back home, took the two laxatives—nothing. So the next week he went back.

"Bowels still no move. Bowels still no move."

"Still don't move, huh? Well, I'm going to double your dosage. This time it's gotta work. Here's four. Go home and come back in two weeks."

So he shrugged his shoulders and went back home and took the four pills. The following week Bowels was a little upset. He came to the doctor's office and said, "Bowels move. Bowels move. Tee-pee full of shit!"

Cold Turkey

If the pilgrims had shot a wildcat
instead of a turkey
we might have been eating pussy on Thanksgiving Day.

Back to Africa

(a)

An old black man wanted to go back to Africa before he died. The passage by boat was $500, and all he had was $499.90. He went to the ticket counter, but he could not get a ticket because he was a dime short. So he stopped another black man passing by.

OLD MAN: Hi Brother, you got a dime to spare? I want to go back to Africa.

BROTHER: All I got is me cigarette change.

A white man overheard when he asked for the dime.

WHITE MAN: Hi Sambo, all you need is a dime to go back to Africa?

OLD MAN: Yes sir, boss.

WHITE MAN: You sure it's only a dime you need to get back to Africa?

OLD MAN: Sure, boss.

WHITE MAN: Well, if that's so, here's a dollar, and take nine other spooks with you.

(b)

There was this nigger that wanted to go back to Africa. He had everything all set, went up to the counter just smiling knowing he was going back to Africa TODAY! Got up to the counter and the man started counting the money. He said, "Sorry, boy, but you ain't got enough money. You're a quarter short." So the man started begging for a quarter to go to Africa. This old cracker overheard him, he said, "Nigger, all you need is a quarter to get back to Africa? HELL, here's fifty cents. Take another nigger with you!"

Ungawa!

Three Russian delegates went to Africa. They wanted to impress the people so that they could take over. They got the chief to gather up all the people, then they started making speeches. They promised to give:

"Toilet tissue in every swamp hole."

And the crowd called out, *"Ungawa! Ungawa!"*

"Hot and cold water in every well."

"Ungawa! Ungawa!"

"Every village will have an oven!"

"Ungawa! Ungawa!"

They made other promises. And they felt so sure that the people would elect them because they had called out so frequently.

As they were walking along, they came across a pile of horse manure. They asked, "What is this?"

The interpreter answered, *"Ungawa."*

The Russian and the Whore

A man came from Russia because he was tired of the women there. On his arrival here in the city, he met a prostitute and took her to a hotel. As she was taking her clothes off he said, "The hair under your arms looks like wool!" She sat down on the chair and he said to her while touching the hair on her head, "This feels like wool!" As she was climbing into bed, opening her legs, he said, "The hair down there on your pussy sure look like wool!" As he said this she sat up in the bed and asked him, "Did you come here to knit or did you come here to fuck?"

Englishman, Black Man

The following is a dialogue between a black man and the woman he is trying to fuck, and an Englishman and the woman he is trying to seduce.

BLACK MAN: Hey baby, what's happenin'?

ENGLISHMAN: Good evening, young lady. How are we feeling today?

BLACK MAN: Mmm, mmm, you's a fine black mama.

ENGLISHMAN: My, my, you are certainly a fair lady.

BLACK MAN: Hey baby, why don't we pop on over to the rib joint and pick us up on some grit?

BLACK WOMAN: Sure 'nuff, baby.

ENGLISHMAN: Would you care for a spot of tea?

ENGLISHWOMAN: I don't mind if I do.

BLACK MAN: Look here baby, I got some reefer up the crib, come on up and we'll fly together, you know?

ENGLISHMAN: Let us two go up to my flat and have cocktails.

BLACK MAN: What? You ain't gettin' off of no draws? Baby, after I done spent my money you better give me some honey!

ENGLISHMAN: I say, why don't we have a go at it.

BLACK MAN: Oh yeah! Hold on—I'm comin'!!!

ENGLISHMAN: I do believe that I am about to arrive.

Chinese Man, Black Man, Jew Man and God

This was when God first made man. He made a Chinese man, a black man and a Jew. He asked the Chinese man what he wanted. The Chinese man said, "Mr. God, man, please give me a restaurant and a laundry."

So God said, "Right-on," and gave him what he wanted. The Chinese man went down to earth and lived happily ever after.

So the black man comes up to God. God said, "What you want, nigger?"

Black man said, "Oh dear God, Mr. Bossman, give me a million dollars, five Cadillacs, an Eldorado, five houses, twenty-five women and a big dick."

So God said, "Right on, you got your wish." The black man went down to earth to live it up.

Then the Jew got up there and said, "Hey God, come here."

God said, "Yea, what you want?"

Jew said, "Ahh, give me that nigger's address."

White Man, Colored Man, Chinese Man in a Storm

A white man, a colored man and a Chinese man were out walking during a storm, and they all took refuge in an old house. There was only one bed in the house but it was a big one, so they all laid down in it. The Chinese man was having trouble getting to sleep when he heard a weird voice saying: "Comin' in the front door, shakin' my ass, Bood-la-ay." The Chinese man looked up wide-eyed and jumped out the window.

Then the white man rolled over and heard a voice saying: "Comin' in the front door shakin' my ass, Bood-la-ay." The white man took a quick look around the room and then ran up the chimney.

Then the colored man rolled over and heard the voice: "Comin' in the front door, shakin' my ass, Bood-la-ay." The colored man pointed to a bowl of beans he had by the side of the bed and said: "You fuck with these beans you gonna be goin' out the back door, lettin' out gas, Bood-la-ay!"

White Man, Black Man, Jew Man and a Can of Beans

There was a white man, black man, Jew man. They were on a camping trip and the white man only had one can of beans. No one else had any food. That night the black man got hungry, so he got up and ate the beans. He didn't want anyone to know he had eaten the beans, so he shit in the can to make it look full of beans, then he went back to sleep. The Chinese man got up hungry, too. He ate what he thought was beans, shit in the can so it would look full and went back to sleep. Then the white man woke up hungry. He ate what he thought were his beans and went back to sleep.

The next morning the Chinese and white man woke up talking about how good the beans had been. The white man said, "But I ate the beans."

The Chinese man said, "No, hell you didn't, 'cause I ate them beans."

The black man looked at both of them disdainfully and said, "Both of ya'all motherfuckers are full of shit."

Colored Man, White Man, Chinese Man and Skunk

A rich man owned a skunk, and he wanted to get rid of his extra money. So he got a white man, a colored man and a Chinese man together and told them that if they could spend one minute with the skunk he would pay them a thousand dollars.

First the Chinese man went in the room. A few seconds later, he came out coughing, wheezing, sputtering and holding his nose. "Phew!" he said to the others, grimacing.

Then the white man went in the room. There was a brief silence, and then the door flew open and the white man came out holding his nose and sputtering, "Phew!"

Then the colored man hoisted his pants, spit on his hands and walked bravely into the room. Thirty seconds went by and all was quiet. The three men outside the room were looking at each other shrugging their shoulders when suddenly the door flew open, and fumes came billowing out of the room. Then the skunk came out coughing and sputtering, holding his nose, and, pointing into the room, said, "Get that stinky black son-of-a-bitch out of there!"

Black Man, Chinese Man, White Man in a Whorehouse

Then there was the time when a white man, a black man and a Chinese man disobeyed all jim crow laws and went to the same whorehouse. But it wasn't race that kept them out. There was a very important prerequisite for entrance: the male organ of procreation had to be of considerable dimensions.

None of the men met the requirements. But they really wanted to get in so the madam took pity on them and gave them some pills to take. She said, "Come back next week after you take these pills and I'll see if you measure up."

So the white man says, "She said to take one, but I want to make sure I get in so I'll take two." So he took two.

And the Chinese man said, "I want to be super-bad, so I'm gonna take five." So he took five.

And the black man said, "I want to be the baddest motherfucker on this earth, so I'm gonna take the whole damn bottle." So he took the whole damn bottle.

So next week the white man went back to the whorehouse and he said, "I took them pills like you told me and I think I'm ready."

The madam said, "Okay, let's see what you got." So he threw it out on the table and she whipped out a yardstick and told him he made it.

Then the Chinese man came in and said he was ready, so she said, "Okay, let's see what you got." He pulled it out, "Whomp!"

She said, "Damn! You go right on in! You damn sho' meet the requirements!"

So the next day the black man came in strutting. The madam said, "What you want?"

He said, "I took them pills and I think I'm ready!"

So she sighed, "Okay, let's see it." And the nigger shouted, "Bring it all in, boys!"

Chinese Man, Colored Man, White Man and the Chimes

A white man, colored man and a Chinese man were walking down the street bullshitting one day when they spied a fine young bitch sticking her head out the window. They asked her could they come up and get a drink of water. After they finished drinking their water they tried to get some pussy. Right when they were about to get over, someone knocked on the door. She said, "You better hide, it's my husband." The Chinese man hid under the bed, the white man got behind the door and the colored man hid in the closet, but his balls got stuck in the door and were hanging out.

The husband was eating when he saw the balls and asked his wife: "What's that hangin' out the closet?"

The woman said, "Oh, that's a new pair of chimes I bought today."

The husband got up and bent down by the colored man's balls and said, "I'm gonna make these motherfuckers ring, then."

He plucked them but nothing happened. He took his fist and hit them, but they still didn't ring. He took his spoon and smacked them—still didn't ring. Then he took a knife and jabbed them—still didn't ring. The husband then picked up a hammer and smashed them, and the colored man cried: "Ding, dong, motherfucker, ding! dong!"

Jew Man, White Man, Black Man and the Judge

There once was a white man, a black man and a Jew. They came upon a parked car and when they looked in, they found a couple screwing. They all screamed, "Uh huh! I'm going to take it to the court . . . take it to the court."

At the trial the judge first asked the white man what he saw the couple doing. When he said, "Fucking," the judge yelled, "$10 fine for cussing in the court."

Next the Jew was asked to say exactly what he saw. He said he saw them fucking. Again the judge yelled, "$10 fine for cussing in the court."

Finally, it was the black man's turn to testify. When asked what he saw in the car he said, "Well, Judge, I'll tell it to you like this:

> There were two legs up
> And two legs down
> And two little butts going 'round and 'round
> They were neck to neck, chin to chin
> Cock out, dick in
> An' if that ain't fucking you can charge me ten."

Black Man, White Man, Chinese Man in Jail

Three men are in jail together in one cell, a black, a white and a Chinese. The wicked jailer wants to play a joke on them, so he says: "If when I measure each of your penis and together they add up to twelve inches, I will let you out of jail."

The black man goes first and he measures six inches. The white next, and he measures five. Now they only have to measure one inch to go free, but before he measures the Chinese is in a corner with his hand in his crotch. The jailer takes his measurement and it's one inch. The jailer, true to his word, lets them out.

The three men are now walking along the road together.

BLACK MAN: Man Oh man, you all see prick, prick at its blackest!
Oh baby! Six inches! Six of the best!
WHITE MAN: Don't forget my five; it helped us to get out of jail.
CHINESE MAN: Remember my inch! Don't forget you all lucky me catch a good cock stand!

Two White Men, Black Man, Devil

There was these three men that was crossing the bridge. These two white guys and this black guy. So they saw the devil. He appeared on the bridge and he says to the first guy, he says, "What your father do?"

And the guy says, "He's an electrician." (You know, white guy.) BOOM! A lightnin' bolt came out of the sky and struck off his dick. POOF!

So he pulls up to the next guy, right? And says to the other white guy, he says, "What your father do?"

He says, "He was a butcher." Man, this flying meat cleaver came out of the sky and WOOP! took it right off.

Then the black fellow came up and he says, "What did your father do?"

He says, "My father was a lollipop maker; you're goin' to have to suck this bad boy."

Black Man, Southerner, Northerner in Hell

There was these three guys, they were all in hell. There was this black guy, and a southerner, and this white guy from New York. So the devil said, "The guy who could tell the best lie could get out of hell."

So he goes to the first guy and say, "All right, let's hear your story."

He said, "Well, I stole all the money out of Fort Knox; biggest robbery in the world."

The guy said, "Man, you're a liar. You stay."

The next guy comes up, says, "I wrestled all the cattle in Texas."

The devil said, "Look, I got a beef burger right here. You're staying."

So the black guy comes up. Devil says, "All right, all right, boy. What's your story?"

The black guy says, "Well, I don't know how I got here. I was sitting here and all of a sudden there came a rumbling and a trembling in the ground. The sky became blood red and all of a sudden when I woke up, my maw was lying on the floor by the stove where she was cooking [*sniff*], beans spilled all over the floor. My papa was lying in the kitchen by the table reading the paper. Just lying on the floor. My sister was combing her hair, the comb was still in her hand. She was lying in the bathroom."

The devil says, "Yeah? And where was you lyin', boy?"

He said, "Well, you see, I was lyin' all the time."

Black Man, White Man, Jew Man in Hell

There was a white man, black man and a Jew man and the three of them went to hell. So the devil told them they could get out if they could think of something he couldn't do. So the white man said, "Race around the world in two seconds." And the devil raced around the world in one second. So the white man had to stay in hell.

The Jew man said, "Drink all the water in the world." The devil drank every drop of water, so the Jew had to stay in hell.

So the devil turned to the nigger. He said, "Well, Devil, I bet you can't guess this." And he pulled out a matchbox, put three holes in it and then farted into it.

"Now, Devil, which hole did that fart come out of?"

The devil pointed to a hole in the matchbox and said, "That one."

The nigger said, "No, this one," and pointed to his asshole.

Jew Man, Chinaman, Black Man in Heaven

Once upon a time three men died and they each went to heaven. There was the Jew, the Chinaman and the Negro. The Jew went to the pearly gates, very happy to have "made it in." Seeing St. Peter, the Jew bowed his head and said: "Greetings, St. Peter! It sure is good to be here."

The Chinaman was also glad to be received into heaven, and when he saw St. Paul, he made the sign of the praying hands, bowed and said: "It's good to be here, St. Paul."

The ole nigger had on a zoot suit, a bee-bop hat and a long gold chain swinging from his side pocket. He came to the gate swinging his gold chain. He looked at St. Peter, gave him the Afro handshake, waved at St. Paul with the black power sign, and said: "Where's my man J.C.?"

Riddles

Q. Who was the first soft drink maker?
A. Adam, he made Eve's cherry pop.

Q. Who was the first carpenter?
A. Eve, she made Adam's banana stand.

Q. When is a girl a virgin?
A. One time out of ten.

Q. What is the first thing newlyweds do when they get to the hotel?
A. They open their drawers and put their thing together.

Q. What is the best thing on a woman?
A. A man.

Q. What is the most useless thing on grandma?
A. Grandpa.

Q. Why is a woman's pants like a donkey's ears?
A. It takes an ass to hold them up.

Q. What part of a girl shouldn't move while dancing?
A. Her bowels.

Q. What is the coldest part of a man's body?
A. His balls, they are always two below.

Q. What is a gentleman?
A. One who can count the hairs on a girl without getting hard.

Q. Why does a rooster crow in the morning?
A. To let the farmer know his cock is out.

Q. A man went to bed with two women. How many animals were in bed the next morning?
A. Three asses, six calves, two pussys and one dead cock.

Q. What is the difference between sin and shame?
A. It's a sin to put it in and a shame to take it out.

Q. What is the hardest thing in the world to do?
A. Put it in soft.

Q. Why is a woman like a frying pan?
A. They both have to get hot before you put the meat in.

Q. What is the difference between a casket and a pussy?
A. One you come in and one you go in.

What an Old Man Said

An old man once said to me:

> "Son, I used to eat my pussy to save my dick
> But now I'm too old to use it."

JOKES ON CHILDREN

I said, shit,
I ain't payin' no $2.59 a yard for felt
when I can go to Billy Joe's and get felt free . . .

What's Wrong, Seymour?

"What's wrong, Seymour?"

"Well, last week I failed my spelling test and Miss Backlash just patted me on the head and said she understood and that according to a man named Jensen I did the best I could. When I got home and showed my mom she beat the tar out of me.

"Today Miss Backlash yelled at me and called me a troublemaker for getting the highest mark in the class on the math test. I thought she would be pleased but she started yelling saying that this same man named Jensen said I wasn't suppose to do better than the white kids.

"I don't know who this Mr. Jensen is but if I ever see him I'm gonna kick him in the face for always getting me into trouble!"

Correct English

(a)

One day little Johnny was going to school and on his way there he had to cross a railroad track. Now little Johnny had a pet dog who would follow him to school, and he would have a hard time trying to get him to go home. This special morning, his pet dog followed him and as Johnny crossed the railroad track, he looked back and saw his dog on the track and he shouted for him to hurry off the track. But disaster struck. So Johnny went on to school.

Later he told his teacher about what had happened. The teacher said, "I'm sorry to hear about your dog. Where did the train hit him?"

Johnny replied innocently, "In the ass."

The teacher angrily retorted, "Johnny, don't you ever utter anything like that in my classroom again. If you must say something like that, say *rectum*."

But Johnny looked at the teacher with puzzled eyes, and said in his child's lisp, "Wreck'd'um, hell! It damn near killed him."

(b)

And then there's the story of Lil' Willie, who either plays hooky from school constantly, or always arrives late for class. One day Willie, arriving late for class, tried unsuccessfully to sneak into the class unnoticed. Willie's teacher asked him why he was late. As usual, Willie told the tallest tale he could think of at the moment. He related how he witnessed an accident and had to assist the police with the investigation. (I might point out that Willie is only seven years old.) It seems that while he was on his way to school, a truck "knocked this dude on his ass," Willie says, and the teacher promptly corrects him and tells him that the word is *rectum*. To which Willie replies, "Rectum, my ass, he damn near killed the motherfucker."

Bad Manners

Teacher prepared school lunch for her kindergarten kids; almost all times, soup, milk and crackers. When she finished, she would say, "Children, your lunch is ready." All marched in and all were seated except Johnny.

TEACHER: What is the matter, Johnny?
JOHNNY: I told you I can't eat that shit.
TEACHER: Oh, Johnny, your language is horrible. I'll have to tell your mother if you say such words again. Go out and stay until I call you.

Johnny went out as he was told.

The next day, time for lunch: the teacher called, "Children, time for lunch. Milk, soup and crackers." The kids came in, all seated except Johnny.

TEACHER: Johnny, I'll not tolerate this nonsense any longer. Tomorrow I'll have your mother out here for lunch and let her see how you carry on.
JOHNNY: My mom don't care.
TEACHER: You just wait and see.

Next day, mom comes to lunch. Lunch is ready. The teacher calls, "Lunch, children." All gathered around. Mom looking on. Johnny came in last, head down.

Teacher said, "Alright Johnny, sit here and eat your lunch."
JOHNNY: I told you three times that I can't eat that motherfucking shit.
TEACHER TO MOM: See? I told you so.
MOM: If he won't eat, fuck him!

Check Her Reaction

This one is about a little kid, see? And his mother and father were separated. And what happened, the kid every once a month did go see his father. So this time, after twelve years, the kid went to see his father and his father wrote out a check real fast and he said, "You know, let me tell you something. You go back and tell your mama," he says, "this is the last check you're goin' to get. I don't have to support you no more, I'm through. You know, son, you just check her reaction. That's all, just check her reaction."

So he said, "Okay," and he went on home and he told his mother. He says, "Mom, you know, here's this check that dad sent." He says, "You know, for twelve years he's been supportin' me and he's not goin' to give me no more checks after this one. But he says something funny. He said to check your reaction when I tell you this."

She said, "Is that what that nigger says?"

He said, "Yeah."

She said, "Well, you go back and tell him for twelve years you weren't his son. And son, just check his reaction."

Grits and Wonder

Jim goes over to his cousin Dick's.

"Good mornin', Dick," said Jim. "How is everything going?"

"Pretty bad," says Dick. "Ain't got no meat for breakfast, just grits and wonder."

Jim said, "What do you mean, 'grits and wonder'? What is wonder?"

Dick answered, "Grits and grease and wonder where the meat's coming from."

Belly Button

Two seven year olds, Jim and Cheryl, were playing.

JIM: Cheryl, may I put my finger in your belly button?
CHERYL: No!
JIM: Ah, Cheryl, please?
CHERYL: Alright ... But Jim! That's not my belly button.
JIM: But Cheryl, that's not my finger either.

Coming and Going

Yesterday that big ole Johnny Brown stuck his hand up my dress and started rubbing between my legs. I said: "What the hell are you doing?" He didn't answer but just kept on rubbing. After a while he stopped and asked me was I coming, and I told him, "I ain't goin' nowhere with you!"

Felt

My momma sent me to the store today to get some felt. I got down there and it was $2.59 a yard. I said, shit, I ain't payin' no $2.59 a yard when I can go to Billy Joe's and get felt free.

I Was Walking Through the Park

I was walking through the park yesterday and two men jumped from behind the bushes, grabbed me and started taking off my clothes. But I wasn't worried; I knew they wouldn't fit them.

The Pocket Book

It was a warm July day in North Carolina. Sister Lane was washing clothes on the scrub board out-of-doors. Now, while she was a-washing, her little boy was crawling and playing in the dirt. The boy found a dime and gave it to his mama to hold on to. So mama took the dime and put it in her pocket and went back to her washing. The boy went back to crawling and playing in the dirt.

In his playing the boy crawled up under his mother's dress. Well, Sister Lane didn't have any drawers on, so when the boy looked up he said, "Ooh, Mama, what's that?"

His mama said, "Oh, that's my pocket book."

So the boy said, "Well, you must have lost my dime 'cause your pocket book is wide open."

Close Your Legs!

A little girl and her mother got on the bus. The bus was crowded and there was only one seat left. The lady sat there. Across from her was a man sitting with his legs spread, taking up two seats.

MOTHER: Baby, go tell that man to close his legs so you can sit down.
CHILD: Mister, my mother said that if you would close your legs there would be room for me to sit down.
MAN: Well, tell your mother that if she had kept her legs closed in the first place you wouldn't be here bothering me now.

A Nickel!

There was this five-year-old girl sitting on the curb, with no drawers on and her legs wide open. This big Cadillac pulled up and a man got out, ran to the girl and gave her five dollars and told her to go tell your mama to buy you some panties. The girl ran to her mama and told what happened and how she got the money. Then her mama decided to go and do the same thing so she could get some money. The very same man pulled up and saw her and said, "Here's a nickel, go buy a net."

How to Kill an Eel in One Easy Lesson

Little Johnny was eight years old and just at the age when he was curious as only boys can be. He had been hearing a lot about courting from other boys, so he asked his mother what courting was. She told him to hide behind the hall curtain some night and watch his sister and her boyfriend.

This Johnny did, and here is how he described it to his mother:

Sis and her boyfriend sat and talked awhile and pretty soon turned out all the lights except the blue one. Then he began to kiss Sis and put his hand in her blouse. Pretty soon they began to kiss and get out of breath. Then he took his hand out of her blouse and put it under her dress. When he did this Sis began to moan and sigh and squirm, and started down the edge of the cot until she was lying down. Then he unzipped his pants and pulled out an eel about eleven inches long. It was standing up and he held it with both hands to keep it from getting away. Sis started to hold him and they both wrestled with the eel for a while. While they were wrestling with the eel, Sis's dress slipped up under her arms. But they kept on wrestling and finally got the scissors hold on it. He helped her by lying on the eel. Soon they got the eel between them and started to crush it. Sis took her arms and legs and wrapped them around her boyfriend. They both started wrestling. . . . . Sis squealed and her boyfriend almost upset the cot with both of them. Pretty soon they gave a moan and a lunge and the both of them stopped moaning. The boyfriend got up, for they had killed the eel because there it hung as limp as could be, and some of its insides ran out.

As Sis and her boyfriend were tired out from the battle with the eel, they sat and talked awhile, and he told her how sweet she was. They started loving and kissing again. They were both surprised, for pretty soon the damn eel came back to life and started another fight. Sis gave a squeal and grabbed it with both hands. They got another hold on it, in record time, and the way they battled this time you could tell Sis and her boyfriend had finally killed the eel, because I saw her boyfriend pull its skin off and take it to the bathroom and flush it down the drain. . . . .

P.S.: Mother fainted.

MISCELLANEOUS

God don't like ugly,
and don't care too much for beauty . . .

Sulky Sailor

I'm a sulky sailor who just got off the ship
I ain't got a dime and I don't give a shit

I'm going downtown to get my roll
And then I'm going back to the ship to grease my pole

On the way downtown I met a farmer's daughter
I said, "Would you gimme just one piece for just one quarter?"

Then I took her to the park and laid her on the grass
As I tried to run my dick up her motherfuckin ass

After a while I was feeling kinda sick
I was aching at the back and dripping at the dick

I went to the doctor and sat on the stool
And I looked him in the eye like a motherfuckin fool

I said, "Doctor, doctor, I'm feeling kinda sick
I'm aching at the back and dripping at the dick."

He said, "I'm sorry, son, but yo time has come at last
'Cause I'm gonna have to cut yo dick from yo motherfuckin ass."

I said, "Doctor, doctor, is that all you can do?"
He said, "No, motherfucker, yo balls go too!"

Old Country Jail

I was standing on the corner
Doing no harm
When 'long came the police
And took me by the arm

He took me around the corner
And rang a little bell
'Long came the wagon
And took me off to jail

Five o'clock that morning
I looked up on the wall
The bedbugs and the roaches
Were playing a game of ball

The score was six to nothing
Bedbugs were ahead
Roaches hit a home run
And knocked me out of bed

Six o'clock that morning
The cook came around
"Coffee and cornbread
Will surely make you strong."

The coffee tasted like tobacco juice
Cornbread was old and stale
And that's the way they do you
In an old country jail.

Stephen Change

Now Stephen was a man like this
When he had no women he used his fist

He stood a hundred women against a wall
And bet a hundred dollars he could use them all

He used ninety-eight, could use no more
His balls were cold, his prick was sore

He went across the street, got an oyster stew
Came on back, and used the other two

HIS WISHES

When I die, bury me deep
Put a gallon of corn at my head and feet
Fold my prick across my chest
Let the whores know I am gone to rest

HIS END

Stephen died and went to hell
Upon meeting the devil he used him well

The devil's imps cringed beside a wall
Shouting, "Get out of here or you'll use us all!"

Little Black Bird

I was taking a dooze under the tree
When a little black bird came and shit right on me
I said, "Don't laugh, little bird, and think you're smart
I knew you was gonna shit; hell, I heard you fart!"

Belgrave

There was a man looking for Belgrave
When he climbed across a dead woman in a cave
Now it took a good pluck
To give a very cold fuck
But look all the money he saved.

Legs in Style

Coca-cola, and legs in style
What's between them makes a man go wild.

Humpty Dumpty

Humpty Dumpty sat on the wall
Humpty Dumpty had a great fall
All the king's horses, all the king's men
Had to help put Humpty's balls back in his pants.

Upside Down . . .

Ladies and gentlemen, hobos and tramps
Bumblebees, mosquitoes and bowlegged ants
We've come before you, to stand behind you
To tell you something we know nothing about

On Wednesday, which is Good Friday
There'll be a ladies' meeting, for men only
The admission is free, so please pay at the door
There'll be plenty of seats, so sit on the floor.

. . . Inside Out

One bright day in the middle of the night
Two dead boys got up to fight
Back to back they faced each other
Pulled out their swords and shot one another

A deaf policeman heard the noise
He got up to kill those two dead boys
If you don't believe my lie is true
Ask the blind man, he saw it too.

When You're Up . . .

When you're up, you're up
When you're down, you're down
When a nigger's up against a cracker
He'll turn him upside down.

. . . When You're Down

Everytime I been down
I tell myself so is the sun
But he gonna be up high
Come early in the morning!

Son

I don't call you son 'cause you mine
I call you son 'cause you shine.

Look into My Eyes

Q: Look into my eyes, what do you see?
A: A simple muthafucka tryin' to hypnotize me.

They Say

They say . . . they want to push for equal opportunity, but *we* think
we look better on the welfare line.

They say . . . we were born shufflin' and talkin' slow, so it ain't
natural for us to want to move ahead too fast.

They say . . . nigga's feet kills grass. I guess that's why it's hard
to find it here in the city.

They say . . . if you give us an inch we'll take a foot—that's how
granddaddy died, behind a foot of rope.

They say . . . those who were born poor were meant to stay poor.
They mean us.

They say . . . being poor don't bother us, because we the happiest
people they ever seen—always dancin' and grinnin'!

Snippets

Everybody knows you have to cook a hog to get lard.

Get up off your rusty-dusty [ashy ass].

The Four F's: Find 'em, Fool 'em, Fuck 'em, Forget 'em.

Clean as the Board of Health.

If there's one thing I can't stand
It's a high-yellow woman with a coal-black man.

Sounds like a P.P. to me [personal problem].

A hard head makes a soft behind.

Your ass don't weigh a ton.

When you move, you lose [Barbershop Rules].

Ain't nothin' comin' to a sleeper but a dream.

You got the dime, I got the time.

Folks as good as the people.

You got a good bottom woman.

Life ain't been no bowl of cherries
It's a pot of beans and they're all cold.

Opportunity is like a man with long hair in front and bald-headed behind: you have to grab hold of it while it's coming to you, 'cause once it passes there ain't nothing to catch onto.

The colored race is like God's bouquet, 'cause you find within it every color arranged like a bunch of flowers.

Times are as hard as Japanese algebra.

White folks is the boss, colored folks is the horse.

"The Great Americans": a story in white-face.

Your eyes are bigger than your belly.

God don't like ugly, and don't care too much for beauty.

Flashes

He be cool as a Maltese kitten tipping across a barbed wire fence.

She's so fine, she'll make your big toe jump.

He be bush-wackin' for days!

Whip it on me, mama!

Ain't this a bitch!

Like a hen breaks wind.

Haul ass!

Buns for days [girl with big behind].

I gots to git over.

Me and you, baby.

Tough titty!

Dere it is.

Swappin' spit.

Hey, brother. What it is?

He's a stone humble runner.

He's a tack-head [hoodlum].

You sho' is a drag.

Dig where I'm coming from?

Cleanest thing since Ajax.

Money talks and bullshit walks.

The hole is greater than the pole.

Man, you just selling wolf tickets [threats].

A Lady!

Girl, what's wrong with your auntie? Heard tell she got all these boyfriends running in and out of her house. Don't you know that starts rumors? Somebody said, I'm not telling who, said she puts out so fine that men from all over come to see her. Last night me and some of the other girls was sitting on the stoop and wouldn't you know this big, fine, sharp, sharp, black-as-tar pearly white-toothed nigger stepped out of this shooooot fine-looking car. Walked up her stairs as if they were made out of the finest silk. All the folks that live in her building said they could hear her cooing all the way into the basement. They also said when that man walked out of there you could see his smile gleaming way over on 100th Street. Johnny said he overheard him say to himself that he had just tasted the finest lady on the East Coast and possibly the whole eastern half of the United States. Now you know anytime anyone call your aunt a lady then he got to be pleased, love-struck or somethin'. Now I betcha your granny, pappy, uncle or mother can't tell her that she ain't the finest fox this side of 79th Street. In fact, they say she's goin' to put an advertisement in the *Daily Bull.* Suppose to read:

> *If you want the hoodoo put on you*
> *And want it to be known who you saw*
> *Then all you got to do*
> *Is stop in at 411 80th Street*
> *And when you come out*
> *People will know you had a ball.*

Freedom

Hard pressed to explain to her little son what freedom is, Sister Wright said, "Son, catch me a bird and bring it here." So the little boy did as he was told and brought a sparrow home. When he woke the next morning, the bird lay on the floor dead. He picked up the bird with tears in his eyes and took it to his mother. His mother looked at him and said, "Son, I don't know what freedom is, but lack of it killed your bird."

CONTRIBUTORS

These materials were mostly collected by students in my classes in African-American literature in 1969–1973 at the Borough of Manhattan Community College (BMCC) of the City University of New York, at Columbia University in New York, and at Swarthmore College in Pennsylvania. Much of it was generated by the collectors themselves as participants in the oral culture; however, the fragmentary and overlapping nature of much of the material, plus the fact that some of it was submitted anonymously, makes it difficult and not especially useful to identify every item with a particular collector. It is therefore fitting that those collectors whose material is included, and who did not expressly prohibit mention of their name, are listed here for a collective attribution and grouped by their institutional affiliation at the time. In addition, collectors and, where known, artists of some of the longer forms are listed separately.

GENERAL LIST OF COLLECTORS

Borough of Manhattan Community College: Carol Austin, Timothy Baskerville, Janeen Bowe, Alice Carlyle, Berniceteen Cox, Teddy Dozier, Brenda Eisbey, Geraldine Greene, Pauline D. Harris, Robert E. Heard, Raymond Heuchling, Adele Hudson, William Jones, Nathaniel Lewis, Paula Martin, James Mitchell, Elma Montgomery, Beatrice G. Myers, James A. Nelson, Claude Ross, Delores J. Smith, Valerie Thompson, Milan Tucker and Wanda White.

Columbia University: Samira Abdu-Samad, Ruth Bates, Jerry Boone, Rachelle V. Browne, Janet Calkins, Margaret Cibulskis, LaVerne Cheri Dalton, Charles Daniel Dawson, Audrey Doman, Darryl Thomas Downing, Gary Friday, Linda Hardwick, Philip Jeffrey Harper, Gerald Harris, David Hathy, Philip S. Hicks, Theresa Hill, Laurence Holland, Norvester L. James, Garrett Johnson, Michael David Johnson, Patrice Johnson, Rita Jones, Edwina Losey, William E. Moore, Dolores A. Nix, Wendy Oldham, Janice Peters, Samuel Powell, John D. Reid, Kenneth Sloan, Ellease Southerland (Ebele Oseye), Bettye Jo Walker, Albert M. Webber and Joan V. Wiley.

Swarthmore College: Sherry F. Bellamy, Steven Bowers, Robert Branch, Andrea Bryant, Priscilla Aquiller Chatman, Chiquita Davidson, Ruth Ann Diamond, Marian L. Evans, Carlton B. Henry, Jacqueline Denise Jones, Michelle

Kelly, Leslie Terese Knight, Margaret Ann Linton, Pierre Miller, Milton Melvin Morris, Larry Gregory Potter, Lorean Simmons, May Akeita Thomas, Vaneese Yseult Thomas, Ernest Williams and Andrea Idell Young.

COLLECTORS AND ARTISTS OF SOME SPECIFIC PIECES

Rapping, Signifying, Boasts and Threats

A Declaration of Friendship: Dolores Nix (Columbia)
If You Don't Like My Apples: Rachelle Browne / Patrice Johnson (Columbia)
When I Die: Kenneth Sloan (Columbia)
Ninety-four Whores: Kenneth Sloan (Columbia)
Three Wine-Ole Bitches: James Mitchell (BMCC)
Fathers and Sons: Claude Ross (BMCC)
Dime: Janeen Bowe (BMCC)

Toasts

The Signifying Monkey

The Signifying Monkey (1): Charles Daniel Dawson (Columbia) / John Inniss; *Artist,* Ronald "Mousey" Wright
The Signifying Monkey (2): Robert Heard (BMCC)
The Signifying Monkey (3): Timothy Baskerville (BMCC)
The Signifying Monkey (4): Charles Daniel Dawson (Columbia); *Artist,* Ronald Roy Coleman
The Signifying Monkey (5): Elma Montgomery (BMCC)
The Signifying Monkey (6): Pauline D. Harris (BMCC)
The Signifying and Pool-Shooting Monkey (8): Lonnie T. Morgan (Minnesota)

Stagger Lee

Stag-a-Lee (1): Audrey Doman (Columbia)
Stagolee (2): Kenneth Sloan (Columbia)
Stagolee (4): May Thomas and Andrea Young (Swarthmore)
Stackalee (5): *Artist,* Steven Bodie of Harlem
Stackolee (6): Janeen Bowe (BMCC)
Stagger Lee and the James Brothers (8): Robert Heard (BMCC)

The Titanic

... And Shine Swam On (1): Dolores Nix (Columbia)
The Titanic (2): LaVerne Cheri Dalton (Columbia)

The Titanic (3):   Charles Daniel Dawson (Columbia) / John Inniss; *Artist,* Ronald "Mousey" Wright
The Tenth of May (5):   *Artist,* Steven Bodie of Harlem
The King, the Queen and the Whore (6):   May Thomas and Andrea Young (Swarthmore)
Shine, the Devil, and His Brother Sammy (7):   Charles Daniel Dawson (Columbia); *Artist,* Ronald Roy Coleman
The Three Women (8):   Carlton B. Henry and Milton Melvin Morris (Swarthmore); *Artist,* Rosiland Plummer
Son of Shine (9):   Carlton B. Henry and Milton Melvin Morris (Swarthmore); *Artist,* Rosiland Plummer

Dolemite: Gary Friday (Columbia)

Death Row: Janeen Bowe (BMCC)

Doriella DuFontaine: Janeen Bowe (BMCC)

Honky Tonk Bud

This is Your FBI (1):   Janeen Bowe (BMCC)
The Hip Cat Stud (2):   Charles Daniel Dawson (Columbia); *Artist,* Ronald Roy Coleman

The Free Snorter: Janeen Bowe (BMCC)

Pete Revere

Pete Revere (1):   Charles Daniel Dawson (Columbia) / John Inniss; *Artist,* Ronald "Mousey" Wright
Big Pete (2):   LaVerne Cheri Dalton (Columbia)

Black Jack Tucker: Elma Montgomery (BMCC)

Invective

Pimpin' Sam: Gary Friday (Columbia)
On the Corner: James Mitchell (BMCC)

Preacher Tales and Parodies

Preacher Man: William E. Moore / LaVerne Cheri Dalton (Columbia)
A Prayer: LaVerne Cheri Dalton (Columbia)
Telephone to Glory: LaVerne Cheri Dalton (Columbia)
The Visiting White Preacher: Andrea Bryant (Swarthmore), "As told by my father"
Fresh Air: Teddy Dozier (BMCC)

I Want to Testify: Andrea Bryant (Swarthmore), "As told by my father"
Make a Joyful Noise!   Robert Heard (BMCC)
Mock Sermon: Beatrice G. Myers (BMCC)
Jonah and the Whale: Charles Daniel Dawson (Columbia) / John Inniss;
    Artist, Ronald "Mousey" Wright

Jokes

Welcome to Muleshoe, Mississippi: William E. Moore (Columbia)
Suicide!   William E. Moore (Columbia)
Southern Hospitality: Ernest Williams (Swarthmore)
Oink!   Teddy Dozier (BMCC)
Help!   William E. Moore (Columbia)
The Nigger Announcer: Philip Jeffrey Harper (Columbia)
The Nigger Ape: Philip Jeffrey Harper (Columbia)
Who is the King of the Jungle?   (a) David Hathy (Columbia); (b) Philip
    Jeffrey Harper (Columbia)
Reno's Comin'!   Philip Jeffrey Harper (Columbia)
You Ain't Shit: William E. Moore (Columbia)
Books and Authors: Ernest Williams (Swarthmore)
The Faggot and the Truck Driver: Geraldine Greene (BMCC)
You Want the Indians to Hate Us?   William E. Moore (Columbia)
Bowels: Leslie Terese Knight (Swarthmore)
Back to Africa: (a) Claude Ross (BMCC); (b) May Thomas and Andrea
    Young (Swarthmore)
The Russian and the Whore: Pauline D. Harris (BMCC)
Englishman, Black Man: Philip Jeffrey Harper (Columbia)
Chinese Man, Black Man, Jew Man and God: Carlton B. Henry and Milton
    Melvin Morris (Swarthmore); *Artist,* Rosiland Plummer
White Man, Colored Man, Chinese Man in a Storm: Philip Jeffrey Harper
    (Columbia)
White Man, Black Man, Jew Man and a Can of Beans: May Thomas and
    Andrea Young (Swarthmore)
Colored Man, White Man, Chinese Man and Skunk: Philip Jeffrey Harper
    (Columbia)
Black Man, Chinese Man, White Man in a Whorehouse: May Thomas and
    Andrea Young (Swarthmore)
Chinese Man, Colored Man, White Man and the Chimes: Philip Jeffrey
    Harper (Columbia)
Jew Man, White Man, Black Man and the Judge: Norvester L. James
    (Columbia)
Black Man, White Man, Chinese Man in Jail: Claude Ross (BMCC)

Black Man, White Man, Jew Man in Hell: May Thomas and Andrea Young
(Swarthmore)
Jew Man, Chinaman, Black Man in Heaven: Bettye Jo Walker (Columbia)
Riddles: Teddy Dozier (BMCC)

Jokes on Children

What's Wrong, Seymour? Steven Bowers (Swarthmore)
Correct English: (a) Andrea Bryant (Swarthmore), "As told by my aunt"; (b)
William E. Moore (Columbia)
Belly Button: Priscilla Chatman (Swarthmore)
Coming and Going: Steven Bowers (Swarthmore)
Felt: Steven Bowers (Swarthmore)
I Was Walking Through the Park: Steven Bowers (Swarthmore)
Close Your Legs! Priscilla Chatman (Swarthmore)
A Nickel! Teddy Dozier (BMCC)
How to Kill an Eel in One Easy Lesson: Teddy Dozier (BMCC)

Miscellaneous

Sulky Sailor: Gary Friday (Columbia)
Old Country Jail: Gary Friday (Columbia)
Stephen Change: William Jones (BMCC)
Little Black Bird: Charles Daniel Dawson (Columbia) / John Inniss; *Artist,*
Ronald "Mousey" Wright
Belgrave: Charles Daniel Dawson (Columbia) / John Inniss; *Artist,* Ronald
"Mousey" Wright
Legs in Style: Rachelle Browne and Patrice Johnson (Columbia)
Humpty Dumpty: Bettye Jo Walker (Columbia)
Upside Down . . . : Bettye Jo Walker (Columbia)
. . . Inside Out: Bettye Jo Walker (Columbia)
When You're Up . . . : Dolores Nix (Columbia)
. . . When You're Down: Dolores Nix (Columbia)
Look into My Eyes: Gary Friday / Kenneth Sloan (Columbia)
They Say: Theresa Hill (Columbia)
A Lady! Lorean Simmons (Swarthmore)